D1104098

Understanding
ISAK DINESEN

Understanding Modern
European and Latin American
Literature

James Hardin, *Series Editor*

volumes on

Ingeborg Bachmann
Samuel Beckett
Thomas Bernhard
Johannes Bobrowski
Heinrich Böll
Italo Calvino
Albert Camus
Elias Canetti
Camilo José Cela
Céline
Julio Cortázar
Isak Dinesen
José Donoso
Friedrich Dürrenmatt
Rainer Werner Fassbinder
Max Frisch
Federico García Lorca
Gabriel García Márquez
Juan Goytisolo
Günter Grass

Gerhart Hauptmann
Christoph Hein
Hermann Hesse
Eugène Ionesco
Uwe Johnson
Milan Kundera
Primo Levi
Boris Pasternak
Octavio Paz
Luigi Pirandello
Graciliano Ramos
Erich Maria Remarque
Alain Robbe-Grillet
Joseph Roth
Jean-Paul Sartre
Claude Simon
Mario Vargas Llosa
Peter Weiss
Franz Werfel
Christa Wolf

UNDERSTANDING

ISAK
DINESEN

SUSAN C. BRANTLY

UNIVERSITY OF SOUTH CAROLINA PRESS

© 2002 University of South Carolina

Published in Columbia, South Carolina, by the
University of South Carolina Press

Manufactured in the United States of America

06   05   04   03   02   5   4   3   2   1

Library of Congress Cataloging-in-Publication Data

Brantly, Susan.
  Understanding Isak Dinesen / Susan C. Brantly.
       p. cm. — (Understanding modern European and Latin American literature)
  Includes bibliographical references and index.
  ISBN 1-57003-428-1 (alk. paper)
  1. Dinesen, Isak, 1885–1962—Criticism and interpretation. I. Title. II. Series.
  PT8175.B545 Z64 2001
  839.8'1372—dc21   2001006785

Contents

Editor's Preface

Understanding Modern European and Latin American Literature has been planned as a series of guides for undergraduate and graduate students and nonacademic readers. Like the volumes in its companion series *Understanding Contemporary American Literature,* these books provide introductions to the lives and writings of prominent modern authors and explicate their most important works.

Modern literature makes special demands, and this is particularly true of foreign literature, in which the reader must contend not only with unfamiliar, often arcane artistic conventions and philosophical concepts, but also with the handicap of reading the literature in translation. It is a truism that the nuances of one language can be rendered in another only imperfectly (and this problem is especially acute in fiction), but the fact that the works of European and Latin American writers are situated in a historical and cultural setting quite different from our own can be as great a hindrance to the understanding of these works as the linguistic barrier. For this reason the *UMELL* series emphasizes the sociological and historical background of the writers treated. The philosophical and cultural traditions peculiar to a given culture may be particularly important for an understanding of certain authors, and these are taken up in the introductory chapter and also in the discussion of those works to which this information is relevant. Beyond this, the books treat the specifically literary aspects of the author under discussion and attempt to explain the complexities of contemporary literature lucidly. The books are conceived as introductions to the authors covered, not as comprehensive analyses. They do not provide detailed summaries of plot because they are meant to be used in conjunction with the books they treat, not as a substitute for study of the original works. The purpose of the books is to provide information and judicious literary assessment of the major works in the most compact, readable form. It is our hope that the *UMELL* series will help increase knowledge and understanding of European and Latin American cultures and will serve to make the literature of those cultures more accessible.

J. H.

Acknowledgments

First and foremost, I am deeply indebted to my long-time mentor, George C. Schoolfield, who directed me to this project, shared his files with me, read the manuscript, and dropped eagerly awaited hints about some obscure references. His generosity is unparalleled. Without him, this book might never have been written. I am grateful to Brad Berkland, who was my research assistant for a summer and was particularly good at finding sources on Africa. Additional thanks are due the American-Scandinavian Foundation, which made it possible for me to visit Denmark and collect some useful materials. My thanks also to the gentle souls who took the time to read parts of the manuscript during its genesis and provided welcome feedback: Donna Brantly, Alida Doll, Sue Janty, Faith Ingwersen, Niels Ingwersen, and Scott Mellor. Finally, I am much obliged to all the students who have enjoyed reading Dinesen with me over the years.

Abbreviations for Editions Used

There is no standard critical edition of Isak Dinesen's work in English. Whenever possible, I have chosen to quote from the editions available in the American bookstores during the preparation of this manuscript, since they are most likely to be the versions consulted by my readers. Readers should be advised that British editions of Dinesen's work were prepared in separate consultation with the author and can contain some substantial differences from the American editions. The Danish memorial edition has come under fire for changing the order of the tales from the originals, but it is the closest thing in Danish to a standard edition. In citing Isak Dinesen's major texts throughout this study, I have used the following editions and abbreviations:

AD   *Anecdotes of Destiny* and *Ehrengard.* New York: Vintage Books, 1993.

CV   *Carnival: Entertainments and Posthumous Tales.* Chicago: University of Chicago Press, 1977.

DG   *Daguerreotypes and Other Essays.* Chicago: University of Chicago Press, 1979.

KBD   *Karen Blixen i Danmark: Breve, 1931–1962.* 2 vols. Edited by Frans Lasson and Tom Engelbrecht. Copenhagen: Gyldendal, 1996.

LA   *Letters from Africa, 1914–1931.* Translated by Anne Born; Edited by Frans Lasson. Chicago: University of Chicago Press, 1981.

LT   *Last Tales.* New York: Vintage Books, 1991.

MU   *Karen Blixen Mindeudgave.* 7 vols. Copenhagen: Gyldendal, 1964.

OA   *Out of Africa and Shadows on the Grass.* New York: Vintage Books, 1989.

OC   *Osceola.* Copenhagen: Gyldendal, 1962.

OMM   *On Modern Marriage and Other Observations.* New York: St. Martin's Press, 1986.

SGT   *Seven Gothic Tales.* New York: Vintage Books, 1991.

WT   *Winter's Tales.* New York: Vintage Books, 1993.

Chronology

A more detailed chronology has been prepared by Frans Lasson and can be found in the American translation of Dinesen's *Letters from Africa, 1914–1931.* In this chronology, I have referred to Isak Dinesen by her real names, Karen Dinesen and Karen Blixen for the sake of bibliographical clarity. Throughout the rest of the book, I have followed American practice and referred to the author as Isak Dinesen.

1885   April 17. Karen Christentze Dinesen is born at Rungstedlund.

1895   March 28. Karen Dinesen's father, Wilhelm Dinesen, hangs himself in a Copenhagen boardinghouse.

1899   Karen Dinesen attends a French school in Switzerland.

1904   Attends the Academy of Art in Copenhagen. Visits Scotland and Oxford.

1905   Visits London. Continues at the Academy of Art.

1907   Debuts as an author under the pseudonym Osceola with the story "The Hermits" and later "The Ploughman," both published in Danish journals.

1909   "The de Cats Family" appears in *Tilskueren.*

1910   Briefly attends a new art college in Paris.

1912   Visits Norway and Rome.
         December 23. Announces her engagement to Baron Bror Blixen-Finecke.

1913   Bror Blixen travels to British East Africa, where funds from Karen Dinesen's family make it possible for him to purchase a coffee farm. Karen leaves on December 2 to join him.

1914   January 14. Karen Dinesen marries Bror Blixen in Mombasa. Not long after the wedding, Karen Blixen learns she has been infected with syphillis.
         August 1. World War I begins.

1915   April. Karen Blixen returns to Denmark for medical treatment.

1916   Dinesen's family purchases an even larger coffee farm. Bror Blixen travels to Denmark and, later, Karen and he return to Africa together.

1918   Karen Blixen meets Denys Finch Hatton. Her brother, Thomas Dinesen, is awarded the British Victoria Cross.

1919   Karen and Bror Blixen visit Denmark. Karen falls ill for five months.

1920   November. Karen Blixen returns to Africa with her brother Thomas Dinesen.

1921   Bror Blixen is dismissed by Karen's family as manager of the farm, and Karen is appointed manager in his stead. The couple separate.

1922   Karen Blixen is disappointed to learn that she is not pregnant by Denys Finch Hatton.

1924   Karen Blixen's mother, Ingeborg Dinesen, visits her in Africa.

1925   Karen Blixen's divorce from Bror is finalized. Karen Blixen visits Denmark.

1926   Karen Blixen returns to Africa. She publishes "The Revenge of Truth" back in Denmark.

1927   Ingeborg Dinesen returns to Africa for a second visit.

1928   Bror Blixen marries Cockie Birkbeck, causing Karen Blixen some social awkwardness, because there are now two Baronesses Blixen. This is felt most acutely when the Prince of Wales visits Kenya.

1929   Karen Blixen returns to Denmark when her mother falls ill. She also takes time to meet Denys Finch Hatton's family in England.

1931   The coffee farm is sold after several years of financial reversals.
        May 14. Denys Finch Hatton is killed when his plane crashes in Tanganyika. Karen Blixen must leave Africa for good. She returns to Denmark to live with her mother and is supported by her brother, Thomas Dinesen, while she prepares the manuscript for *Seven Gothic Tales.*

1934   *Seven Gothic Tales* appears in America under the pseudonym Isak Dinesen and receives warm reviews. The book also appears in England later that year.

1935   *Seven Gothic Tales* is released in Denmark.

1937   *Out of Africa* is published in Denmark and England.

1938   *Out of Africa* appears in America.

1939   January 27. Karen Blixen's mother dies at age 82. Blixen continues to reside at Rungstedlund.

1940   Karen Blixen travels to Berlin as a correspondent for the Danish newspaper *Politiken.*
        April 9. The German occupation of Denmark begins.

1942   *Winter's Tales* is published in America, England, and Denmark.

1943   Farah Aden dies, making it difficult for Blixen to maintain contact with the people from her farm. Blixen does not learn of his death until after the war.

1944   *The Angelic Avengers* appears in Copenhagen under the pseudonym Pierre Andrézel.

1945   Clara Svendsen begins working for Karen Blixen as her secretary.

1946   Karen Blixen undergoes a spinal operation to treat the chronic pain she suffers as part of the physical aftermath to her syphilis. Bror Blixen is killed in a car accident.

1951   Karen Blixen makes trip to Greece and Rome.

1952   Mau Mau rebellion occurs in Kenya.

1953   Karen Blixen tries to arrange to be sent to Kenya as a correspondent, but her health and a lack of financial support thwart her plans.

1955   Karen Blixen undergoes a serious stomach operation at the age of seventy.

1957   *Last Tales* is published in America, England, and Denmark. Blixen is made an honorary member of the American Academy of Arts and Letters.

1958   *Anecdotes of Destiny* appears in America, England, and Denmark. Karen Blixen creates the Rungstedlund Foundation, which will preserve her home as a bird sanctuary funded by the revenues from Blixen's work after her death.

1959   January 3 to April 17. Blixen makes her only visit to the United States.

1960   *Shadows on the Grass* appears in England and Denmark.

1961   *Shadows on the Grass* appears in America.

1962   September 7. Karen Blixen dies at home in Rungstedlund. Kamande Gatura, Ali Hassan, Ahmed Farah Aden (Saufe), and Mohamed bin Juma (Tumbo) are each granted five thousand crowns under the terms of Blixen's will.

Understanding
ISAK DINESEN

CHAPTER 1

Understanding Isak Dinesen

Dinesen's tales have been described as puzzles, labyrinths, three-dimensional spaces, and multilayered texts embedded with new clues to be discovered upon each rereading. Dinesen included "blank pages" in her texts, moments where the narrator falls silent and the reader's imagination is expected to fill the gap. For these reasons, each reader's experience of a Dinesen text is likely to be different; hence, the inappropriateness of suggesting a definitive reading. Nevertheless, the more a reader becomes aware of the hints, clues, allusions, and hidden meanings in the text, the deeper will be the reader's understanding.

Reading analyses is no substitute for a reader's own meeting with the text, and I assume that my audience has already read for themselves the texts under discussion. Chapter 1 contains some general observations about understanding Isak Dinesen and the nature of the Dinesen text. The subsequent detailed readings of individual texts will occasionally refer to the larger thematic issues raised here.

In the preparation for this book, as many secondary works as possible in English, Danish, Swedish, German, and French have been consulted. The most useful and intriguing observations and interpretations are presented along with my own insights for the reader's consideration. In the best case, the reader will feel that he or she has spent time discussing these texts with a group of particularly well informed and observant friends. Scholars may wish to use this book to refresh their memories about the copious secondary literature that has been produced about Dinesen. In addition to skimming the cream off the secondary literature, an effort has been made to scan Dinesen's interviews and correspondence for her own comments about her fiction. The 1996 publication of *Karen Blixen i Danmark: Breve, 1931–62* (Karen Blixen in Denmark: Letters, 1931–62) provided much material along these lines that had not been readily available before. Dinesen did not like to comment upon her own stories, especially not in public, but on occasion she felt provoked by "inaccurate" readings and set the record straight in her private correspondence. I will be treating Dinesen as an especially astute and interesting interpreter of her own fiction, but the reader must decide whether he or she wishes to accept Dinesen's words as authoritative.

Dinesen wrote most of her texts in English and recast them into Danish later. It is difficult to speak of translations, since she allowed herself much more creative liberty than a translator would claim. Occasionally, she inserted new phrases and paragraphs into the Danish versions. Again the issue of authority raises its head: which is the authoritative text, the English or the Danish? Susan Hardy Aiken has suggested that Isak Dinesen and Karen Blixen, as she was known to her Danish readers, are two different, but intricately intertextual, authors, and much can be said in favor of this position.[1] Since most of the audience for this book will be reading the texts in English, I will treat the English versions as primary and mention significant variations in the Danish texts that might be of interpretive import. Unlike Dinesen, I do not demand any foreign-language competency from my readers and have translated my sources myself, unless otherwise indicated.[2]

Dinesen put a great deal of effort into constructing her seemingly effortless tales: "I know the whole story before writing the first word. I actually carry my stories in my head for a long time, before I write them. I tell them and retell them to myself."[3] No doubt this method of construction helped to create the sense of orality that many of her tales possess. Although Dinesen insisted on her status as a storyteller along the lines of Scheherazade of the *Arabian Nights,* Robert Langbaum gently protested the identification of Dinesen's stories with tales from oral tradition: "Yet her stories cannot—in spite of her own claims to the contrary—really be classed with the sort of stories you can tell orally. The complexity of pattern, the need to read backward and forwards, would make the stories impossible to take in by ear."[4] When Dinesen performed some of her shorter inset tales before audiences, witnesses claim that she had memorized the stories, since her performance did not vary from the written text. Dinesen's tales are so carefully crafted that small variations might have changed the import of the tale entirely.

Dinesen paid considerable attention to the details in her work: "I am really quite extraordinarily conscientious as an artist!—many things I have rewritten fifty times.—Will my potential readers have some sense of this, and will they, in that case, think it has been worth the trouble?" (*KBD,* 1:87). Among these carefully worked-out details might be a gesture or a blush. Several critics have noticed the significance that body language or physiological responses can have in Dinesen's tales.[5] Dinesen may have borrowed this technique from the Icelandic sagas, several of which she had virtually memorized as a child. Although the robust Vikings of the sagas seem to bear little resemblance to Dinesen's refined aristocrats, she nonetheless learned important lessons in narrative reticence from the saga narrators: "The sagas never explain, they tell what has happened and leave it to the reader to decide why. Many of the nineteenth century's greatest authors, from Thackeray to J. P. Jacobsen, stand by the reader's side and keep him strictly on the right path. I can not say whether one method is better than the other, even if I myself prefer the form of the sagas" (*KBD*, 2:406). For example, the saga narrator would not presume to state that King Eirik Bloodaxe was angry with Egil, even though the latter had killed his son. Instead, the saga describes how Eirik flushes dark red when he learns that Egil has come to York, and the reader can make a good guess at his feelings. Dinesen's omniscient storyteller is prepared, on occasion, to enter the mind of her characters, but more often the reader must deduce from a blush or an agitated gesture when something of emotional significance has transpired.

Although Dinesen received little formal education, her knowledge of world literature exceeds that of many scholars, let alone the average reader. Dinesen makes frequent use of allusions to literature and art, and occasionally these asides seem to be merely decorative. Many times, however, the references can be of profound significance. The scholar Bernhard Glienke has brought considerable expertise and energy to bear in tracing the literary allusions in Dinesen's work in *Fatale Präzedenz: Karen Blixens Mythologie* (1986, Fatal precedence: Karen Blixen's mythology). For anyone who can read German and Danish, Glienke's inventory of allusions is invaluable, and it has proven a rich resource for the present study. Explaining all the allusions in Dinesen's works is too vast a task, so that in this book only allusions that have a direct and significant bearing on the interpretation of the tales will be treated.

Allusions can provide a type of compression, enabling Dinesen to invoke an entire literary tradition or thematic context with just a phrase. A reference to Lord Byron brings with it a wealth of associations to Gothic literature, dark romantic heroes, and changing social attitudes about love. Sometimes allusions, when traced to their source, contain clues for deciphering the text. For example, Agnese in "The Roads Round Pisa" makes up an apparently harmless anecdote about Joseph and Potiphar's wife. When compared to the original biblical tale of seduction and betrayal, it seems that the point of Agnese's anecdote is that she, too, has been seduced and betrayed. In some cases, Dinesen uses allusions to transgress the boundaries of her own text and link it with other fictional worlds. Dinesen dreamed at the end of her life of creating a work called *Albondocani,* which was to consist of one hundred independent, but interlocking, tales. The resulting effect would have been a work that, like the *Arabian Nights,* provided an intricate tapestry of life and destiny. This idea must have been alive even at the outset of her literary career, since she makes frequent intertextual references to her own work as well as to world literature. Dinesen's entire oeuvre is connected by a network of allusions, so, in a sense, one might argue that she actually completed *Albondocani*.

Several attempts have been made to place Dinesen in the context of various literary movements, but as yet, there seems to be little consensus. Jørgen Gustava Brandt may have hit the nail on the head when he jokingly described Dinesen as "very old-fashioned, completely up-to-date, and way ahead of her time."[6] Particularly in the early years of her reception, Dinesen was viewed as something of a literary anachronism, since her work so profoundly engages the literature of previous centuries. Dinesen designated some of her tales as gothic, and the influences of romanticism on them are especially strong. In later years, Dinesen playfully enhanced her reputation as a literary anachronism by claiming to be three thousand years old. Nonetheless, her work does not simply replicate the literature of prior ages, but, rather, enters into a dialogue with the literary traditions of the past.

Some critics think of her as unique with no particular connection to trends in contemporary literature. One critic wrote, "Her work shoots up suddenly like a coral reef from unknown depths. No traffic from the great mainland of writing travels to this isle of palms."[7] In the 1930s, the dominant literary trend in Denmark was social realism, and her writing could hardly seem further removed from the Danish mainstream. In Dinesen's view, "Realism is for those with no imagination."[8] She was more interested in private issues of existence than in current events or political views. Dinesen was, however, well-informed about contemporary literature, and her literary choices were made as a response to the world around her.

Modernism began to make its presence strongly felt in Denmark after the Second World War, when Dinesen was already an established artist. Seen from a European perspective, Dinesen has been associated with modernists like Eliot, Yeats, Mann, and Joyce because of her use of symbols and her search for aesthetic order against the background of modernist chaos.[9] Each of these authors relied heavily on myth as an organizing principle. James Frazer's *The Golden Bough* (1922) and the writings of Carl Jung (1875–1961) contributed to that trend in early modernism. Frazier examined common mythic structures in belief systems around the world. Jung drew from similar sources to advance his theories on the collective unconscious. Dinesen's emphasis on the human need for stories, particularly stories from the past, might justify Dinesen's inclusion in this company.

The brand of modernism that came to Denmark in the postwar years reflected a suspicion of literary traditions, fondness of stylistic experimentation, and pessimism. Dinesen struggled with the modernism practiced by young Danish authors, many of whom were guests in her home: Thorkild Bjørnvig, Jørgen Gustava Brandt, Ole Wivel, and others. Dinesen's strong reliance upon past literary tradition set her apart from them. In describing the current generation of 1965, Dinesen lamented to a friend: "But they hate the past and want to break with it; not that one can blame them too much. The near past to them is nothing but a long history of wars, which to them is without interest. It may be the end of a kind of civilization."[10] Dinesen felt that a connection with the past was essential to creating identity. A person with no memory, she observed, does not know who he is (*DG,* 21).

Dinesen was a great proponent of narrative order and found experiments with narrative disorder foreign to her literary tastes. She complained to one interviewer about writers who had taken "a string of scattered impressions and observations and put them together and called it a book."[11] Dinesen also had little patience with the general pessimism that afflicted the younger generation of writers, and especially little with Martin A. Hansen, whose name she turned into the following anagram: "Han er min satan" (He is my Satan). Dinesen told another interviewer: "Here around Rungstedlund, young poets sit in small lovely houses and write about Angst. . . . 'But don't they have a right to?' asked my friend Harry Martinson. . . . 'Who has given you the idea that there should not be dangers in life?' I had to reply. . . . I believe it is natural for mankind to live in the proximity of danger. It has been mankind's lot for thousands of years. One *must* have courage to live."[12] Dinesen felt that the creative powers of imagination could transform the world: "If a sufficiently attractive illusion can be created, the reality automatically follows" (*OMM,* 37).

In recent years, postmodern theory has provided a vocabulary for discussing Dinesen's texts that seems to suit the purpose exceptionally well. Robert Langbaum noted a quality of Dinesen's writing that he called "the gayety of vision," and Dinesen herself referred to it as a sense of fun.[13] The postmodern term would be "playfulness." The complexity and artistry of Dinesen's tales tend to make many readers and critics approach her work with veneration and sobriety. Dinesen despaired when she felt she was being taken too seriously, "I do often intend a comic sense, I love a joke, I love the humorous."[14] She chose Isak as part of her pseudonym because it is Hebrew for "the one who laughs." The attentive reader will come across a number of jokes in Dinesen's writings, some of them quite scandalous. In 1956, the critic Harald Nielsen was offended by a line in "The Poet," in which "old maids grow hyacinths in tall glasses so that they may watch the roots" (*SGT,* 406).[15] A contemporary reader might not think twice about this line, but someone familiar with the Victorian Age's ability to find a chair leg indecent will make the connection between hyacinths and phallic symbols. It is a mistake, however, to assume that Dinesen's own sensibilities were Victorian. She referred to D. H. Lawrence as a Puritan, and stated about herself, "I have very little sense for what people in general find shocking."[16] Two other terms from the postmodern vocabulary that have been applied to Dinesen's work are "disruptive" and "subversive," but it is wise to bear in mind that her disruptive subversions are often quite subtle.

Dinesen's fiction places great emphasis on art, masks, and storytelling, and the weight lies not on the reality behind the work of art, but on the work of art itself. Although this prioritizing of art has many times been described as Dinesen's aestheticism, from a postmodern perspective her work could be described as antireferential. Several characters in Dinesen's tales achieve a sense of identity by creating a story about themselves, and it is irrelevant whether the story is true or not. One Dinesen commentator has observed, "Storytelling recreates and affirms the human process of constructing reality."[17] Dinesen insisted that her tales were fantastic products of her imagination. She explained once in an interview, "The origin of my stories often contains a real fact, which has been lived. But it is only the particle around which the pearl is born. It does not have any significance, we cannot even see it."[18] The mask is more important than the face behind it.

Dinesen grew irritated on occasion when asked about the meaning of her tales, and, especially, whenever critics tried to find meaning outside the text in the author's opinions or life. Her texts employ many elaborate devices to undermine narrative authority: embedding tales within tales, employing unreliable narrators, using pseudonyms, and so forth. Each of these devices is a well-known trick of romantic irony, which postmodernism has cheerfully adopted. Dinesen once cited with approval an Italian reviewer of "The Monkey": "He wrote that it all sounded quite plausible, that a lady should become a monkey— Why couldn't that happen?—but that the author herself exists, *that* we refuse to believe."[19] Another means of evading a sense of narrative authority is to avoid closure, leaving the reader to decide what will happen next. Meaning in a Dinesen text is generated in an interaction between the reader and the text, not laid down clearly and officially by the author. This general evasiveness and playfulness are all qualities of the postmodern.

The critic Grethe Rostbøll has called Isak Dinesen postmodern because of a similarity between Dinesen's approach to dualisms and Jacques Derrida's thinking on the same issues.[20] Derrida argues that dualisms like man/woman have traditionally implied a power hierarchy, in which one is implicitly better than the other. Both Derrida and Dinesen challenge such power hierarchies. Dinesen's work is riddled with dualisms: man/woman, rich/poor, north/south, wild/domestic, master/servant, God/Devil, comedy/tragedy, and so on. The dynamic interaction of opposites is central to Dinesen's texts. In *Shadows on the Grass,* Dinesen writes, "Two homogeneous units will never be capable of forming a whole, or their whole at its best will remain barren. Man and woman become one, a physically and spiritually creative Unity, by virtue of their dissimilarity. A hook and an eye are a Unity, a fastening; but with two hooks you can do nothing" (*OA,* 378). Although Dinesen looks for "Unity," or a type of reconciliation, between opposites, it is not at the cost of compromising the integrity and identity of either part of the dualism. In most cases, Dinesen does not prioritize one part of the dualism over the other. Both are equally necessary. Occasionally, however, Dinesen does allow her personal biases to shine through, as in the case of aristocrat/bourgeois. Dinesen clearly favors the former over the latter.

An important dualism that Dinesen alludes to frequently in her work is that of the Apollonian/Dionysian. Nietzsche described these two elements and their relationship to art in *The Birth of Tragedy* (1872). The god Apollo represents order, boundaries, logic, and rationality. Dionysus, the god of wine, represents intoxication, chaos, passion, and inspiration. A work of art dominated by the Apollonian element will be sterile, overemphasizing structure and form. A totally Dionysian work will contain an overabundance of emotional impact but cannot be comprehended. The best art, argues Nietzsche, contains both elements. Dinesen works this theme into several of her texts. For example, it is said of the Cardinal in "The Deluge at Norderney," "To his great power of imagination he joined a deep love of law and order" (*SGT,* 6). This is a sign that the Cardinal possesses considerable artistic powers. In "The Cloak," Angelo, overwhelmed by his passion for his master's wife, goes to see a statue of Dionysus. He has been thrown out of balance by the Dionysian and must regain contact with the Apollonian before he can become a great artist. Although Dinesen may have a weak spot for the Dionysian ("Dinesen" is etymologically related to "Dionysus"), she acknowledges the necessity of both elements.[21]

After reading several stories by Dinesen, one sees certain character types emerging. They are by no means carbon copies of one another but bear a distinct family resemblance. These types become another connective element in Dinesen's writings, enabling the reader to follow themes from one story to another. The newcomer to Dinesen's fiction would do well to keep an eye out for these characters, so, a brief description of some of the most common character types may be useful. The list includes—but is not limited to—the aristocrat, the bourgeois, the artist, the Diana, the witch, the caryatid, and the blossom.

Dinesen's apparent fondness for aristocrats was partly responsible for her initial negative reception in Social-Democratic Denmark, but Dinesen's endorsement of the aristocrat was not necessarily a political move. Robert Langbaum has argued, "It is because their cause is so hopeless in a political sense that she can use their obsolete virtues as a stance from which to understand and criticize modern values."[22] Others have claimed that being an aristocrat in Dinesen's world is more a state of mind than a class distinction, and someone like Emmanuelson in *Out of Africa* can behave like an aristocrat even though he is a penniless unemployed actor. The aristocrat is characterized by fearlessness, style, wildness, imagination, risk-taking, a respect for tradition and culture, and a sense of honor peculiar to the category. Malin Nat-og-Dag of "The Deluge at Norderney" is an excellent representative of the aristocrat. She is proud of her family name and traditions, does not fear dying in a hayloft, upholds a sense of style and decorum even under adverse circumstances, and has prodigious powers of imagination. The aristocratic code of honor is displayed in "The Pearls," where Alexander is willing to fight and die for his country but avoids paying his tailor. The Old Lord of "Sorrow-Acre" must keep his word of honor even if it costs a woman her life.

The opposite of the aristocrat is the bourgeois. If an aristocrat has money, he or she has inherited it. The bourgeois have earned their money through their own skills. Aristocrats are frequently penniless, whereas the bourgeois person may have money in abundance but is afraid of losing it. The bourgeois values security, stability, material goods, domesticity, convention, and morality. There are few major Dinesen characters who are bourgeois, so the bourgeois point of view is often presented by minor characters. The primary task of the bourgeois in Dinesen's tales is to disapprove of the aristocrat. Pastor Rosenquist in "The Monkey" is a spokesperson for bourgeois values; hence, he is appalled by the sudden fortuitous change in the old Count's circumstances. Stability and a clear system of punishment and reward are to be preferred. Peter Skov in "The Pearls" speaks disapprovingly of a lavish gift given as a grand gesture by one who could not afford it. The bourgeois point of view, which Dinesen took to be the dominant view of her age, is rarely seen in a positive light.

The artist has a great deal in common with the aristocrat, and the two categories often overlap. The artist nevertheless transcends class and can be found in any station of life. Sacrifices may be demanded of the artist: a nose, both feet, a few fingers, a family, or a voice. The artist is driven by the artistic impulse. For the sake of art or the artistic gesture, the artist is willing to spend ten thousand francs or give away a priceless pearl and may take a life or give his or her own. The medium of the artist can be painting, sculpture, food, singing, acting, dancing, or storytelling, but the artist's canvas can just as easily be life itself. Both Pellegrina from "The Dreamers" and Cardinal Salviati from the *Albondocani* suite in *Last Tales* take to manipulating artistically the destinies of others. Manipulating destiny is a risky undertaking that may well fail, as Councillor Mathiesen's fate in "The Poet" illustrates. The ultimate artist in Dinesen's writing is God. In

Seven Gothic Tales, God is presented metaphorically as the puppet master who pulls the strings of destiny in order coax his human puppets into presenting a satisfying performance. The Book of Job is one of the most frequently invoked allusions in Dinesen's work. Job asks the standard question of theodicy, "Why do bad things happen to good people?" or in other words, "Why me?" God responds with a catalogue of his achievements as Creator. God is an artist and good and bad are aesthetically necessary. The human artist by virtue of her or his artistic talent possesses greater insight into the workings of the divine artist than other more mundane mortals.

The Diana, the witch, the caryatid, and the blossom are all types of female characters in Dinesen's fiction that have been commented on by different critics at various times, and there has not always been consensus about them.[23] These character types do not cover all women in Dinesen's fiction. These categories are bound by class and pertain primarily to the women of the affluent bourgeoisie and the aristocracy. These designations are rather fluid and can sometimes represent different stages in one woman's life. Childerique of "The Caryatids" goes through all four, and, in fact, category-shifting in general is common among female characters.

The Diana takes her name from the goddess of the hunt in Greek mythology. Diana was a chaste goddess who had Actaeon torn apart by his own hounds for daring to spy upon her while she was taking a bath. She is also associated with the moon. In Dinesen's fiction, the Diana is often a tomboy who enjoys traditionally masculine sports like the hunt. She values her independence and chastity and is occasionally forced to defend herself from masculine intrusions. The figure is associated with strength, power, and, at times, innocence. The Diana figures are not particularly interested in being women and carry a phallic bow and arrow. Although Dianas abound in Dinesen's tales, perhaps the best example is—despite her name—Athena from "The Monkey." Athena is large and strong, and she enjoys hunting and riding. She is willing to fight to retain her independence, as Boris discovers at the cost of his two front teeth. In representing a stage along life's way, Dianas are most commonly adolescent girls who resist coming of age and marrying. Dinesen shows a great deal of sympathy for the Diana in her tales, and she once wrote to her sister, "All my life I have cared more for Diana than Venus; I am both more attracted to her type of beauty, as I have seen it portrayed in statues and paintings, and also I myself would prefer Diana's life to that of Venus, however many rose gardens and dove-drawn coaches she might have" (*LA,* 382).

In her essay "Daguerrotypes," Dinesen described the witch as a woman who "existed independently of a man and had her own center of gravity" (*DG,* 33). Whereas the Diana is commonly on the defensive against the world, the witch is an aggressor. Unlike the Diana, the witch may be sexually active, and so being, can be seen as threatening by men. She has her own sources of power, which are symbolized by the phallic broomstick. Many men fear her. During Malin Nat-og-Dag's life, she moves from being a fanatical Diana to being a witch. Her role as a sexual predator is purely imaginary, but disturbing enough to make society blunt its sense of jeopardy by considering her mad. Her name and her fortune make Malin beholden to no man. Unlike the other categories, witches can transcend the restriction of class, as evidenced by Simkie, the gypsy in "Caryatids, an Unfinished Tale." Susan Hardy Aiken has described the witch as "a figure of subversive female potency and creativity whose craft was analogous to that of the woman writer."[24] Dinesen enjoyed enacting the role of witch in her later years.

The Diana and the witch resist the expectations of patriarchy. The caryatid and the blossom work within that system of expectations. The image of the caryatid derives originally from Greek architecture, where female figures were used as pillars to hold up the roofs of great buildings. The caryatid has been trained to uphold patriarchy and tradition. If she is married, the caryatid will focus her energy on producing a male heir to ensure the continuance of the family name. If she is not, the caryatid will dedicate herself to supporting the memory of the male heir and the honor of the family, as in the cases of Fanny and Eliza in "The Supper at Elsinore" or Martine and Philippa in "Babette's Feast." The personal cost of being a caryatid can be great. The original caryatids are, after all, made out of stone. Caryatids are either frigid or sexually dissatisfied. They subordinate their entire lives to maintaining patriarchy.

Although the role of caryatid did not appeal to Dinesen personally, she nonetheless had respect for the type. In an interview, Dinesen once pointed to a family album that covered her family history for three hundred years. She commented, "But it only tells us about the men. Their deeds and lives are described painstakingly with all the details we can muster. There is nothing about the women, only a dry comment about how this man married this or that woman. But if I look at the family letters and whatever else we have of documents, I find the women to be extraordinarily powerful forces behind the work of the men."[25] Dinesen's tales go far in filling the silence about the role of women in previous generations.

At a superficial glance, the blossom may appear identical to the caryatid. The blossom is aware of the rules of patriarchy and gives the appearance of observing them. Like the caryatid, she can be married and have borne children to carry on the family line. The difference lies in the blossom's taste for subversion. The type is referred to as a blossom because so many of these women are compared to flowers and are paragons of feminine beauty. Unlike the caryatid, blossoms are capable of erotic love, and this capacity is indicated by their tendency to blush. A blossom obtains the object of her desire by transgressing the rules of patriarchy, even while seeming to maintain them. Ulrikke in "A Country Tale" is a blossom. She is in love with Eitel and has even borne him a daughter, but she is married to an old man on the neighboring estate. Although meant to be sacrificed to the life of a caryatid, Ulrikke has found a way to personal fulfillment by disregarding patriarchy's obsession with legitimacy. The blossom subverts patriarchy from within, but she does not resort to open rebellion like the Diana or the witch. The figure of the blossom perhaps stems from a hope that some of the caryatids listed in the family trees managed to have a little fun.

This introduction far from exhausts all of the themes that run throughout Dinesen's work. Many more will be dealt with as they arise in the individual analyses. A thorough understanding of Isak Dinesen will involve close readings of individual texts combined with an appreciation of the themes and motifs that connect the entire body of work. Understanding Isak Dinesen is an ongoing process, not a task that can be completed. Part of the pleasure of reading Isak Dinesen is the prospect of stumbling across something new. Her tales can profitably be read over and over again.

CHAPTER 2

Seven Gothic Tales

Isak Dinesen was forty-nine when *Seven Gothic Tales* appeared in 1934. She had a wealth of life experience behind her, and the sophistication and maturity of her English-language debut is striking. Dinesen often said that if she had not lost the farm in Africa, she would never have become a writer. She had published a few tales in Danish journals under the name Osceola, but for many, *Seven Gothic Tales* represents the beginning of Isak Dinesen's literary career. When Isak Dinesen left Africa in 1931, she had already completed "The Roads Round Pisa" and "The Monkey." The other five tales were finished in Denmark. Originally, Dinesen intended to publish nine tales under the title *Tales of Nozdref's Cook*. Nozdref's Cook is a character out of Gogol's *Dead Souls* (1842). In the Danish edition of *Seven Gothic Tales,* Baron von Brackel notes that the modern world appears to be created the way "Nozdref's Cook made soup—a little pepper, salt, and herbs, whatever was around—and 'some flavor or another will come out of it'" (*MU,* 1:99). Evidently, Dinesen decided against comparing her collection to a culinary hodgepodge. The original nine tales would have included "The Caryatids, an Unfinished Tale," and "Carnival," but Dinesen felt that the contemporary references in "Carnival" would disturb the tone of the volume. "The Caryatids" was saved for later publication.

Instead of this being a "hodgepodge," there is reason to think that Dinesen took great pains over the composition of the collection as a whole. Her American publisher, Robert Haas, convinced Dinesen to change the order of the tales from what she had originally proposed. Dinesen's feelings about the order of the stories was strong enough that when given the opportunity, she saw to it that the British and Danish editions of the tales were ordered according to her original concept:

USA	England
Deluge at Norderney	The Roads Round Pisa
The Old Chevalier	The Old Chevalier
The Monkey	The Monkey
The Roads Round Pisa	Deluge at Norderney

The Supper at Elsinore	The Supper at Elsinore
The Dreamers	The Dreamers
The Poet	The Poet

Ole Wivel has pointed out that the original order causes the collection in Denmark and in England to be framed by two stories involving Augustus von Schimmelman.[1] "Roads Round Pisa" was one of the first stories written for the volume and contains reflections upon destiny and art that perhaps were meant to provide a hint about how the rest of the tales in the book should be taken. There is something of a mirroring effect in "The Roads Round Pisa." The beginning and the end of the tale resemble each other. If the original order of the tales is maintained, then this same sort of mirroring occurs in the collection as a whole, with the presence of Augustus von Schimmelman at the end, pointing back to the beginning of the collection. Judging from Robert Haas's letters, "The Deluge at Norderney" was the American publisher's personal favorite, so he chose to begin the volume with a tale that had grabbed his attention.

In part, Dinesen wrote *Seven Gothic Tales* in English for economic reasons, since the English-language book market is much larger than the Danish. Dinesen also said she chose to write in English because she felt comfortable expressing herself in that language after seventeen years in Kenya. In addition, Dinesen felt that the English public would be more sympathetic to her tales, since, in her view, the English-speaking countries possessed a stronger tradition of fantastic literature than Denmark. In 1923, Dinesen wrote to her mother about the American writer James Branch Cabell and his novels *Jurgen* (1919) and *The Cream of the Jest* (1917) which she characterized as "full of fantasy, and all this has made me wonder whether a new direction in literature is about to develop, making use of fantasy" (*LA,* 164). In England, she pointed to Lewis Carroll's *Alice's Adventures in Wonderland* (1865) and David Garnett's *Lady into Fox* (1923) as examples of fantastic literature.[2] As far as her Danish audience was concerned, Dinesen felt, "We have few or no fantastic books here at home. We have Ingemann's *The Sphinx* and Heiberg's *Christmas Jests and New Year's Fun,* but who remembers them? I was afraid that people, after reading my book, would ask: 'What is the meaning of what you write?' There is no meaning, and there should not be a meaning. It is dream. Fantasy!"[3]

Dinesen eventually decided to publish *Seven Gothic Tales* in Danish, but after auditioning several translators she decided to recast the book into Danish herself. The Danish edition is not, strictly speaking, a translation, since Dinesen has allowed herself to "improve" some of the tales in Danish. Many of the changes are minor, but some are substantial. Anyone interested in a detailed comparison of the English and Danish versions should consult Elias Breds-dorff's essay on the subject.[4]

Dinesen's reception in the United States was enthusiastic beyond all expectation. The United States was in the grip of the Great Depression, and one American reviewer began by quoting Dinesen's "The Poet": "When one is tied down heavily enough to an existence of care, it becomes pleasant to think of careless times and people" (*SGT,* 359).[5] The American reviewers embraced the imaginative qualities of the book: "*Seven Gothic Tales* has burst upon us from a gray literary sky."[6] It may be worthy of note that 1934 was also the year *King Kong* was released in theaters. Other films released in the 1930s include *Frankenstein* (1931), *The Mummy* (1932), and *Lost Horizons* (1937). Exotic locations and strange happenings were welcome because they could remove the reader from the harsh realities of the everyday. British reviews were also warm, "This belongs to the company of the world's great books."[7] Even so, one English reviewer found the style "pompous."[8]

Dinesen's misgivings about how the Danish audience would receive her book proved to be well founded. The predominant literary mode in Denmark was social realism. The public debate of contemporary social issues had not raged as strongly since the days when Georg Brandes called the Modern Breakthrough into being in the 1870's. Dinesen's imaginative tales set in the previous century were quite different from what most Danes were reading. Svend Borberg described Dinesen as a flamingo-red orchid in a cabbage patch, and Swedish reviewer Mario Grut compared her to "a crane in a dance with sparrows."[9] The most notorious of the Danish reviews accused Dinesen of "snobbism, the fantastic, and perversity."[10] The negative Danish reviews upset Dinesen. Svend Borberg, with a good dose of irony, suggested one reason for Dinesen's being subjected to such a beating by the Danish critics: "It was naturally very cheeky, not to say brash, of Isak Dinesen—alias Baroness Karen Blixen—to conquer the world first with her book *Seven Gothic Tales* and then come to Denmark with it. As a Danish author she should have felt obligated to ask here at home first if she was worth anything."[11] This was simply the beginning of an uneasy relationship between Dinesen and her Danish public that would last throughout her career. Even so, in 1999, the readers of the large Danish daily newspaper *Politiken* voted *Seven Gothic Tales* to be the third most important Danish work of the twentieth century.

The choice of *Seven Gothic Tales* as the title for the English work and *Syv fantastiske Fortællinger* (Seven fantastic tales) as that of the Danish is the result of a canny assessment of her potential audiences and the literary traditions with which they might be familiar. "Gothic" appeals, of course, to the English Gothic and "fantastic" is a word that draws one's thoughts towards the German romantic, as in *Fantasiestücke in Callots Manier* (1814–15, Fantasy pieces in the manner of Callot) by E. T. A. Hoffmann. In a Danish interview, Dinesen called *Seven Gothic Tales* a nonsense book: "I don't know another word for books in which all sorts of fantastic things happen. You probably know Hoffmann's Tales? It is something of the same sort, but not really the same."[12] With some reason, Dinesen felt her Danish interviewer would be more familiar with a reference to German romanticism, rather than the English Gothic. When asked why she chose the phrase "Gothic Tales," Dinesen answered, "Because in England it places the stories in time and implies something that both has an elevated tone and can erupt into jests and mockery, into devilry and mystery."[13] Both English and German traditions left their mark on Dinesen's writing, as she explained to her friend Bent Mohn: "I know more about the English 'Gothic' than German romanticism, but there are also works in that [tradition] which have meant a lot to me" (*KBD*, 1:500).

In English, the term "Gothic" has several associations, and Dinesen's critics have found a use for a number of them from time to time. The Goths were Germanic barbarians who attacked the Roman Empire. With reference to the sometimes subversive qualities of Dinesen's texts, Susan Hardy Aiken playfully suggests that Dinesen might be considered "a 'barbarous' marginal force that continually imperils the [traditional] center."[14] The Gothic also refers to an elaborate type of medieval architecture, and some critics have found similarities between the architecture of a Gothic cathedral and the complex construction of Dinesen's narratives: "The architecture of the . . . stories permitted the author to stop, at any moment, and add on a flying buttress or a whole new wing."[15] Dinesen herself specified, however: "I didn't mean the real Gothic, but the imitation of the Gothic, the Romantic age of Byron, the age of that man—what was his name?—who built Strawberry Hill, the age of the Gothic revival."[16]

The period of the English Gothic, roughly located between 1790 and 1830, came close on the heels of the Age of Reason. Many of the notable contributors to the Gothic were women: Ann Radcliffe, Mary Shelley, and the Brontë sisters. Dangerous and irrational forces seem to be at large in the Gothic, no doubt as a protest against the rationality of the era that preceded it. The Gothic is characterized by an interest in the past and exotic locations. Eric Johannesson has speculated, along with others, that the motive behind such a change in scene is to "liberate the imagination from the fetters which too familiar an environment imposes upon it."[17] The typical Gothic hero is a man with a secret past who rejects the moral claims of society—a Byronic rebel. All of these features are familiar elements in Dinesen's writing.

Sibyl James has written an important essay on Dinesen's relationship to the Gothic, in which she notes some significant points upon which Dinesen differs from the traditional English Gothic.[18] Gothic narrators often resort to preachiness. Evil villains assault the innocent heroine's virtue, but society's conventional morality is ultimately affirmed. Dinesen, on the contrary, is anything but preachy, and her villains are likely to be the conventionally minded. The Gothic usually resolves the supernatural into the natural: there is not a ghost, but a madwoman in Rochester's attic; Frankenstein animates his monster with galvanic energy, a scientifically acceptable principle at the time. Dinesen does not worry about confining herself to the plausible: prioresses turn into monkeys and vice versa. Dinesen does not use her supernatural effects to scare her readers, which was one of the main projects of the Gothic. The supernatural for Dinesen simply represents freedom of the imagination.

The styles of the English Gothic and German romanticism overlap a great deal. Both relish the fantastic. The Gothic ruin that engages the spectator's imagination finds its counterpart in the romantic textual fragment. The English Gothic and German romanticism share a common source of inspiration in *The Arabian Nights* and Boccaccio's *Decameron* (1353). German romantic authors spent a good deal of time theorizing about a short-story art form they called the *Novelle* (novella), developed on the model of Boccaccio's tales. According to Goethe, the novella should describe an extraordinary event, and August Schlegel thought the story should contain a distinct turning point. In general, plot in the novella is more important than character. E. T. A. Hoffmann and Adelbert von Chamisso, two writers deeply admired by Dinesen, are among the foremost creators of German novellas. Dinesen has learned a few tricks from her favorites.

Peter Schlehmihl, a character from a famous tale by Chamisso, makes a brief appearance in Hoffmann's "A New Year's Eve Adventure." In much the same way, the fictional Augustus von Schimmelman would surface in Dinesen's *Out of Africa,* or Henrik Ibsen would make a cameo appearance in "The Pearls." "Real" and "imaginary" worlds become linked, and the dividing line is blurred.

German romantic writers were also fond of irony and literary masks. Hoffmann's "Don Juan" is allegedly written by a traveling music enthusiast. Adopting a literary mask enables the author to relinquish narrative authority and forces the reader to assess the bias of the narrative. The narrative says one thing but may imply another, and the reader must be attentive to catch the nuances. This effect, which engages the participation of the reader in deciphering the text, is known as romantic irony.

Few authors do romantic irony better than Dinesen's countryman, Søren Kierkegaard. In *Either/Or* (1843), Kierkegaard, writing under the pseudonym of

Victor Eremita, claims to have found two manuscripts in a desk, and he deduces they are written by two different people, whom he calls "A" and "B." Among "A's" papers there is another text called "The Diary of a Seducer;" which may or may not be written by "A" under the name Johannes. Similarly, Karen Blixen, writing under her pseudonym Isak Dinesen, nestles tales within tales within tales. The reader is consistently thwarted in her or his attempt to locate an ultimate voice of authority. Dinesen took such great pains to distance herself from the events in her tales that she was annoyed by the prospect of readers asking, "Did you really mean it? . . . Have you experienced this yourself?"[19] These narrative connections between Kierkegaard and Dinesen have been examined at length in an essay by Eric Johannesson.[20]

"The Deluge at Norderney"

The first paragraph of "The Deluge at Norderney" skillfully sets the stage for this tale and the tales that follow. Perhaps this is why Robert Haas chose to begin the American edition with it. Dinesen describes "the romantic spirit of the age, which delighted in ruins, ghosts, and lunatics," that stood in contrast to what had delighted the Age of Reason: "the harmony of a philosophic system" (*SGT,* 1). The Danish edition states further, "the romantic age found its harmony in contrasts" (*MU,* 1:249). The interplay of contrasts is a theme that will be explored throughout the story. One such contrast touched upon at the outset of the tale is the difference in the lots of men and women in the upper class of 1835. Old gentlemen partake of "political and dynastic discussions" (*SGT,* 2). These men control society and are concerned with the continuance of the male line and the family name. Their wives "become one with nature" and "gaze straight up at the full moon" (*SGT,* 2). The women, who appear to be more greatly moved by the forces of nature, contain the possibility of transgression. Should they give in to nature and have an affair in that "lonely hollow in the downs," the dynastic plans of the old gentlemen will be disrupted.

Susan Hardy Aiken has suggested that the deluge that follows dissolves the boundaries between contrasts: "The deluge is a countercreation, a devolution that undoes the order of hierarchical oppositions—heaven and earth, sea and dry land, day and night (and implicitly 'male and female')."[21] The title's nod at the biblical deluge points to the themes of transition and impermanence. In 1835, European history has reached a pivotal point: old ways are giving way to the modern. The Cardinal/Kasparson and Malin Nat-og-Dag discuss the tragic/heroic fate of the vanishing aristocracy at great length. According to Dinesen's original concept, this story should be placed in the dead center of the collection. As such, it would form a transition from the somewhat lighter tone of the earlier tales ("Roads Round Pisa," "The Old Chevalier," and "The Monkey") to the darker tone of the subsequent stories ("The Supper at Elsinore," "The Dreamers," "The Poet"). On several levels, "The Deluge at Norderney" signals change and the suspension of normal boundaries: anything can happen.

The flood leads to the assembly of the four main characters in a hayloft to spend the hours until dawn (and rescue), conversing and telling stories. This framework for the telling of stories is classic in many respects. The baroness in Goethe's *Conversations of German Emigrants* (1795) insists that stories should show they are being told "in good society." Scheherazade told her tales to the court of the caliph and the storytellers of the *Decameron* were all noble ladies and gentlemen. Malin Nat-og-Dag's maid is excluded from the circle of the hayloft because her presence would affect the tone of the stories to be told. In both *The Arabian Nights* and the *Decameron,* the storytellers are spinning their tales in order to keep death at bay. Scheherazade is threatened with execution if her tales fail to intrigue the caliph enough to let her live another day, and the ladies and gentlemen of the *Decameron* are fleeing a plague in Florence. Death surely awaits in the shadows of the hayloft of Norderney and may take center stage at any time "like . . . some fine Italian tenor" (*SGT,* 16).

The composition of the party in the loft is in many respects full of contrasts, and yet symmetrical. There are two young people and two old, two women and two men. The young man dislikes being an object of scrutiny; the young woman desires to be seen. The old man is an ex-gigolo pretending to be a cardinal; his counterpart is an old maid of strictest virtue imagining herself to be a harlot. The two women are fiercely proud of their noble birth; the two men are apparently bastards stemming from the lower rungs of society. All four residents of the hayloft are at first glance sexually "innocent," Jonathan and Calypso because of their youth, the Cardinal and Malin Nat-og-Dag by choice. The Cardinal is a saint; Malin takes her name from a French word for the devil (*le malin*). "Malin" is also the Swedish counterpart to the Danish "Malen," a shortened form of "Magdalene."[22] This allusion to the sainted prostitute of the Bible suits the mixed character of Malin Nat-og-Dag.

When they find themselves alone in the loft, "as if they had been four marionettes, pulled by the same wire, the four people turned their faces to one another" (*SGT,* 13). If, as originally planned by Dinesen, *Seven Gothic Tales* had begun with "Roads Round Pisa," which contains an important reference to a marionette play, this line might have seemed more significant than it does taken alone. These characters are in the hands of destiny. They must try to keep the ideas of the divine author clear and play their roles to the utmost. The four are also engaged in a masquerade in which masks are both created and laid aside: "Not by the face shall the man be known, but by the mask" (*SGT,* 75). The skill that goes into the creation of a mask can only be appreciated if we get a glimpse at what lies behind it.

Jonathan Mærsk is the first who is called upon to tell the story of his life. Jonathan is young and has been much confused by life. Arranging his experiences into a story, a work of art, will prove therapeutic for him: "Perhaps I shall understand it all better when I can, at last, give words to it" (*SGT,* 28). Jonathan's tale is of a fall from innocence. He is raised in "the garden of Assens" by the skipper Clement Mærsk and his wife, Magdalena. Skipper Mærsk represents the sea and his wife the earth. Both manage to live in harmony with their attentions focused on tending either the cargo of a ship or the plants, flowers, and insects of the world. They have little need of or interest in money or in "making things happen." Rasmus Petersen, Jonathan's "friend" plays the role of the snake in this garden, by introducing him to the world of society and self-consciousness. When Jonathan learns that he may be the illegitimate child of the Baron Gersdorff and that society only cares about him because of his social position, he experiences his fall from innocence: "I thought of the garden of Assens, but it was closed to me forever. Once you have eaten of the tree of knowledge, and have seen yourself, gardens close themselves to you. You become a person of fashion, even as did Adam and Eve when they began to occupy themselves with their appearance" (*SGT,* 35).

Jonathan sinks into a deep melancholy, and his behavior, against his will, begins to emulate a series of literary clichés. Jonathan earns the nickname Timon of Assens, a reference to the title character of Shakespeare's *Timon of Athens,* who is a notorious misanthrope. The Baron Gersdorff seeks to make him "the glass of fashion, and the mold of form," which is a description of Hamlet taken from act 3, scene 1. When Jonathan is contemplating suicide, he falls into another literary/romantic trend. After the publication of Goethe's *The Sorrows of Young Werther* (1774), suicide pacts became fashionable. The German author Heinrich von Kleist committed suicide together with Henriette Vogel in 1811. Thus Jonathan cannot even commit suicide without his last moan becoming *"le dernier cri"* (literally "the last moan" and idiomatically "the latest fashion") (*SGT,* 38). Skipper Mærsk sends Jonathan to be cured by salt water, and as the flood waters continue to rise, Jonathan may be cured of his despair once and for all in a manner not intended by his father. The Bath at Norderney becomes, to borrow a pun from Aiken, Jonathan's last resort.[23]

There is an unresolved mystery at the heart of Jonathan's story: is he Baron Gersdorff's son or isn't he? The Baron offers Jonathan "a finder's fee for the summer of 1814," which suggests that this is when he would have met Jonathan's mother (*SGT,* 30). Since Jonathan's mother was a sailor's wife, she would have often been left alone and she could have encountered the Baron because of their common love of plants. The fact that Jonathan's mother is named Magdalena, after a biblical woman of experience, may indicate that she does have something of a past. An argument against the Baron's paternity is that Malin Nat-og-Dag apparently does not believe in it. When she claims Calypso as her daughter, it is because "I am making her, as much as my old friend Baron Gersdorff ever made you" (*SGT,* 40). In other words, the bond is one of imagination, not biology.

One of the striking aspects of this question is that Jonathan's legal father, Skipper Mærsk, does not care about Jonathan's true paternity: "Leave the women's business alone. . . . Here you are, Jonathan, a seaworthy ship, whoever built you" (*SGT,* 38). This is not the only unconventional response of Skipper Mærsk, who also reburies a pirate's treasure for exercise. Mærsk's association with the sea has left him free of the values cherished by society and represented by Baron Gersdorff. The two fathers stand in stark contrast to each other. Skipper Mærsk wants nothing but happiness for his son. The Baron Gersdorff wants to see himself in his son, to be resurrected in him, hence his choice of new name for Jonathan: De Résurrection. Despite being a man of fashion, Baron Gersdorff has shown a certain lack of imagination in creating himself. As a writer, he is only able to imitate other writers. The Baron wants Jonathan to show him the original Baron Gersdorff, but all he gets is a series of reflections from other sources, as Jonathan's behavior "after the Fall" indicates. Jonathan is drawn into the self-conscious, self-reflective circle of the Baron, from which he can see no release. The uncertainty of Jonathan's paternity is essential because it leaves open to him the possibility of escape.

Malin Nat-og-Dag quickly perceives the contrast and the symmetry of Jonathan's fate when compared to that of Calypso. As a male, Jonathan has been raised with a sense of self-evident authority; thus, he compares himself to God when describing his experiences: "This was, I thought, what Lucifer had really done to God: he had looked at him, and had made the Lord feel that he himself was being judged by a critic" (*SGT,* 34). Jonathan does not care much for the sensation of being weighed, judged, and criticized. Malin replies to this sentiment, "You talk, Timon, of Lucifer offending God by looking at him to see what he was like. That shows that you worship a male deity. A goddess would ask her worshiper first of all: 'How am I looking?'" (*SGT,* 45). The fate of male and female are quite different in this society. A woman's worth is closely linked with her appearance and her validation by the male gaze. She is raised to be an ornament and to be looked at. The story that Malin tells about Calypso serves as a contrast to Jonathan's tale and is about the consequences of not being seen at all. Further, Calypso's story is a tale of contrasts—male/female, Dionysian/Apollonian—that have been thrown out of balance.

Count August von Platen-Hallermünde (1796–1835) is an actual German poet, who was known to have been homosexual. Beyond this, the tale is pure fantasy. Dinesen uses the Count as a representative of extreme self-absorption. Robert Langbaum succinctly characterizes the Count's condition as "the inability of a mind to love anything beyond its own diagrammatic imprint upon the external world. To love women and wild animals, you have to believe in the concrete reality of objects other than the self."[24] The Count gives himself up to a monoculture based upon his own tastes. He surrounds himself with men—no female creatures of any kind are welcome within the walls of the enclave. He engages in mathematics and philosophy, academic disciplines traditionally associated with male logic. He is taken as "an Apollo himself," a representative of order (*SGT,* 49). His castle is meant to invoke the times of the Crusades, an age in which women were left behind and men rode off to impose their worldview on the Holy Land and to exterminate those who thought differently. This exaggerated male culture denies the value of anything feminine or different, and in this atmosphere, Calypso is raised. The result for her is, understandably, a sense of annihilation and worthlessness.

Despite the message of her environment, it is clear that Calypso possesses great power, a fact Malin underscores by comparing her to an assortment of mythic women. Calypso is the name of a nymph who holds Odysseus captive to her charms for seven years. Calypso is compared to Psyche, a woman so lovely she made Venus jealous. She is Ceres, the goddess of nature's generative power, who has borrowed a lightning bolt from Jove. She is Judith, the Jewish heroine who defeats an army with both her personal charms and a sword. By altering the personal pronoun in Paul Gerhardt's hymn—"Against me [God] who can stand?"—Calypso assumes the role of God (*SGT,* 50). To be saved, Calypso must be brought to a realization of the power within her.

Calypso believes in her own worthlessness and is prepared to cut off her breasts in order to become part of the male culture that has denigrated her. On her way to carrying out her purpose, Calypso finds herself in a special place, which Aiken describes as "a concealed, subversive feminine space, the grandmother's— literally, Great Mother's—womb/room."[25] In this place, she finds a painting that teaches her what her environment has concealed: her body is not disgusting, but beautiful; young women are to be admired, not shunned. The mirror in the room, the glance of the fauns and satyrs, enables her to see herself for the first time. The values she has learned are overturned in this place: "The god Dionysos himself, who was present, looked her, laughingly, straight into the eyes" (*SGT,* 48). This validating glance makes Calypso conscious of her own power and robs the Count of his. When she looks upon him again, he has become "a poor little doll stuffed with sawdust, a caricature of a skull" (*SGT,* 49).

Not all critics have interpreted Calypso's epiphany in front of the mirror positively. Marilyn Johns Blackwell suggests that Calypso's experience results in "an acknowledgment that woman's function is purely sexual, that the roles available to her to play out are severely delimited, that she is an object to men, and that the transforming gaze comes not from God, but from males, who function as surrogate deities in women's lives."[26] In other words, Calypso's realizations only result in her submission to her male-defined role in society. According to Aiken's interpretation, however, Calypso has discovered her own female subjectivity, the ability to create herself. As Aiken see it, "Calypso's jubilant self-recognition leads not to fragmentation, alienation, and acceptance of the law of the father as the price of identity, but to 'a great harmony' . . . and a repudiation of that law."[27] Calypso is able to overcome the burdens her uncle has placed upon her by denying her value and to choose her destiny for herself. If her choice of marriage to Jonathan seems to some fairly traditional, it is nonetheless her choice and considerably better than self-mutilation.

Jonathan's story contains the unresolved mystery of his paternity, and Calypso's tale raises the question of whether these events took place at all. Just as Jonathan tried to understand himself by making his life into a story, Malin attempts to perform the same service for Calypso by showing her herself in a tale. Malin appears to be successful: "But still the story, correct or not, was to the heroine herself a symbol, a dressed-up image of what she had in reality gone through, and she acknowledged it by her clear deep glance at the woman" (*SGT,* 46). A mirroring effect is taking place. In Malin's tale, Calypso gazes into a mirror to find herself reflected in a painting, a work of art. In the loft, Calypso again sees herself reflected in a work of art, Malin's tale. Through this hall of mirrors the truth has been communicated, even if it has nothing to do with the facts.

With her considerable powers of imagination, Malin is able to create a harmony out of the contrasting destinies of the two young people. Her tale teaches Jonathan that there are worse martyrdoms than being scrutinized. The Count's extreme self-absorption might have served as a cautionary tale to young Jonathan, who has been happiest in his life when he was not thinking of himself. Malin offers him a path back to the garden of Assens, where his pleasant task was to look after things. He will now look after Calypso, and the Baron's wealth and title will only assist him in that task. Calypso's needs will be met by becoming the focus of Jonathan's attentions. The solution reconciles them both to their destinies:

> "Oh Jonathan," said Miss Malin, "are you going to thank the Baron, upon your knees, that he took the trouble about you?"
>
> "Yes, Madame," said the young man.
>
> "And you, Calypso," she asked the girl, "do you want him to look at you forever and ever?"
>
> "Yes," said the girl. (*SGT,* 52)

This exchange unites the two characters quite as much as the ceremony which the Cardinal invents.

The figure of the Cardinal/Kasparson is another example of contrasts that form a unity. One is an aristocratic man of God, the other an actor of uncertain origins, and yet they form a sort of partnership. The duo is compared to Don Quixote and Sancho Panza, one of the many master/servant pairs of world literature commonly invoked by Dinesen. Kasparson's revelation toward the end of the story—that he has killed the Cardinal in order to impersonate him—is a shocking narrative moment and is a typically "Dinesenian" device that makes us reevaluate all that has gone before. Aage Henriksen has reported that Dinesen once remarked to a guest, "I suppose you have understood that the two characters of the Cardinal and Kasparson are one and the same person."[28] This provocative remark need not be taken literally—in fact a number of details from the text would speak against it—but figuratively, there may be something to it. We are told of the Cardinal, "To his great power of imagination he joined a deep love of law and order" (*SGT,* 6). The Cardinal himself is something of a reconciliation of opposites, and Kasparson serves the side of his character that is imagination.

Once the revelation of Kasparson's identity is made, one might look back and see that there have been signs all along that the Cardinal is the actor/valet Kasparson. The moment when the Cardinal/Kasparson bows before the applauding ladies is indeed filled with exquisite irony, since Kasparson the actor is allowed a curtain call for his best role. To urge the farmers back to the task of rescue, he resorts to a coachman's vocabulary, *"Eh bien, Allons, allons"* (Oh well, let's go, let's go), words comfortable in the mouth of Kasparson the servant (*SGT,* 8). When he regains consciousness after passing out in the loft, the Cardinal/Kasparson "stared wildly at them, and put his hands to his head" (*SGT,* 16). He is concerned that his bandage, his mask, has been removed. Malin mentions in passing the fashion of men wearing tight trousers requiring the services of two valets to draw them on, and the Cardinal adds, "And a difficult job even at that" (*SGT,* 25). These are the words of a valet.

The sense in which the two are one may lie in Kasparson's reference to act 3 of Adam Oehlenschläger's *Axel and Walborg* (1810). In the play, the lovers Axel and Walborg have been separated by king and church, and the only way that Axel's friend Vilhelm can see to bring them together is to commit fraud in a good cause. He intends to impersonate the ghost of St. Olaf in order to frighten away the people in the church, so that Walborg can be whisked off to a ship in the harbor. The question is raised as to whether impersonating a saint is a sin. Vilhelm defends himself:

> [Fraud? And who has said, it is fraud?]
> My honored lord, St. Olaf comes in person,
> He puts me on, he drapes himself in me.
> I am his ghost, the larva of his spirit;
> The transient shell of an immortal mind . . .
> (*SGT,* 75)[29]

Using Vilhelm's words, Kasparson is claiming, in a sense, to be possessed by the spirit of the Cardinal, possessed like a hollow vessel that the Cardinal might use to work his own good deeds. He, too, is committing fraud for a good cause. Kasparson claims, "The Cardinal would have recognized himself in me" (*SGT,* 74). Perhaps this is what Dinesen meant when she claimed that the Cardinal and Kasparson were the same person. The Cardinal's spirit has been at work through Kasparson.

Kasparson is a liminal figure who defies normal categories of thinking. Conventional gender expectations do not signify: his stepfather was a eunuch who raised Kasparson to be a courtesan of wealthy men, and later in life Kasparson became the lover of the dowager principezza of Pisa. He is one of several Dinesen characters who has *ballon,* an unusual quality of lightness enabling him to defy the laws of gravity. He has been a barber of Seville, merging art and life by means of this operatic reference. Kasparson evades the categories of class. He is a member of the proletariat, a servant, but as the king of France's half-brother he has the noblest blood of anyone in the loft. Kasparson's mother was Johanne Händel-Schütz, a well-known actress of the time. Actors and actresses during this historical period were generally ambiguous figures, able to associate with high society, but not really belonging to it. His father is the Duke of Orléans (1747–93). A member of the high aristocracy in France, the duke renounced his title in support of the French revolution and adopted the name of Phillippe Égalité. Despite his efforts on behalf of the revolution, Phillippe Égalité was nevertheless guillotined. His son, Louis Phillippe (1773–1850), was later proclaimed

Citizen King in 1830. This is the man Kasparson refers to as his little brother. It is the height of irony in the story that Kasparson, the proletariat, should become the strongest spokesman for the old aristocracy. Even his noble relatives have rebelled against it.

Kasparson is a great impostor, having taken his name from Kaspar Hauser (1813–33), a foundling picked up by Nuremberg police and accepted by some as the prince of Baden. He died from stab wounds received when called to a rendezvous with the promise of information regarding his parentage. Like Kasparson, Kaspar Hauser was willing to give his life to prove his (false) identity. Unlike Kaspar Hauser, Kasparson has been willing to commit murder in order to achieve the role of his life. Why? The answer may lie in the inset story, "The Wine of the Tetrarch."

Hans Holmberg has given a masterful reading of "The Wine of the Tetrarch" in which he demonstrates the carefully crafted tension between Christian and heathen values through the contrasting figures of Peter and Barabbas.[30] For Peter, the sign of the cross is a symbol of the burdens one must bear for the sake of belief. For Barabbas, the cross is a piece of wood nailed together by carpenters that he is physically strong enough to have carried to Golgotha. To Peter, the wine of the Last Supper represents the blood of Christ and the promise of salvation. To Barabbas, it is only wine that may or may not taste good. The two, Peter and Barabbas, never seem to communicate. They remain in their separate spheres at the end of the story.

The story is a tragic one for Barabbas. As Langbaum has pointed out: "Barabbas, Judas, Pilate, Caiaphas fascinate Isak Dinesen as the tragic figures in the divine comedy of the passion. They were tragically sacrificed, their suffering is endless, in order to make possible Jesus's comic sacrifice, the happy outcome of which was never in doubt."[31] Barabbas has been deprived of his destiny because Jesus has literally died in his stead. Existence means nothing to him. Dinesen herself wrote, "The point is that, for Barabbas, it was a greater misfortune to miss his crucifixion, than it would have been for him to be crucified" (*KBD*, 1:169). This is the key to the connection between this tale and Kasparson's fate: "Should I have lived on as the servant for whom the lord had died?" (*SGT*, 74). Donald Hannah explains, "Kasparson tells the story, 'The Wine of the Tetrarch,' to underline the change his life has undergone: he has murdered the real Cardinal in order to save himself from the same fate as confronted Barabbas. He has at last found a purpose in life, and taken his redemption into his own hands—by rejecting the doctrine of atonement in refusing to allow the lord to sacrifice his own life for his servant."[32]

Many readers still find themselves appalled by Kasparson's crime, but is there any sign that the text vindicates him? If one reads the story backwards, certain details emerge that might point in this direction. Once his mask has fallen, Kasparson claims, "They have seen the face of God in my face. They will tell you, after tonight, that there was a white light over the boat in which I went out with them" (*SGT,* 76). His prediction is confirmed if we return to the beginning of the story where the narrator tells us, "Many years after, in the minds of the peasants, it seemed that his company in their dark despair had shed a great white light over the black waves" (*SGT,* 5). Moreover, the deluge is known as "the flood of the Cardinal," indicating that Kasparson has indeed carried off his role successfully (*SGT,* 4).

It is not traditional to deal with Malin Nat-og-Dag last in an analysis of "The Deluge at Norderney," in part because she is one of the first characters introduced by the omniscient narrator. In many ways, Malin is as central a figure as the Cardinal/Kasparson and runs less of a risk of being upstaged by Kasparson if dealt with last. Malin Nat-og-Dag's name (Night-and-Day) invokes the theme of contrast that runs through the entire story. She acts as the evening's hostess and through the power of imagination creates the harmonious union of Jonathan and Calypso. When she was young, the strict beliefs of the protestant sect of Herrnhutenism and the mores of her time enforced upon her a fanatical virginity, and she was as eager as any Diana to have men torn to shreds for desiring her. In this culture, woman has "one center of gravity. . . . She might poison her relations and cheat at cards with a high hand, and yet be an *honnête femme* as long as she tolerated no heresy in the sphere of her specialty" (*SGT,* 17). As long as she remains chaste, Malin is an honest woman. Malin becomes freed from her defensive posture by menopause: "what changes all women at fifty: the transfer from the active service of life—with a pension or the honors of war, as the case may be—to the mere passive state of looker-on" (*SGT,* 20). Woman's reproductive ability constitutes the weight of their role in this male society, but passive uselessness does not seem to suit Malin. With a power of imagination seen by some as madness, Malin creates a life of jaded experiences for herself where there have been none. Instead of a Diana, Malin casts herself as a witch, a powerful being dangerous to men. She is more than Kasparson's equal when it comes to imagination and enacting a role.

In a letter to Aage Henriksen, Dinesen wrote of Malin's relationship to Kasparson and her view of the end of the tale,

She [Malin] stands quite "symmetrically" opposite Kasparsen [sic], in as much as Kasparsen, who is depraved, finds his final self-realization in the role of a saint, whereas she, who is a sort of eternal innocent, . . . has had to realize herself in the likeness of the Great Whore. When Kasparsen at last confesses his guilt with pride, she confesses . . . with a sort of proud modesty . . . her eternal innocence or purity, her Diana nature. The author's (surprisingly) optimistic worldview shows itself here in that the two meet in trust and harmony, "in light," which may be taken, because of the story's structure, as salvation. (*KBD,* 2:214)

Thus the story returns, in the end, to the harmony of contrasts invoked at the beginning of the Danish edition of the tale.

But there is an issue as yet unresolved: Do they survive the night or do they not? The answer is up to the reader. On the one hand, the fact that the flood is known as "the flood of the Cardinal" implies that Kasparson's masquerade was never discovered by the world at large, which may mean he drowned. Malin's words to Kasparson before he kisses her are a delicious double entendre: "Fils de St. Louis, montez au ciel!" (Son of St. Louis, ascend to heaven!). They might be interpreted colloquially as "Let me take you to heaven, baby!" but these are also the words reputed to have been spoken to Louis XVI by the priest who escorted him to the guillotine. Death may be at hand. The narrative then informs us: "So the proud old maid did not go unkissed into her grave" (*SGT,* 78). This sounds ominous, but the question is whether that grave is an imminent watery one or not. The final line of the tale, delivered in French, is a significant phrase from *The Arabian Nights:* "At that moment in her story, Scheherazade saw the sun rise, and discretely fell silent" (*SGT,* 79). Scheherazade has saved her life for another day by telling stories, and the openness of the narration will keep her alive. Our characters have also spent the night swapping tales, and perhaps the openness of their fate will rescue them as well. In a stimulating essay, Elisabeth Bronfen has pointed out that in Dinesen's tales closure very often means death.[33] Some readers will no doubt feel that the individual tales of the characters possess enough closure to doom them, but for others, the open ending will at least keep the characters alive in our imaginations.

"The Old Chevalier"

The focus of "The Old Chevalier" seems to be the ideas and attitudes of a bygone era. A contrast between the past and the present is set up in the frame of the tale. Although Baron von Brackel narrates most of the story, he is evidently speaking to a young man ("you young men of the present day," *SGT* 93) sometime during the 1920s to judge from the modern fashions characterized as "a few perpendicular lines, cut off before they have had time to develop any sense" which invoke a flapper's costume (*SGT,* 93). The events of the tale take place in 1874.

A theme of transience is struck at the outset with an invocation of the *danse macabre,* a medieval motif that represents the skeletal figure of death dancing with a string of figures whose ages range from newly born to extreme old age. Charles Camille Saint-Saëns's (1835–1921) symphonic poem, *La Danse Macabre,* composed the same year as the events of "The Old Chevalier" take place (1874), helped to revive the theme at the end of the nineteenth century. Both Ibsen and Strindberg used the motif in their late plays. Within the first three pages of "The Old Chevalier," there are no less than twenty-one references to age, not even counting the one that occurs in the title of the text. An emphasis is placed on the transitoriness of physical beauty. Baron von Brackel is described as having been "a sort of ideally handsome youth . . . although no trace of the past beauty could be found in his face" (*SGT,* 81). Brackel says of the lover who tried to poison him: "Her great beauty, unless some rare artist has been able to preserve it in color or clay, now probably exists only within a few very old brains like mine" (*SGT,* 82). The Baron then mentions that he had first met her when they were staying with "other gay young people who are now, if they are alive, faded and crooked and deaf" (*SGT,* 82). These references serve to give a strong impression of the passage of time and the sense that the Baron is giving us a glimpse into a world slipping beyond our reach.

As usual, Dinesen draws upon literary sources to help set the historical stage. She makes references to Byron, Baudelaire, and the *fin de siècle.* In the journal *Gil Blas,* Hans Brix noticed tales resembling aspects of "The Old Chevalier." In one, a young starving girl is fed with delicacies at her lover's table, and in another, a wife competes with her husband in infidelity.[34] Brix also detected several references to the poetry of Emil Aarestrup (1800–1856) woven into the text. The Baron remarks, "Our poets of those days would tell us how a party of young beauties, behind the curtains of the bathing-machine, would blush and giggle as they 'put lilies in water'" (*SGT,* 96). This is a reference to one of Aarestrup's ritornelles, brief three-line poems in which the poet often compares a lady's charms to flowers. Aarestrup is known for the eroticism of his poetry and his use of color, both of which help to set the tone of the Baron's tale.[35]

The Baron begins his story with a tale that "has nothing to do with what I was going to tell you" (*SGT,* 81). This is a statement that begs to be questioned. The episode in which the Baron's mistress tries to poison him constitutes a counterpoint to the ensuing encounter with Nathalie. Susanne Fabricius was the first to note that "here the young man gets the opportunity to experience the position women are placed in as objects, manipulated by foreign motivations."[36] Gurli Woods agrees that in this episode there is something of a gender reversal; the mistress takes all the initiatives.[37] Grethe Rostbøll notes that the Baron casts himself in the role of Desdemona, whereas his mistress assumes that of Othello.[38] The Baron's mistress is in competition with her husband, and her relationship with the Baron is a battle in which fortresses must be burned so that the enemy cannot take possession. This conflict between the sexes stands in stark contrast to the harmony the Baron will experience with Nathalie.

The Baron's description of his mistress then segues into an account of the early days of the "emancipation of women." Although the Baron appears to express sympathy for the movement, it is perhaps not unfair to assume that it provokes deep fears in him as well. The anxious projection of the *femme fatale* in turn-of-the-century art arose in tandem with women assuming more power in society. The Baron's mistress makes an attempt to be a "fatal woman" when she offers him poison and he suspects her of being a werewolf who might "go down on all fours and snarl at me" (*SGT,* 84). She is the monsterous woman feared by the *fin de siècle*.

There is considerable scholarly disagreement about the continuation of "The Old Chevalier," and the crux of the matter is what we should think about the Baron's behavior towards Nathalie. One group of critics sees him as a hero, whereas the other views him as a failure. The difference of opinion is no doubt caused by ambiguities inherent in the text, and each reader must form her or his own opinion.

To the first group of critics, the encounter between Nathalie and the Baron is an erotic idyll, a moment of perfection in an otherwise flawed world. According to Thomas Whissen, the two achieve this perfection by playing in a sort of game: "The contract between them is seen as a liberating rather than a restraining force because it allows the players to don a mask and thus enjoy all the freedom a disguise permits."[39] There is something profoundly musical about Nathalie, who begins to sing before she even speaks in the haven of the Baron's room. She plays the guitar and sings two songs for him, one of which he cannot understand because it is in a foreign language: "These words that I did not understand seemed to me more directly meaningful than any I had ever understood" (*SGT,* 101). It is as though the Baron is caught in Kierkegaard's "Immediate Stages of the Erotic," where the erotic principle is best expressed through music. The moment is immediate, erotic, and musical. The idyll cannot last forever and reality eventually intrudes. According to Kierkegaard, language is in conflict with the immediate: "Language involves reflection, and cannot, therefore, express the immediate. Reflection destroys the immediate, and hence it is impossible to express the musical in language."[40] Nathalie's first statement in direct discourse is "I must go back," followed by "And you will give me twenty francs, will you not?" (*SGT,* 101, 102). Her words break the immediate spell of the evening.

The Baron clings to the magic as long as he can and thinks of her request in terms of a fairy tale. He feels he must rise to the occasion and give Nathalie the money she asks for, even though it is a ridiculously small sum considering what she has given him. Eric Johannesson explains, "As a result of his fidelity to this code of chivalrousness the Baron loses Nathalie. He has observed the rules of the game: he has paid the price. He has accepted the jest in the spirit in which it was offered. By respecting the pride of his partner the Baron has made the relationship end as it began: within a magic circle of freedom, grace, and beauty."[41] The Baron's parting gesture is thus seen as heroic, completely against his own inclinations.

The context of this entire tale is a debate about "forsaking an inclination for the sake of principle" (*SGT,* 81). The connection between this moment in which the Baron pays Nathalie and the original discussion is made clearer in the Danish version of the text, which includes a few lines not present in the English: "There was nothing in the world that I feared more, that was less according to the wishes of my own heart, than to give her twenty francs—but the wishes of my own heart, I was finished with that. And that was, of course, what we were talking about, you and I, to begin with" (*MU,* 1:111). Dinesen may have wished to point out the importance of this moment of chivalry through her choice of title. "The Old Chevalier" echoes the word "chivalry" in the same way that the Danish title, "Den gamle vandrende Ridder" echoes the Danish counterpart "ridderlighed." The Danish title possesses further connotations as well. "Den gamle vandrende Ridder" (The old errant knight) invokes images of Don Quixote, a figure in the grip of a chivalric code that is outmoded. The Baron's chivalrous sacrifice is difficult for him and will leave him bereft, but he has learned a valuable lesson.

Sara Stambaugh interprets the consoling glance that Nathalie bestows upon the Baron as she leaves him as a good sign that "the Chevalier has learned to look beyond woman as symbol and to see her fundamental humanity."[42] The skull that the Baron imagines must belong to Nathalie is similarly a symbol of their common humanity. Brix connects the skull scene with another ritornelle from Aarestrup, in which a young lady promises her skull to her lover as a gift: "Not a *memento mori,* but a Remember, I lived!"[43] Nathalie has indeed etched herself in the Baron's memory forever.

If this reading of events seems convincing, the arguments amassed on the other side of the controversy are also compelling. Several critics are upset by the Baron's thoughtlessness and self-absorption in his behavior towards Nathalie, a woman in obvious distress. He treats her as a gift to him by a friendly fate, not as a person. Gurli Woods sees in the digression about the man who does not care whether his cook loves him or not as long as he makes a good omelette, an attitude in which, "Love is thus equated . . . with the consumption/delivery of food and wine, and the individual behind the 'product' does not matter."[44] Whereas the

Baron may have felt himself objectified in his relationship to his former mistress, his relationship to Nathalie seems more natural and harmonious because, "Now von Brackel takes all the initiatives. He tells Nathalie/Eve to eat and to undress. It is he who finishes the undressing of her as if she were a doll, etc."[45] This objectification of Nathalie has unleashed some genuine indignation among certain critics. Grethe Rostbøll writes, "It went as it should: The Man took what was offered to him and all his words about emancipation and women's equality were forgotten when it really counted."[46] Another ritornelle by Aarestrup invokes the key word of this tale and might support such readings:

Hvor hans Manere ere ridderlige!   How his manners are chivalrous!
Kun skade, at han ene Øje skeler,   A pity that he leers with one eye,
Og at hans Handlinger er lidderlige. And that his actions are lascivious.[47]

These lines point to the discrepancy between the hollow conventions of good manners and the more telling nature of deeds.

The Baron's behavior in offering Nathalie the twenty francs is not seen as an act of chivalry by Susanne Fabricius: "[He has] thus ruined her life and his own chance for understanding. . . . A conventional action scarcely thought through is later rationalized into a ritual act of duty."[48] We recall that the Baron himself felt that if he had had more imagination he might have devised a strategy that would have enabled him to "keep" Nathalie. He himself feels a sense of failure. Susan Hardy Aiken concurs with Fabricius: "Far from simply ratifying the chivalric code the Baron invokes and the androcentric 'aristocratic' worldview that generated it, the story renders them problematic, enacting their ultimate bankruptcy by showing that, under the guise of adoration, they objectify the beloved woman as an eroticized/idealized prize to be won by the lover, a sign within his discourse, a means to his own self-reflections."[49] Marianne Juhl and Bo Hakon Jørgensen are convinced that von Brackel does not have Dinesen's sympathy. According to their interpretation, the Baron should have followed his inclination for the girl, and his choosing "duty" was a big mistake.[50] Moreover, the tendency among these critics is to see the Baron's fantasy about encountering Nathalie's skull as ghoulish. Because he cannot have her, he wishes her dead.

There are also some hints in the text that, after his experience with Nathalie, the Baron may give in to his own homosexual tendencies. Even before this, we have been told that he thought more highly of his mistress's husband than he did of her. The Danish word is a bit stronger. The Baron "elskede" (loved) the young man more than his wife (*MU*, 1:86). The Baron identifies with Orpheus, who loses his wife Eurydice by looking back as he leads her out of the underworld. According to Fabricius, after this devastating loss Orpheus practices homosexuality.[51] Orpheus is also subsequently torn apart by women. The skull that the

Baron fantasizes as belonging to Nathalie is compared to that of Antinoüs, the Emperor Hadrian's homosexual lover. These details are suggestive and may be interpreted to mean that once the ideal of Woman has dissolved before his eyes, Baron von Brackel no longer wants anything to do with women.

A particular challenge in "The Old Chevalier" is assessing the reliability of the Baron as a narrator. The initial narrator of the tale describes the Baron as "least of all . . . ingenious" (*SGT,* 81). The Baron himself seems aware of his own lack of imagination in handling his parting from Nathalie. Dinesen's choice of names is rarely random, and Aiken has pointed out the German root of Brackel means "waste" or "refuse."[52] These details might make the reader want to take what the Baron says with a good deal of salt. Nonetheless, many critics have wanted to cite this tale as a typical expression of *Dinesen's* views on women. There is no doubt that Dinesen is very effectively exploring the attitudes of a bygone era, but it is dangerous to assume that the Baron's opinions are also those of the author.

For example, inspiration for the clothing digression was traced by Tom Kristensen to a reference in Wilhelm Dinesen's *Hunting Letters* (1889–92): "The secret power of the feminine is implication."[53] Much has been made by Judith Thurman and others about Dinesen's attachment to her father, and thus one might easily draw the conclusion that Dinesen shares a nostalgia for this mysterious view of women. However, Dinesen writes to her aunt,

> Father writes in . . . "Hunting Letters": "however enchanting a well-formed feminine leg may be when revealed by an incautiously lifted dress, there is nothing in the least alluring in being presented with the whole leg, right up to the knee"—no doubt presuming by this pronouncement to have demonstrated to all decent sensible women the reprehensible foolishness of these skimpy skirts, as if it were unthinkable for us really to *want to run* and be free of clothes impeding our movements. (*LA,* 263)

Although Dinesen can appreciate the aesthetics of the clothing worn in the nineteenth century, she would not choose such apparel for herself.

Dinesen's single utterance about this text does not go very far towards settling the controversy. She comments on the story in a letter to Johannes Rosendahl in the context of a larger discussion of Nemesis: "Simply and briefly I can say that the concept contains ideas of price and commodity, a theory that it pays to buy something at as high a price as possible, or that one cannot 'get off cheaply,'—this seems quite foreign to modern people, all of whose efforts often center upon getting off cheaply.... "The Old Chevalier" attains a sort of satisfaction, or peace, in understanding that he cannot 'get off cheaply,' and by paying the price" (*KBD,* 1:391). This would seem to indicate that, in Dinesen's view, the chevalier's act is indeed chivalrous and meant to be seen as heroic. Perhaps the consoling glance from Nathalie is intended to excuse the Baron's earlier self-absorption as a by-product of his youth—he is only twenty. It may be going too far, however, to assume a full-fledged endorsement of the Baron and the world in which he lives. One should perhaps take note of the different fates of the two women in the Baron's life. The emancipated mistress lives to be a contented old lady. Nathalie is swiftly destroyed by life. Together with the multiple hints that the Baron's worldview is dated, these different destinies may point to the untenable nature of an idealized view of women. Perhaps Dinesen does not seek to approve or disapprove the Baron's worldview, but merely to understand it.

There remains one more noteworthy feature about the reception of "The Old Chevalier." In the years after this tale was published, some male readers found it unsettling that Dinesen was able to describe "the physical perfection of a beautiful young woman with the same eyes as a man."[54] Otto Runge wrote to Dinesen: "Your narrator here in some wonderful way becomes one with the reader's mind. I don't understand how something like that can be created by a woman" (*KBD*, 1:150). What Brix and Runge experience with a degree of amazement, Harald Nielsen viewed with disgust: "That Baudelaire in the poem to his black mistress lets his thoughts follow where his senses are already at home, is not surprising, but what sort of interest drives a woman to lift the skirts of her sisters— and especially at the same time that she is praising their virginity?"[55] In other words it is acceptable to Nielsen for male authors to regard women as sexual objects. Since he assumes that such depictions can only stem from sexual desire, he feels that there is something perverse about a woman writer describing her own sex in a sensual fashion. Dinesen's narrative cross-dressing has disturbed Nielsen's assumptions about gender. If nothing else, Dinesen's writing illustrates that we should not be comfortable about our gender assumptions.

It is also worthy of note that—although the dividing line is not absolute— there is a general tendency for the readers who approve of the Baron to be male and those who disapprove to be female. It may be that approval or disapproval of the Baron's behavior depends upon with whom in the story the reader identifies. The reader seeking resolution and authority from the author will find that she has successfully hidden herself behind several layers of narrative masks. The reader, male or female, may try the Baron's point of view on for size, and if it does not fit, he or she can imagine what the feelings of the silent Nathalie might be. The reader is left to draw his or her own conclusions about the experience.

"The Monkey"

In the case of "The Monkey," some of the most ingenious readings of the text have been performed by scholars publishing in academic journals or other venues not easily accessible to the general public. Annelies van Hees and William Mishler have exposed a number of the tale's secrets, inspired by the analytical tools of psychoanalysis, and Dag Heede has thrown fresh light on some of the troubling gender issues the story evokes. The following treatment of the tale draws on the work of all three of these scholars as well as others, but is especially indebted to Annelies van Hees's sensitive literary detective work.

The ending of "The Monkey" contains a startling revelation. The Virgin Prioress, whom we think we have known throughout the tale, turns out to have a double nature. She is able to exchange shapes with her monkey. The majority of Dinesen's tales, although they suggest fantastic possibilities, remain within the realm of the plausible and do not resort to such overtly supernatural devices. The scene is shocking, and we are forced to reevaluate everything we thought we knew about the events preceding the metamorphosis. This narrative twist is similar to, though even more spectacular than, the Cardinal revealing himself to be Kasparson at the end of "The Deluge at Norderney."

Eric Johannesson has pointed out that the theme of doubles is common to Gothic literature, listing the examples of "Menardus in *Die Elixire des Teufels,* or Ambrosio in Lewis's *The Monk,* or Stevenson's *Dr. Jekyll and Mr. Hyde,* or the jeweler in Hoffmann's *Mademoiselle de Scudery.*"[56] In each of these stories, the person with a double nature is male, and one side is most certainly bad, while the other is good. Conventional morality prevails when the evil side of the character is destroyed. In David Garnett's "Lady into Fox" (1922), a story Dinesen once mentioned in an interview as a good example of the fantastic, a Victorian woman is inexplicably transformed into a vixen.[57] Her husband tries to adjust but grows increasingly distressed as more and more of her animal nature takes over, and the ex–Victorian angel goes so far as to run away, mate, and have a litter. The transgressions of the wife are ultimately punished when she is torn apart by hounds. In typical fashion, Dinesen has reinscribed the traditions of the Gothic. The Prioress and her monkey are not destroyed at the end of tale; conventional morality has not been confirmed, and it is not at all certain that one side is better than the other.

The emblem of this doubleness is the Wendish idol described by the Count, "the goddess of love had the face and facade of a beautiful woman, while, if you turned her around, she presented at the back the image of a monkey" (*SGT,* 130–31). Athena raises the question, "But how . . . did they know, in the case of that goddess of love, which was the front and which was the back?" (*SGT,* 131). Athena's remark, which questions the hierarchy of such dualisms, is much in keeping with the theme of the harmony of contrasts so prevalent in Dinesen's tales in general.

As Hans Brix pointed out, Dinesen could have learned about this Wendish idol, called "Sieba" or "Siwa," from Bernhard Severin Ingemann's *Grundtræk til en Nord-Slavisk og Vendisk Gudelære* (1824, Fundamentals of a North-Slavic and Wendish mythology).[58] Ingemann was one of Dinesen's favorite authors, and the double aspect of "Siwa" is described in a footnote to his *Valdemar den Store og hans Mænd* (1824, Waldemar the great and his men), a copy of which, much used, is in Dinesen's library at Rungstedlund.[59] According to Ingemann, all Wendish gods possessed a double nature, one dark and one light. Siwa was traditionally depicted as a woman with long hair holding an apple in one hand and grapes in the other. (Note that the Prioress serves Boris pears and grapes when he first arrives at the convent.) The other side of the idol depicts "a brash triumphant monkey."[60] Whereas Ingemann sees the woman as a representative of innocence, he says of the monkey, "Just as the monkey on the whole is mankind's most disgusting distortion, so it is especially, as is known, the natural image of lust and unchaste indecency."[61] Like his other romantic/Gothic compatriots, Ingemann is certain that one side is good and one side is bad. Dinesen takes a different view. To Robert Langbaum, Dinesen said, "When men by way of their conventions have got themselves into difficulties, then let the monkey in, he will find the unattainable solution."[62]

Looking back over the tale, it is difficult to tell at any given time with whom one has been dealing. When Boris first arrives, it is stated that the monkey had been missing for a few weeks, usually a sign that the Prioress has transformed herself and left the convent in charge of her monkey familiar while she enjoys a freer life. The same Prioress who greets Boris with the pears and grapes of the "front" of the idol, speaks with passionate feeling of forests and trees. Athena has seen the monkey in the place where Cupid stood just a few days earlier, and the monkey crosses Boris's path on the way back from his proposal visit. Is this the "real" Prioress, or not? The Prioress's private dining room has "just lately" been redecorated in a style that would appeal to a creature from Zanzibar. A heavy incense is being burned, perhaps to mask the scent of the monkey. When Boris is refused by Athena, the Prioress goes "up to the window, as if she meant to throw herself out" (*SGT,* 138). When the Prioress turns around again, "She was all changed" (*SGT,* 138). Marianne Juhl and Bo Hakon Jørgensen construe this transformation as the moment when the monkey takes over, but this "change" is nothing like the metamorphosis that occurs in the final scene of the story.[63] The monkey certainly seems to have the upper hand during the seduction supper, as body language would indicate: "From time to time she made use of a little gesture peculiar to her, of daintily scratching herself here and there with her delicately pointed little finger" (*SGT,* 144). The Prioress also savors the cloves from Zanzibar, which is another hint at who is in control. In the final scene, after the metamorphosis, we are presented with "the true Prioress of Closter Seven" (*SGT,* 162). William Mishler has noted that when assessing an appropriate translation of this phrase into Danish, Dinesen rejected Valdemar Rørdam's suggestion "den rigtige" (the correct, rightful) and chose instead "den virkelige" (the real, true).[64] Rørdam's term would have implied a hierarchy, a moral judgment on which side of the Prioress was the right side. Even if presented with the "true" Prioress, some readers may still be in doubt as to what that means.

Dag Heede has made the amusing suggestion that in the light of the Prioress's metamorphosis, if we consider "the cornucopia of pets present in the enclosed building, the uncanny suspicion arises that perhaps all the women from time to time change into their pets and vice versa."[65] The menagerie includes parrots, cockatoos, dogs, cats, a deer, and "a white Angora goat, like that of Esmeralda" (*SGT,* 109). The reference is to Victor Hugo's *The Hunchback of Notre Dame* (1831), in which Esmeralda is suspected of being a witch and her goat, an animal familiar. The hint does point to strange powers that may dwell in these "superfluous" women who have been set aside in a cloister. Closter Seven is more coven than convent.

The event that instigates the intrigue of the tale is Boris von Schreckenstein's need to escape a scandal. Although not stated explicitly, it is clear that Boris has been accused of homosexuality and needs to get married in order to repair his social reputation. In this society such matters are not discussed unless in euphemisms. The old librarian, when pressed as to the nature of the scandal, begins to talk about Greece. The connection lies in such texts as Plato's *Symposium,* in which love between men is treated as natural and positive. The cloistered women, however, associate Greece with coiffures and fashions from their youth, creating some delightfully comic confusion. The point of the scandal does seem to sink in eventually and disrupts the entire worldview of the women of the convent. They have been raised to consider women objects of desire to all men, and their entire social existence has been based upon it. Dinesen includes the almost wistful line: "Had they known that it might ever be called into question, all these lives, which were now so nearly finished, might have come to look very different" (*SGT,* 112).

Dag Heede has suggested that Dinesen uses Boris's homosexuality as "a way of representing the normal, not as natural, but as a construction, one single, possible version of reality among a multitude of others. . . . Boris is not only the most 'normal' person in the text, but as the focus of the story, the person whose thoughts and views . . . the reader follows, and who is the most obvious person for the reader to identify with."[66] The very existence of the idea of homosexuality creates a disruption in the minds of the convent women, which could also be described as the realization that what they had taken for normal and natural may instead be a mere social construction. This realization opens up limitless possibilities for living. The text of "The Monkey" does not express much sympathy with Boris's accusers, described as being "sanctimonious" and acting "under the pretense of moral indignation"(*SGT,* 111). Heede goes so far as to state: "Homosexuality is used here more than anything else as a positive anti-bourgeois metaphor, a way of rejecting the dull, settled life of 'supporters, fathers-in-law, authorities on food and morals.'"[67]

The Prioress decides on a match between Boris and Athena upon the receipt of a mysterious letter. The message no doubt contains the news that the Count has won his lawsuit, making Athena a particularly wealthy young heiress. Moreover, the Count's lawyer also has a monkey from Zanzibar, so perhaps the jungle telegraph has been at work. The choice of Athena surprises Boris since from his childhood both his mother and his aunt "had been joining forces to keep him and Athena apart" (*SGT,* 118). Why? Mishler argues convincingly that the possibility exists that Athena and Boris are brother and sister. The Count was a special admirer of Boris's mother in days gone by. When he greets Boris it is with the words: "Boris, my child . . ." (*SGT,* 124). Dinesen specifically rejected Rørdam's translation of "Boris, min Dreng . . ." (Boris, my boy) in lieu of "Boris, mit Barn!" (Boris, my child), perhaps in order to underline the suggestion that the Count might be Boris's father.[68] When the Count writes that he had hoped to see Boris's features in the unborn generations to follow, the Count might at the same time be seeing his own genotype through Boris as well as Athena. Incest, along with homosexuality, is yet another socially disruptive force brought into play in this tale. No wonder Pastor Rosenquist, the spokesperson for conventional morality, seems completely at a loss.

According to van Hees's analysis, Boris's homosexuality is the result of his Oedipus complex.[69] He has become so bonded to his mother that sexual relations with another woman would constitute a betrayal. Boris has just come from his mother and "a row of wild scenes which his mother's love and jealousy had caused" (*SGT,* 114). The Count comes to represent the father in this Oedipal triangle. Upon first sight of the Count, Boris thinks, "This old man knows all, and is going to kill me" (*SGT,* 124). After proposing, Boris feels like Don Giovanni waiting for the Commendatore. Don Giovanni is the notorious seducer of Mozart's opera, who is punished at the end by the stone replica of one of his victims' fathers. This, then, is another image of paternal retribution. Boris is repeatedly afflicted with the sense that something is wrong. He prefers to think of Athena as a skeleton, a desexualized being, and not a threat to his relationship to his mother. On his way to seduce Athena, Boris recalls some lines from Aeschylus's *Eumenides* in which Orestes asks for Athena's help as he is being brought to trial for the murder of his mother. He is thus expressing his fear of what this encounter will mean for him. Sex with another woman is tantamount to the murder of his mother and betrayal. After the botched seduction, Boris again invokes lines from Aeschylus, which are erroneously attributed to Euripides in the English text, but correctly identified in the Danish. This time, Boris quotes Orestes' words thanking Athena for helping him be acquitted of the crime of matricide. Boris no longer needs to feel guilt about becoming involved with another woman.

If Boris is unnaturally bound to his mother, more than one interpreter has felt that Athena is unnaturally bound to her father.[70] This may be what the Prioress implies with her scandalous anecdote about the Holy Family visiting Paris. The Duchess of Berri is rumored to be pregnant by her father, and even though she expostulates to the Virgin, "You would never have done it," in some sense the Virgin has been impregnated by her Father in heaven (*SGT,* 144).

Athena takes her name from the virgin goddess of wisdom, but she is more specifically a Diana, and as the Prioress tells us, Boris would make a fine Actaeon. According to the legend, Diana had Actaeon torn apart by his own hounds for daring to spy upon her taking a bath. Athena is six feet tall, able to do a chin-up on a hunting horn—lifting both herself and her horse off the ground—and defiantly virginal. She is compared to carnivora: a lioness and an eagle. When she stands on one leg like a stork, she is emulating the Masai warriors Dinesen knew in Africa. Athena is the typical adolescent heroine identified by Robin Lyndenberg, one who perceives marriage and maturity as equivalent to a loss of freedom.[71] "From being a success at court, a happy, congratulated bride, a mother of a promising family, good Lord, deliver me" (*SGT,* 142). She is perfectly happy with her tomboy existence and does not want anyone to take it from her.

During the first chat Athena has with Boris, they look up and see the constellation of the Great Bear. The story of the Great Bear can be found in Ovid's *Metamorphoses.* Callisto, a nymph in Artemis's (Diana's) hunting party, is loved by Zeus, and so the jealous Hera transforms her into a bear. When Callisto's son, Arcas, is about to kill her, Zeus turns them into constellations. Being transformed into a constellation is a common means of escaping physical jeopardy in Greek mythology. The very name of Closter Seven, which alludes to the constellation of the Pleiades, invokes another such tale. Zeus turns the seven daughters of Atlas into the Pleiades in order to save them from the amorous pursuit of Orion. Sexual attention is another form of physical jeopardy, and the image is a suitable one for a cloister. Later, when Athena is told she will have a child, she stubbornly announces, "My father will teach him astronomy" (*SGT,* 158). For both Athena and Agnese in the "Roads Round Pisa," the study of the stars takes them away from earthly cares and becomes a metaphor for escaping amorous attention.

Athena is a partisan of the French Revolution and she recites for Boris some lines from a French song by Auguste Barbier. The text describes a horse that eludes its masters, originally a metaphor for the French Revolution. Annelies van Hees notes that Athena no doubt sees herself as the mare, "which no hand has touched and no one has managed to saddle."[72] She no doubt also identifies with the bear who kills five men before she is taken. Athena identifies with wild, powerful animals and is distressed to hear the story of the African elephant that dies in a cage. She is afraid, with reason, that the Prioress wants to subdue her and put her into a cage, which is why the tale is the main *faux pas* of the evening. Long before Boris appears on her doorstep Athena has made it abundantly clear she will not relinquish her virginity without a fight.

The scene in which Boris and Athena engage in combat is riddled with symbolic import. Boris approaches through a hall with a black and white tiled floor, and he emerges into a pink and crimson bower: "Of all the memories which afterward Boris carried with him from this night, the memory of the transition from the coloring and light of the corridor to that of the room was the longest lasting" (*SGT*, 151). This event will signal a transformation for Boris, a type of rebirth. He moves from a space where black is black and white is white to a very feminine space where such clear distinctions are absent. Dag Heede reads this space as a womb:

> The whole room was hung with rose silks, and in the depths of it the crimson draperies of the four-poster bed glowed in the shade. There were two pink-globed lamps, solicitously lighted by the Prioress' maid. The floor had a wine-colored carpet with roses in it, which, near the lamps, seemed to be drinking in the light, and farther from them looked like pools of dark crimson into which one would not like to walk. (*SGT*, 151)

The room is being viewed through Boris's eyes, and of course he is the "one" who does not feel comfortable walking into this space.

The only unfeminine object in the room is Athena, who looks like "a sturdy young sailor boy about to swab the deck" (*SGT*, 152). Athena defends her virtue with considerable vigor. Annelies van Hees, Bill Mishler, Anders Westenholz, and Grethe Rostbøll all agree that when Athena knocks out Boris's two teeth it is a symbol of castration.[73] Curiously, this seems to make Boris happy. According to van Hees, his castration obviates the necessity for Boris to be unfaithful to his mother. The struggle goes on and ends with a kiss that disgusts them both. There is something out of proportion in Athena's reaction to the kiss. It is "as if he had run a rapier straight through her" (*SGT,* 154). The kiss is a symbolic consummation that saps the virgin warrior of her strength in an almost magical way, not altogether unlike the way in which Samson is deprived of his strength by having his hair cut off. Athena is later compared to Samson, but a Samson who has regained his strength again (*SGT,* 159).

The discussion the morning after is quite comic. The Prioress takes it for granted that the rape has been committed, and Athena is too ignorant of the birds and the bees to know whether one can get pregnant from a kiss or not. Even though the Prioress extorts from Athena the promise to marry Boris, Athena still remains true to her Diana nature and promises to kill Boris at the first opportunity. At this juncture there is a tapping at the window, and shortly thereafter the remarkable metamorphosis of the Prioress and the monkey takes place. Boris, Athena, and the reader are all quite startled, and Dinesen has her little joke by having the monkey sit on the bust of Immanuel Kant, author of *The Critique of Pure Reason* (1781). What has just happened exists beyond the limits of reason, and Kant can't help us. Interpretations of what this scene means for the two young people vary widely.

Hans Brix seems to feel that the Prioress's subjugation of the monkey has instructed Athena that she must subject herself to Boris.[74] Langbaum feels the scene makes Boris and Athena "ready for human love," by which he must mean that they have in some sense been "cured."[75] Juhl and Jørgensen believe that the two have learned that the relationship between men and women must be sexual, and thus, these critics also endorse the notion of a cure, as does Vibeke Schröder.[76] Mishler also seems to subscribe to the couple's experiencing a psychological liberation from their respective complexes.[77] Van Hees feels that the scene has caused Boris and Athena to accept their sexuality as it is and also to realize that they can marry in any case.[78] Dag Heede sees a happy ending, "in an 18th century view, that the two combine in a reasonable, sensible union, where they probably will do little damage to another."[79]

Indeed, Boris's homosexuality and Athena's desire to remain chaste are not in conflict, as the Prioress has already noted: "She will have nothing . . . and you will give nothing. It seems to me, in all modesty, that you are well paired" (*SGT,* 137). Athena and Boris can keep up appearances and enjoy a certain sort of freedom within the circle of their marriage. Closter Seven is the namesake of Kloster-Zeven, which is famous in history as the site for the signing of a treaty between England and France in 1757, in which England capitulated to France and agreed to remain neutral in the European arena for the rest of the Seven Years War. Thus, Closter Seven seems a suitable spot for generating peaceful agreements. Athena does not need to kill Boris, and they can probably get along in the future.

A fan wrote to Dinesen requesting clarification of "The Monkey," and Dinesen's response is worth quoting at length:

> With regard to the tale "The Monkey," I am, as always when a reader asks me what a story means, quite uncomfortable, since I feel the only honest answer would be: "There is no meaning." I think it would be a shame if an author could explain a story better with outside information than it explains itself! I believe that when I wrote "The Monkey," I thought of the situation as follows: The Prioress has a monkey that is very close to her and in whose company she needs to take refuge from her limited life in the cloister. Every now and then she feels such an attraction and need for a free life in nature that she changes shape with the monkey and for a while is absent from the cloister, where the monkey takes charge. As a young girl, I myself had a beloved dog about which I had a similar fantasy. If one is looking for a deeper meaning to the story, it would probably be this: When human relations become unusually complicated or completely mixed up, let the monkey come. It is monkey-advice and monkey-help that Boris gets in the cloister; only when, through these methods, a way out can be glimpsed and darkness begins to lighten, does the Prioress come back and resume her place. The monkey has plainly chosen a criminal path upon which the Prioress would not have set foot, but in its solution there is salvation for Boris and, it should be understood, also a promise of a more human happiness for Athena. This is not a good explanation, but you are free to come up with a better one. (*KBD*, 2:433)

Dinesen's words about salvation for Boris and a more human happiness for Athena are sufficiently vague, so that interpreters are free to continue to speculate.

At the beginning of the tale, Boris fantasized about how his aunt would take the news of the scandal, and he weighs possible reactions in the form of Latin phrases. *"Et tu Brute"* (You too, Brutus!), which is an exclamation that marks betrayal: "How could you!" *"Ad sanitatem gradus est novisse morbum"* (It is a step towards health to recognize sickness) anticipates the Prioress's perception of Boris as a deviant who needs to be healed. *"Discite justitiam moniti, et non temnere divos"* (Be warned, learn justice and learn not to despise the divine) is an important phrase since it appears again, without the warning note, as the last line of the story. Since at the beginning of the tale, Boris and the reader both think of the Prioress as a defender of moral rectitude, the admonition Boris anticipates would be something like "Follow the rules of Christian behavior." By the end of the story, our understanding of the Prioress has changed and we realize that the divine forces at play have been pagan. The original *"Discite . . ."* quote is from Virgil's *Aeneid,* not a Christian text at all. The divine in "The Monkey" embraces the two-sided, double nature of Siwa. The second time the phrase is invoked, it might be construed: "Learn justice and embrace both sides of the divine." The revelation at the end of the story forces us to reevaluate not only this phrase, but the entire story. Repeating a phrase whose significance has changed is a technique that Dinesen will use again in "Alkmene." It is a device that makes the reader reexamine her or his assumptions. The sentence has not changed, but after experiencing the story, the reader has. The reader's expectations and understanding of this fictional world have altered—another metamorphosis has taken place. Now everything must be reexamined and reinterpreted.

"The Roads Round Pisa"

The "Roads Round Pisa" was one of the first stories that Dinesen completed for *Seven Gothic Tales,* and it was meant to be the first story in the collection. One critic suggests that "The Roads Round Pisa" may earn this pride of place because it "appears in thematical concentration as well as in narrative structure as virtually archetypal for the tales of the book."[80] The construction of the story is ingenious, and the first-time reader, like Augustus von Schimmelman, may not always be clear about what exactly has happened in the text. Such readers make take comfort in the fact that the tale even managed to confound such an experienced reader as Professor Hans Brix, prompting Dinesen to write him a long, detailed letter in 1950, pointing out what she considered errors in Brix's reading of the tale in his book, *Karen Blixens Eventyr* (1949, Karen Blixen's Tales).

The tale is constructed rather like a puzzle. Toward the end of the tale, Carlotta reflects: "Life is a mosaic work of the Lord's, which he keeps filling in bit by bit" (*SGT,* 215). Each of the nine sections of the tale contains information important for solving the mysteries of the action, and when the final piece falls into place, the moment of epiphany arrives. The big picture, the central plot, should become evident. In this way, Eric Johannesson has compared "The Roads Round Pisa" with "The Roads of Life" in *Out of Africa.* In that illustrated tale, a man experiences all sorts of misfortune during the night, but when he wakes up the next morning, he sees that his movements have drawn the pattern of a stork. Thus, both tales are existentially comforting: if at any given moment life seems meaningless and harsh, wait, and the significance of it all will become clear in the end. Carlotta also says, "I was told never to show a fool a thing half finished. But what else does the Lord himself do to us during all our lives?" (*SGT,* 215). The significance of a life or a tale is not clear until it is over.

Dinesen has been clever about embedding the textual clues that will lead to a final epiphany, and many readers have missed them. Casey Bjerregaard Black has suggested that the road in "The Roads Round Pisa" is a symbol for the search for truth, and the ironic narrative games that Dinesen plays as she leads us down the road may qualify as postmodern.[81] Susan Hardy Aiken would probably agree. She has argued that "To travel the roads round Pisa, then, is to traverse, both literally and psychologically, a 'feminine' space where randomness, coincidence, and irregularity replace the orderly connections and progressions of the masculine *civitas* as of narratological order and authority."[82] In Aiken's gender-sensitive reading of Dinesen's texts, she describes these two locations Pisa/Around Pisa as masculine/feminine. The roads round Pisa are where things happen and meaning is generated. The tale dwells on Pisa itself for not much more than a paragraph. Both Aiken and Black might agree that, in "The Roads Round Pisa," it is not possession of the truth that counts, but the search that signifies.

The first section of the tale introduces us to Augustus von Schimmelman. Most of the action of the tale is seen and interpreted by Augustus, who does not appear to be the most perceptive and reliable of observers. Else Brundbjerg has unearthed the interesting detail that Augustus's *alma mater* in Ingolstadt possesses at least one other fictional alumnus: Dr. Frankenstein from Mary Shelley's *Frankenstein* (1818).[83] Perhaps one is to understand by this Gothic "in-joke" that both men majored in Colossal Egotism. Despite his initial denial, Augustus's fixation with mirrors seems to indicate a high degree of self-absorption. In an earlier draft of the tale, Dinesen meant to call him Herman von Spiegelhausen (Herman from the house of mirrors), but opted for the more subtle Augustus von Schimmelman (Augustus, the man of mold).[84] None of these appellations should inspire the reader with confidence. Despite his flaws, Dinesen reprises this character two other times in her writing, in "The Poet" and *Out of Africa*.

Instead of calling Augustus a house of mirrors, Dinesen has him reflect upon the phenomenon in the first chapter. A hall of mirrors is a source of distortion: "So your own self, your personality and existence are reflected within the mind of each of the people whom you meet and live with, into a likeness, a caricature of yourself, which still lives on and pretends to be, in some way, the truth about you" (*SGT,* 166). Augustus believes that a true mirror of the soul can exist in the soul of a friend. In other words, for Augustus, the purpose of friends is to show him himself, a rather narcissistic purpose for a good friend. When his wife looks for her reflection in his eyes, all she sees is that his gaze is fixed upon her new diamond earrings. Augustus reflects himself in others, but does not seem willing to function as a mirror in return, hence the tragic mismatch in his marriage. Based on Augustus's behavior throughout the story, the reader should feel free to question the philosophies that Augustus puts forward. He is in existential limbo.[85] He ponders, "I do not know what to do with myself or my life. Can I trust to fate to hold out a helping hand to me just for once?" (*SGT,* 167). Fate will answer Augustus's question loudly and emphatically in a few moments, but will Augustus understand he has been answered?

Augustus contemplates a smelling-bottle that belonged to a maiden aunt of his father's and notes that this bottle prompted him to travel to Italy. The hand of fate, or the puppet master, has already begun to pull the strings. The smelling-bottle will return at the end of the tale as an omen that Augustus has been in the grip of great forces. Dinesen ends the section with a metafictional wink at the reader. Augustus wonders if in a hundred years people will be reading about him and what they will think about him. Augustus would like to use the reader as yet another mirror.

A coach accident occurs right before Augustus's eyes, and as he approaches the victims, he sees what he takes to be an old man. Once a bonnet with curls could be clapped on his head, "the old man was transformed into a fine old lady of imposing appearance" (*SGT,* 169). This is a clear example of how the omniscient story narrator is limiting the reader to Augustus's horizons of perception. He is mistaken about what he sees, and so is the reader. This incident is also one of many instances of gender ambiguity in the text. As usual, Dinesen disrupts and challenges the conventions of gender. A person's appearance is not necessarily a clue. The old lady, Carlotta, requests Augustus's aid in getting a message to her granddaughter Rosina: "Tell her . . . that I cannot lift my right hand, and that I will bless her" (*SGT,* 170). Carlotta also assures Augustus in no uncertain terms that there is a God, thus answering his question of a moment ago.

Carlotta goes on in the next section to tell her story. She says that she has only loved three people in her life and that she has never cared for anything male, leaving us to further ponder Carlotta's indeterminate gender. Carlotta also has had a terrible fear of childbearing and has managed to arrange things so that the possibility will not arise. The nuts and bolts of these arrangements are left to the reader's imagination. One of the three Carlotta has loved is her stepdaughter, Anna, who runs off with a soldier and dies bearing Rosina. Rosina is another of Carlotta's beloved three. In order to protect Rosina from the prospects of childbearing, Carlotta marries her off to the wealthy Prince Pozentiani. Pozentiani's name is misleading (it is spelled Potenziani in the Danish edition), since he is anything but potent: "a caprice of nature had made him, although an admirer of our sex, incapable of being a lover or a husband" (*SGT,* 172–73). Although another sexually indeterminate character, Pozentiani's inability to have sex with Rosina makes him the perfect match in Carlotta's eyes.

Carlotta and her granddaughter, Rosina, become caught in a generational shift. In the eighteenth century, marriage among the upper classes was an issue of family honor, politics, and money. Love did not enter into the negotiations. The nineteenth century saw the introduction of the romantic notion that love should be the major prerequisite for marriage. Carlotta wants to choose Rosina's husband for all the practical reasons that are traditional. Rosina wants to marry her cousin Mario for love. Rosina, as her name might indicate, is a blossom figure, a type of feminine beauty in Dinesen's fiction, who is compelled by erotic love and who does not mind cheating law and order just a little in order to achieve her erotic desires. Lord Byron is commonly associated with the introduction of this new idea about love and marriage, so it is appropriate that Rosina receive aid from her friend Agnese, who likes to dress up as Byron.

Rosina tries to escape but is caught by Carlotta. They each make a vow in a church, and Carlotta promises, "I swear that as long as I can lift my right hand I am not going to give my blessing to any marriage of yours, except with the Prince" (*SGT,* 175). Thus, Carlotta's loss of the use of her right hand in the accident is a significant injury, since it is a sign that God takes these promises seriously. A month after her marriage to the Prince, Rosina is able to prove that she is a virgin and receive an annulment; whereupon she marries Mario. She is now expecting a child. Augustus undertakes to bring Carlotta's message to Rosina and adds some lines from Goethe's *Faust* to a letter he is writing that may make us hope that Augustus is on the right track: "A good man, through obscurest aspirations, / Has still the instinct of the one true way . . ." (*SGT,* 178).

"The Roads Round Pisa" is relatively silent about what transpires between Rosina and the Prince during the one month of their marriage, but Dinesen suggests in her letter to Hans Brix that it was not at all uneventful. Dinesen mentions Emile Zola's novel *Rome* (1896) as an inspiration for the part of the intrigue whereby Rosina is able to achieve the annulment of her unhappy marriage by proving her virginity. Dinesen comments that, between the moment Rosina announces that she wants an annulment and her final journey to Rome, "a great battle has taken place between husband and wife. Potenziani [sic] has tried to convince or force Rosina to give up her intentions, but she has clung to them with an unbelievable strength" (*KBD,* 1:562). She cites the detail that Rosina has been crying on the occasion that Agnese is playing chess with the Professor who was to talk to Rosina about her duties. Moreover, Dinesen points to Pozentiani's line, "When she was frightened or angry her face, her whole body, blushed like an oleander flower" (*SGT,* 206), as an indication that "something in his behavior can have been offensive to his young wife" (*KBD,* 1:565). These still waters seem to run deep indeed.

Augustus stops at another inn on his way to Pisa and learns from the innkeeper that he is about to be joined by Prince Pozentiani and Prince Giovanni Gastone, a remarkable coincidence, considering the tale he has heard the night before. Such remarkable coincidences abound in this tale, leading one to suspect that the forces of fate have taken more than a casual interest in events. Prince Giovanni, called Nino, shares a name with the famous seducer Don Giovanni and is also a great ladies' man, although he remains popular in the region. He is a particular patron of the language, traditions and art of Tuscany. The innkeeper inserts one important detail in his catalogue of Prince Nino's qualities, the significance of which is not clear until later in the story. Nino's mood had changed lately, and "he had been known to say that a miracle had crossed his way and made him believe in miracles" (*SGT,* 180). Something has happened to Nino that he cannot explain rationally.

Augustus also meets Agnese, another incredible coincidence, but mistakes her for a boy for quite some time. The reader shares his misperception. Once Augustus discovers he is speaking to a woman, his manner towards Agnese changes completely. He is ruled by the conventions that govern behavior between the sexes in this society. Significantly, Agnese does not change her behavior towards Augustus at all. Augustus's views on clothing are quite the opposite of Baron von Brackel's in "The Old Chevalier." The Baron prefers the concealing layers of feminine dress for women, whereas Augustus thinks that trousers are the only rational sort of apparel for either gender.

Agnese confides in Augustus that something has happened to her that she could not turn into poetry and she is caught in the memory of that one hour of her life. She is on her way to Pisa to study astronomy. In the case of Athena in "The Monkey," the study of astronomy is a symbol of the desire to escape physical jeopardy, that of sexual attention in particular. Like Athena, Agnese appears to be another Diana figure, adopting masculine dress and uninterested in the erotic attentions of men. Agnese compares the roles of the sexes to that of hostess and guest. Augustus dismisses the crude guest who "takes what he can get and goes away" and instead describes the guest who wants to be diverted, impress his own personality upon his surroundings, and find a meaning for existence (*SGT,* 185). In a nutshell, Augustus has described what he wants out of life and what he expects from others, not only from women. Agnese then remarks that the hostess wants to be thanked. As the story unfolds, we will learn that Agnese has indeed been the victim of a crude guest and has not been thanked. Agnese quickly exits when Prince Pozentiani and Prince Nino enter the inn.

"The Story of the Bravo" is essential as a clue to decoding the mysteries of the text, but first Pozentiani engages in a digression about Vincenzo Monti (1754–1828), an Italian author who also created a literary treatment of Don

Giovanni. Monti's tirade against Monsignor Talbot has been cited as an expression of Dinesen's aesthetics. In essence, human beings are the raw material that might inspire the creation of literary greatness, such as Odysseus, Don Quixote, or Don Giovanni. Great art confers immortality, although there are no guarantees that real life does: "When the statue is finished in marble or bronze, he [God] breaks us all up" (*SGT,* 188). In Dinesen's tales, art often functions as the great justification or consolation. When Job asks "Why?" God responds with the answer of an artist, "It is aesthetically necessary." A horrible experience can be accepted if viewed aesthetically as part of a great tragedy.

Whether Monti is speaking for Dinesen or not might be questioned, especially in light of the fact that Donald Hannah has traced these sentiments to a similar passage in Pirandello's *Six Characters in Search of an Author* (1921): "He who has the good fortune to be born a living character may snap his fingers at Death even. He will never die! Man . . . The writer . . . The instrument of creation . . . will die . . . But what is created by him will never die."[86] Pirandello's play is a modern metafictional romp, and in this passage a fictional character lays claim to immortality by virtue of being fictional. Dinesen makes a playful gesture by placing almost the same words in the mouth of an author. (Could Monti have been the author Pirandello's six characters were looking for?) Dinesen's intertextual gestures connect her fictional world with other fictional worlds. In this case, Dinesen also shows her approval of Pirandello, whom she once called "an Einstein in literature!" (*LA,* 232).

"The Story of the Bravo" is not about what it seems to be about. In that story Prince Pozentiani accuses Nino of having betrayed him. From details revealed later in the story, it appears that Prince Pozentiani has foreseen the possibility of Rosina's gaining an annulment if she remains a virgin and considers that he might not mind an heir from a Ducal house. Therefore, he has persuaded his friend to rape his wife, Rosina, perhaps by offering to pay off Prince Nino's debts, just as the nobleman in the tale pays off the bravo. Nino believes he has raped Rosina, expressed obliquely as, "if a man be dead who has had my stiletto in his heart three times, up to the hilt" (*SGT,* 190). One does not need Freud's help with that image. Since Rosina is able to prove her virginity, Pozentiani's logical conclusion is that Nino has lied to him when he said he committed the deed. Nino's only explanation for Rosina's virginity is a miracle.

Dinesen elaborated on Nino's position in her letter to Brix:

Of Nino it can be said, for the enlightenment of any truly interested reader, that his circumstances at the Osteria really *were* desperate. He feels that he has been seduced into a deed of darkness, whereby he has lost his temporal and eternal salvation, by his former best friend, whom he still deeply admires. At the same time, he understands he cannot refute his friend's accusation of betrayal. He [Nino] has himself . . . said that a miracle has crossed his path and persuaded him to believe in miracles, which is to say, that in his eyes, heaven has intervened and taken the part of the victim. But he could hardly convert the Prince to this belief. His entire soul is at once fraught with tension and completely paralyzed, and he sees no other way out but death. Augustus comes . . . to believe during his conversation with him "that he was clinging to the fatefulness of the coming hour with a passionate tenderness." (*KBD*, 1:566)

Nino's response to "The Story of the Bravo" is as an art critic: "I think that as a story yours was too long, and even yet it has had no end. Let us make an end tonight" (*SGT*, 192). He throws wine into Pozentiani's face, thus precipitating a duel that will end in death for one of them. Elizabeth Bronfen has made the observation that closure is death, so it will take a death to bring about the end of the story.

Agnese calls Augustus out of the inn to ask what the quarrel has been about. She has him repeat "The Story of the Bravo" twice, "and stopped him to have certain words and figures repeated to her" (*SGT*, 195). Her expression indicates that she too has experienced a deadly insult, and she wonders if it is possible that Nino and Pozentiani will both be killed in the duel. Later in the tale, Prince Nino asks Agnese, whom he takes for a young man, to act as second at the duel when the Prince's other friend becomes ill. Agnese agrees and responds with an apocryphal anecdote about Joseph granting Potiphar's wife a favor. In the biblical tale, Potiphar's wife has done Joseph a great wrong by accusing him of attempted rape and having him thrown in prison. Agnese's tale is therefore about someone who has been wronged being in the position to grant a favor to the one who has wronged him. In granting Prince Nino this favor, Agnese is in essence doing the same thing: Nino has wronged her in some way.

Agnese takes Augustus to watch "the immortal *Revenge of Truth*," a marionette comedy. This is another of Dinesen's intertextual jokes, since *The Revenge of Truth* is a marionette comedy she herself wrote as a young woman and published in 1926. The paraphrase of the play in "The Roads Round Pisa" is not an exact description of Dinesen's original play, but very close. Aage Henriksen has written an important essay connecting Dinesen's use of the marionette theme to Heinrich von Kleist's romantic view of marionettes in his essay "On the Marionette Theater" (1810).[87] In Kleist's essay, marionettes are praised over human dancers because they can completely subject themselves to the will of the puppet master. Human dancers reflect upon their actions and so their movements will be imperfect. Something of this message is communicated to Augustus, who indeed has a tendency to reflect too much: "The truth, my children, is that we are, all of us, acting in a marionette comedy. What is important more than anything else in a marionette comedy, is keeping the ideas of the author clear" (*SGT*, 199). Because of the remarkable coincidences we have already seen in this tale, there is a strong sense that divine forces are pulling the strings of fate.

Donald Hannah has pointed out that Dinesen's play, despite being called a marionette comedy, has only been performed by live actors. Hannah has explored the connections between Dinesen's play and the *commedia dell'arte* tradition.[88] *Commedia dell'arte* is an improvised dramatic art form from Italy. There is no script. Actors are given their roles, which indicate certain character types, and they are given a plot. The rest is improvised. Dinesen's character Mopsus at one point runs amok in *The Revenge of Truth* and wants to subordinate the entire play to his ego.[89] He relents when he realizes this would not be aesthetically satisfying. "Keeping the ideas of the author clear" makes more sense in connection with *commedia dell'arte* than a marionette play. Thus human beings are all improvisational actors, and we must play our roles to the utmost keeping the idea of the author/God clear. Hannah found the following sentiment among Dinesen's notes: "Every human being . . . believes in God—*in a guiding principle in the universe. It depends then on which God he believes in.*"[90] The reader is free to name this guiding force whatever he or she cares to: God, puppet master, author, fate . . .

At dawn, the morning after the marionette comedy, the time for the duel has come. Before Prince Nino and Prince Pozentiani pull their triggers, Agnese steps forward and tells a tale that has the impact of a speeding bullet. She explains that for one hour she exchanged places with her friend Rosina. Once she has delivered her speech, the scene is described as follows: "They all stood perfectly immobile, like a party of little wooden dolls placed on the terrace of the inn, in the middle of the great landscape—Augustus and the old doctor, because they did not know what this speech meant; the old Prince and Giovanni, because they were too deeply impressed to move" (*SGT*, 206–7). They appear as marionettes on a stage. Augustus does not understand what has happened, but the attentive reader realizes that this is the last piece of a puzzle that has tormented three lives. Nino raped Agnese by mistake during the hour she took Rosina's place, so there has been no miracle and Nino has not betrayed Pozentiani. There is no longer a need for the duel.

A duel is fought however, between Pozentiani and God. Pozentiani laments, "Too small I have been, too small for the ways of God" (*SGT*, 207). Pozentiani has tried to manipulate the destinies of others in his favor, thus usurping the prerogative of God. Closure is death and Pozentiani has seen the design of his life. Agnese's tale supplies the last piece of the pattern, which proves fatal. A few moments later, Pozentiani "took hold of his pistol, as if on guard against a greater enemy," and then he dies (*SGT,* 207). His last word is Carlotta's name, leaving us to wonder about the relationship between these two androgynous characters. The bullet he fires almost strikes Augustus, but there is still no sign he has understood what he has witnessed.

In the next section, Augustus goes inside, and for the first time the reader is not bound to Augustus's perception of events. Prince Nino and Agnese, rapist and victim, are left to confront each other. Aiken has noticed the similarity of Agnese's name to *agnus* "lamb," as in *agnus dei* (Lamb of God), the synonym for an innocent sacrifice. Agnese is "a feminized Lamb of God—a surrogate sacrifice whose 'blood' has been shed in another's stead."[91] A cock descended from biblical times crows, an image of betrayal, since it recalls the cock crowing three times when Peter denies Christ. Agnese is compared to Daphne, a nymph who escaped the amorous attentions of Apollo by being turned into a laurel tree. The experience of the rape petrified Agnese and confined her to that one hour of her existence.

Prince Nino resorts to the language of Dante, probably the best choice he could make. Both Nino and Agnese possess a deep love of Italian poetry and are able to use Dante's verses to express the inexpressible. In the Danish edition, the verses are quoted in Danish, but English readers must brush up on their Italian. The stanzas are from Dante's *Purgatorio* and the first (canto 30: 34–39) consists of Dante's words to his beloved Beatrice, expressing his awe of her. The next stanza (canto 31: 85–89) voices repentance, guilt, and regret that the one he loved must now be his enemy. Agnese responds with Beatrice's words of forgiveness (canto 33: 31–36). The title of this section is "The Freed Captive." Nino's apology and her forgiveness have released Agnese from being captive to that one hour in her life and now she is free to do whatever she chooses.

Augustus finally makes it to Pisa and completes his mission. As mentioned earlier, his activities in Pisa itself seem of relatively little consequence compared to the events on the roads round Pisa. Augustus travels to Carlotta's country estate in order to receive the thanks of the family. His view of the estate is masked by a sudden thunderstorm. Carlotta, Rosina, and the baby are compared to the holy family, with the father, Mario, relegated to the role of the Magi. The baby is something of a divine child, the bright spot at the center of the mosaic, the point of all the intrigue. Carlotta has finally learned to love something male and attained harmony.

Carlotta then produces the final resounding coincidence of the story. The third person she had loved in her life turns out to be Augustus's beloved great aunt, and the mate of his aunt's smelling-bottle is produced with a picture of his home estate. If the thunderstorm had not drawn a curtain across the landscape, Augustus might have recognized Carlotta's estate on his own smelling-bottle. Augustus has not been a mere incidental player in these events. Fate/God has prepared a lesson for him and drives it home with a series of thundering omens, including the traditional sign of a covenant between God and man, a rainbow. Why does he not share this information with Carlotta? Does he understand?

Critics are fairly united in the opinion that Augustus does not understand and that by looking into the mirror at the end of the tale, he is back where he started. Casey Bjerregaard Black's assessment sums up the critical sentiment nicely: "By failing to create a story, the materials for which lie readily at hand, Augustus condemns himself to a peripheral, parasitic, and shadow-like existence, which we see confirmed in 'The Poet.' . . . Augustus's refusal to share his insight with the old woman and thus make 'a tale which she would forever have cherished and repeated' . . . becomes a colossally egotistical blunder."[92] In the context of her letter to Johannes Rosendahl about Nemesis, Dinesen characterizes Augustus as one of the characters who wants to "get off cheaply" and thus will not embrace his fate (*KBD,* 2:12). The one dissenting critical voice belongs to Hans Holmberg, who interprets the mirror as a symbol for truth. In Holmberg's view, the fact that Augustus looks at himself in the mirror indicates that he has finally learned the truth about himself.[93]

As the first story in the British and Danish editions of *Seven Gothic Tales,* "The Roads Round Pisa" introduces the reader to the important themes of fate, marionettes, and the relationship between art and life. Moreover the text might cue the reader as to Dinesen's narrative games and the circumstance that all is not what it seems, useful knowledge for deciphering the subsequent tales. The fact that Dinesen reprises Augustus's character in other works indicates that his particular type continued to occupy her.

"The Supper at Elsinore"

The tone of "The Supper at Elsinore" is somewhat darker than the previous tales in the collection. Orson Welles claimed it was his favorite Dinesen story.[94] The physical setting of the tale was quite familiar to Dinesen, who lived at Rungsted in the inn that had sheltered the Danish poet Johannes Ewald, who is remembered by Madame Baek. The perilous route from Elsinore to Copenhagen passed right by Dinesen's window. From that same window Dinesen had a view of the sound where the privateers fought and which has frozen over to allow Morten to return from hell. Elsinore has been an appropriate place to spot ghosts since the first act of *Hamlet.* Like *Hamlet,* "The Supper at Elsinore" is a tale of incest and frustrated love that leads to tragedy.

It has been common among scholars to think of "The Supper at Elsinore" as the story of the thwarted lives of Fanny and Eliza. As young women of the early nineteenth century, their lives have been tightly controlled. Their brother Morten has been able to live a life of adventure, whereas the two sisters have been confined to their cages, like the birds to which they are so often compared. The conversation at Fanny's birthday party clearly illustrates the views men have of women, which have shaped the lives of these sisters. Given a pair of wings, Fanny would fly, even if she needed to use a broomstick. The Bishop instructs her that she may have the wings of an angel, as long as she never considers flight and remains on a pedestal. He invokes the example of Lilith as a cautionary tale, "neither husband nor angels can master her" (*SGT,* 240). The theater director goes on to compare women to poetry, rather than prose. The words of poetry must "stand, walk and behave according to difficult and painful laws" in order to be beautiful (*SGT,* 241). Prose, which is unregulated by such rules, is the language of political action, not a domain for women. The commodore compares women to sailing ships, dependent upon the wind and the hand that steers them. "The beastly steamships," he claims, "may well be a species of witches of the sea—they are like self-supporting women" (*SGT,* 241). The message in each of these comparisons is the same: Women should remain passive and under the control of male expectations. The two sisters have deeply internalized this message and feel "that the final word as to what you are really worth lies with the other sex" (*SGT,* 237).

Fanny and Eliza have become celibate caryatids, like the sisters in "Babette's Feast." Their entire lives have been dedicated to maintaining patriarchy in the form of their family honor. They try to make right the mess that Morten has left behind him and have dreams of him returning from his travels with honor. Even so, they are aware that their family is doomed. The De Conincks all bear a resemblance to a death's head. The male heir has absconded and been hanged. The sisters' task is not to marry and reproduce but to bear the burdens of the family even as they slowly fade from existence.

Robert Langbaum noticed the incestuous undertones that run between the three siblings, but Annelies van Hees, through a very careful reading, has made the case quite clearly. As usual, the narrative of this tale creates uncertainties. The perspective of the tale often seems to be that of Madame Baek, but the perspective shifts unnoticeably and without warning. Madame Baek is said to be a very different sort of character from the two girls, so one may question her understanding of their circumstances. In her heart, she believes that Fanny and Eliza never marry because of "the doom which hung over the breed," but "toward the world she held the theory that they had not been able to find any man worthy of them except their brother" (*SGT,* 218). Annelies van Hees argues that this theory Madame Baek holds out to the world as a sort of mask for the true reason, is, in fact, the real reason.[95] She has gotten it right without knowing it. Both Fanny and Eliza are in love with their brother, Morten, and that love will lead to the doom of their family.

Morten's name even incorporates *le mort* (death).[96] He is compared to Hamlet, Bluebeard, Sinbad the Sailor, and the Flying Dutchman, the myths of each of which are incestuous, according to van Hees's psychoanalytic reading.[97] Sinbad, Odysseus, who is also mentioned in the tale, and the Flying Dutchman are all sailors on a quest. Sinbad undertakes seven fantastic voyages. Odysseus is on a quest to return to Penelope, his faithful wife. The Flying Dutchman, according to the German poet Heinrich Heine, is condemned to sail eternally, but every seventh year he goes ashore to be married and can only be saved by the faithfulness of a woman. Morten has been absent for thirty years and has married five times, so Morten's identification with the Flying Dutchman legend is mathematically possible. Van Hees argues that if Morten's mistress, Katrine, is counted as a common-law wife, then Morten's return to his sisters is a journey to see if the magical "seventh wife" has been faithful to him.

Morten left without a trace on the eve of his wedding to Adrienne. Madame Baek speculates about what might have happened: "Had he begged her to take him and hold him, so that it should no longer be in his power to leave her? . . . Or had she yielded, and found the magic ineffective?" (*SGT,* 230). Later, during Morten's speech on God's ability to say no, he uses some suggestive phrases when thought of in this context: "I thought of those great, pure, and beautiful things which say no to us. For why should they say yes to us, and tolerate our insipid caresses? Those who say yes, we get them under us, we ruin them, and leave them, and find when we have left them that they have made us sick" (*SGT,* 267). One could interpret this to mean that perhaps Adrienne had yielded to Morten and the magic was ineffective. He remains bound to the "noble, proud woman" who says no to him: his sister. When Fanny reproaches Morten for his treatment of Adrienne, he responds by reminding them of a comic song from the French Revolution. According to Langbaum, "The point seems to be that just as Marat had only the shirts he had stolen from the aristocrats, so Adrienne never had an existence to destroy."[98] Adrienne is thus dismissed.

Morten is concerned to learn whether his sisters have married. As he goes on to describe his career as a pirate, his relationship to his ship, *La Belle Eliza,* emerges as a vicarious sexual relationship with his sister, Eliza. Morten explains, "I fell in love. . . . And she was somebody else's, so I could not have her without cheating law and order a little" (*SGT,* 259). Eliza belongs to the world of patriarchy and convention and breaking the incest taboo is not taken lightly. It turns out that Eliza has known for some time what the name of his ship was and the thought has brought her joy: "Oh, you burghers of Elsinore, did you see me dance the minuet once? To those same measures did I tread the waves" (*SGT,* 261). When Morten loses his ship, he metaphorically loses his ballast, that which lends him stability and ties him to the earth. He is unable to sleep and states, "I shall never lay me down to rest until I can sleep once more on her, in her, *La Belle Eliza*" (*SGT,* 263). The eroticism of this comment is blatant.

When he is about to be hung in Cuba, Morten requests one more minute of life, "I will think, with the halter around my neck, for one minute of *La Belle Eliza*" (*SGT,* 268). Hans Brix saw in this motif an echo from Emil Aarestrup's poem "Skjøn Ellens Elsker" (1838, "Lovely Ellen's Lover.")[99] The poem tells the story of a man's obsession with the lovely Ellen that causes him to leave wife and child and become a thief and a murderer. The final stanza reads:

> He lay his head on the block—
> No mercy was granted him.
> As the executioner grabbed his hair—
> Hold—he cried—just a second!
> It was only, lovely Ellen,
> because it pleased him
> still under the executioner's axe
> to think once more of you![100]

Morten, too, has deserted his wife-to-be and become a thief and a murderer. In Aarestrup's poem, it is clear the deeds are inspired by a woman. In Morten's rendition, the deeds have been inspired by the ship, *La Belle Eliza.*

Dinesen commented on the moment of execution to Hans Brix:

> Morten thinks, with the rope around his neck, not about the girl Eliza, but honestly and truthfully of his ship. But this ship has become for him a sort of symbol of his sister, or through it she has become a myth for him— through the ship *La Belle Eliza* the two of them have reached full understanding. The relationship is rather clear to Eliza herself and seems, according to her nature, quite natural: This is, what she has gotten out of life, that she, as *La Belle Eliza,* has attained a real existence, has been loved by, and has been the destiny of, her brother. (*KBD,* 1:518)

The confirmation of all she has suspected of her relationship to Morten brings a blush to Eliza's face, the typical Dinesen sign of erotic excitement, and she is compared to "a chaste, flaming bride" (*SGT,* 262).

But what about Fanny? Hers is the truly tragic destiny in this tale. The two sisters have been a pair all their lives, yet they are described in different terms. Eliza is *la Beauté* (Beauty), a swan, fair, well-dressed, and less clever. She is the perfect ornament and inspiration for Morten. Fanny is *l'Esprit* (Spirit), a wing-clipped bird, dark, not beautiful, but clever. Both sisters have longed for a life of action away from Elsinore. Even Eliza says to Morten, "How I have wished that I were you," instead of "How I have wished that I were *with* you" (*SGT*, 255). Eliza, in a sense, has been with Morten the whole time. Fanny, whose sympathies are with Lilith, has become embittered by her life. When Fanny learns that Morten comes from hell, her heart leaps, as though she might be pleased that he is being punished for what he has done to her. She reproaches Morten, something which Eliza never does, "We are old maids, all on your account. Nobody would have us" (*SGT*, 257). When Eliza comments that the circle is complete, Fanny adds "the vicious circle" (*SGT*, 268). For Fanny there is no moment of affirmation at the end of the tale. She is shut out of the relationship between Morten and Eliza, even though she has dedicated her life to them. Fanny is miserable and complains of the cold in her maiden bed. Her expression, "to hell," may be directed in bitterness at her brother, although she regrets it in the last moment: "Take me with you!" (*SGT*, 269). Fanny's life has been wasted.

In her letter to Johannes Rosendahl about Nemesis, Dinesen described in negative terms those who want to get off cheaply, not pay the full price their destiny demands of them. In this letter, the De Coninck sisters find themselves in interesting company: "The Councilor in 'The Poet,' the Misses De Coninck, Count Schimmelman and Emilie in 'The Dreaming Child' all want to 'get off cheaply' and only discover—or in the case of the Misses De Coninck and Schimmelman, will only discover—harmony by paying the full price" (*KBD*, 1:391–92). The Councilor and Schimmelman are not particularly admirable characters. There is an implied reproach in Dinesen's comments. Perhaps the De Coninck sisters should have staged a full-scale rebellion, rather than submitting to their tame, vicarious, uneventful lives.

"The Dreamers"

"The Dreamers" is perhaps the most personal of Dinesen's *Seven Gothic Tales*. She has said very little about the tale itself, except when Thorkild Bjørnvig charged, "You are Pellegrina," Dinesen replied, "Yes, I am. . . . The loss of her voice corresponds to my loss of the farm and Africa."[101] "The Dreamers" was the first tale that Dinesen wrote after leaving Africa and returning to Denmark. Readers can easily seek for themselves the biographical parallels Dinesen points to with her remark. When considering Dinesen as a reader of her own texts, one might infer a rather sympathetic stance toward the character Pellegrina. Not every analyst of the tale has shared such a sympathy.

Truman Capote came up with the idea of filming "The Dreamers" with Greta Garbo in the role of Pellegrina. Dinesen was thrilled, as she wrote to Robert Haas, "I am more happy than I can tell you about the idea of Greta Garbo taking the part of Pellegrina. I have always thought her by far the greatest film actress of all, and I feel that she can do this part as I have seen it myself when I wrote the story. I hope and wish that the dream may become a reality!" (*KBD*, 1:391–92). Garbo was not willing to break her isolation for this sensational comeback, so Dinesen expressed herself willing to settle for Ingrid Bergman, directed by her husband Roberto Rossellini. Neither of these projects ever made it to the screen.

The structure of "The Dreamers" is complex, even by Dinesen's standards. The initial frame of the tale describes three men, Said, Mira Jama, and Lincoln Forsner, traveling on a dhow from Lamu to Zanzibar in 1863. This frame is something of a curious cultural inversion of Joseph Conrad's *Heart of Darkness* (1902). Conrad's famous novel begins with four European men on a boat at anchor on the Thames and leads into a story of the mysteries of the "Dark Continent." Lincoln is the only European on the dhow, and he tells his African/Arabic audience a tale of Europe that will seem exotic to them, "But as to names and places, and conditions in the countries in which it all took place, and which may seem very strange to you, I will give no explanation. You must take in whatever you can, and leave the rest outside. It is not a bad thing in a tale that you under- stand only half of it" (*SGT*, 279). The tale of Pellegrina is presented in thoroughly European dress, but the foreign audience of the tale provides a cultural disloca- tion. Moreover, the world of the storyteller Mira Jama is that of *The Arabian Nights*. The European Pellegrina will find herself translated back into that idiom by the end of the tale.

From within this frame, Lincoln begins a story set twenty years in the past, the climax of which takes place in the Swiss Alps, a liminal space where the North meets the South. Lincoln soon digresses to a flashback, the story of how he met Olalla and how he came to be searching for her months later. He meets two companions, Friedrich Hohenemser, alias Pilot, and the Baron Guildenstern, who each has a story to tell about Madame Lola and Rosalba respectively. At this point, the reader is reading tales within a tale within a tale. After a chase up the mountain, Pellegrina's mysterious companion, Marcus Cocoza, finally tells the story of the opera singer, Pellegrina Leoni.

As in "The Deluge at Norderney," "The Monkey," and "The Roads Round Pisa," a vital piece of information is withheld from the reader until the end—in this case Pellegrina's identity—which compels the reader to reevaluate all that has gone before. Pellegrina has played the roles of all three of these women: Olalla, Madame Lola, and Rosalba. The reader's interpretive skills are further challenged by the multiple narrative layers in the tale and the unreliability of the narrators. Pellegrina does not speak directly in this story. The reader only sees her as she is mediated through the eyes of the men around her. There is ample reason to question whether these narrators understand what has happened. Lincoln is mistaken when he believes "Olalla" is fleeing from Marcus. Pilot may not have actually killed the Chaplain of the Bishop of St. Gallen (he passed out immediately), and his leg was probably never broken. The Baron believes he has seduced Rosalba, whereas there are signs that Rosalba/Pellegrina has stage-managed the entire scene. Marcus's relationship to Pellegrina is unusual and one may question whether he has revealed everything. "The Dreamers" is a tale of many mysteries which allows interpreters much room for speculation.

Some interpreters have chosen to focus on the outer frame of "The Dreamers." According to Gargi Roysircar Sodowsky and Roland Sodowsky's existential interpretation, the tale of Pellegrina is told to instruct Said who in his "narrow role of avenger" must be saved from "his inauthenticity."[102] Pellegrina's acceptance of her loss and the contingencies of existence become a positive parable that Mira Jama translates into more familiar terms in the "Sultan Sabour of Khorassana." Since the Sultan's faithful slave has had his nose and ears cut off, the parallel with Said and Mira Jama is clear. The story is meant to help Said prepare for the possibility of failure.

Anthony Stephens feels that Pellegrina's story has been told for the edification of Mira Jama. Mira Jama has apparently lost his ability to tell stories. Lincoln's tale is a story of coping with loss: "Pellegrina Leoni must be deprived of the attribute which has up till now defined her, namely her singing-voice, before she can participate in the stories of Lincoln, Pilot, and Guildenstern as Olalla, Madame Lola, and Madame Rosalba. Mira Jama, in like fashion, having initially lost his role as storyteller, has to complete this process by becoming the audience for Lincoln's story—in other words: participate in a complete exchange of roles himself—in order to emerge at the end with his narrative gift restored."[103]

Mira Jama lost his ability to tell tragic stories when he lost his ability to fear. Since then he is unable to inspire fear in others. Since Mira Jama does not tell stories of poverty and unpopularity, he says he will tell funny stories when he resumes his narrative career. A comic vision of the world is left to him. Loss as a prerequisite for artistic production is a theme that runs throughout Dinesen's work and is described in the metaphor of the coffee tree that has lost its taproot. The tree will not bear fruit, but will flower more richly. Mira Jama has lost his nose and ears, just as the shoemaker/storyteller in "The Pearls" has lost his feet.

57

Judith Thurman refers to this as a Faustian sacrifice and adds to the list of such artists Marelli, the *castrato,* and Cardinal Salviati from "The Cardinal's First Tale" and Malli from "The Tempests," who have each renounced normal human love.[104]

The frame of "The Dreamers" is also significant in that it discusses the theme of dreaming. Mira says that in his dreams "the world creates itself around me without any effort on my part" (*SGT,* 276). In *Shadows on the Grass,* Dinesen describes her own joy of dreaming in terms similar to those used by Mira Jama. She explains: "For we have in the dream forsaken our allegiance to the organizing, controlling and rectifying forces of the world, the Universal Conscience. We have sworn fealty to the wild, incalculable, creative forces, the Imagination of the Universe" (*OA,* 439). Dreaming, in a sense, becomes surrender to the powers of imagination. Mira Jama claims that Lincoln dreams "awake and walking about. You will do nothing yourself to choose your own ways: you let the world form itself around you" (*SGT,* 277). Moreover, Mira states, "For really, dreaming is the well-mannered people's way of committing suicide" (*SGT,* 277). "Suicide" literally means "the murder of the self." One can commit suicide by perpetrating an act of violence against oneself, but that leaves a mess for others to clean up. Dreaming one's way through existence also entails a death of the self, but one has instead relinquished a stake in a single identity and stopped trying to sculpt one's own fate. The world forms itself around the dreamers, and they allow the Imagination of the Universe to take them where it will. Lincoln says that it is Pellegrina who has taught him to dream in this way.

Said stands in contrast to this mode of existence. He is a man of action. He is young and the world is drinking him in. The tale implies that Said will be a part of dramatic events: "Of Said's revenge, in the end, other tales have told" (*SGT,* 272). If Lincoln's tale is meant to educate Said, it does not seem to have achieved its purpose. In a letter correcting the Swedish translation of the tale, Dinesen observed about the end, "Said did not lie down to sleep, because he had too much to think about, but Mira, who has surrendered himself to fate and who finds comfort in dreaming as soon as he sleeps, lay down to sleep" (*KBD,* 1:173). The last line of the story informs us that Lincoln joins him in sleep.

The story of Pellegrina herself, in addition to its autobiographical undertones, constitutes an ingenious rewriting of Gothic traditions. After prolonged exposure to the Gothic, readers will begin to notice that the heroes, dark and tormented as they may be, have led much more interesting lives than the heroines. Heroines are virginal angels in the house, confined to quarters and swaddled in a straitjacket of moral convention. Even though things may come out all right in the end, women of the Gothic tend to spend much of their time being victimized.

Heroes, on the other hand, have generally defied moral convention, but the secret sins in their past only lend them a brooding attractiveness. Women with sexual experience are dangerous, occasionally madwomen, and most often punished by the end of the story. These appear to be the rules of Gothic fiction. In creating a fictional alter ego, Dinesen was not about to cast herself in the role of helpless victim. She had, in fact, always imagined herself in the role of the dark hero, taking the name of Lord Byron as a pseudonym in her youth. Dinesen felt at home with the Gothic, and no doubt relished the challenge of breaking the rules without shattering the expectations of the genre. In "The Dreamers," Dinesen manages to create a female dark hero, something which the original Gothic did not produce.

As part of her Faustian career, Pellegrina enacts the roles of whore, revolutionary, and saint, which Susan Hardy Aiken has called, "Three of the most overdetermined versions of 'woman' in Western patriarchal culture."[105] She has played these roles voluntarily, allowing the men in her life to read her according to these predetermined categories. Lincoln wants to lead her from a life of sin, the Baron from a life of virtue. Just as each man wants to possess Pellegrina and subordinate her into a role of his choosing, Pellegrina disappears.

In the case of Olalla, we see one of the categories of women in Gothic fiction being rewritten. Dinesen may have taken the name from a short story by Robert Louis Stevenson, "Olalla" (1885). The original Olalla is a Gothic victim trapped in a house with her degenerate relations and doomed to a life of celibacy, so as not to pass on the family madness. Dinesen's Olalla is a charismatic woman of experience who lavishes her favors on Lincoln. Olalla makes being a whore seem a pleasant and useful occupation, a sentiment totally at odds with the conventional morality of the Gothic. Lincoln finds Olalla when he slips the attentions of his old tutor, who is taken up with "the ancient Priapean cult of Lampsacus" (*SGT,* 282). Priapus was said to be the son of both Dionysus and Aphrodite, and his symbol was the phallus. Metaphorically, Lincoln himself goes to worship this deity when he enters the brothel. With typical Dinesen humor, it is noted that Lincoln first goes to the brothel with a party of theologians and has a difficult time searching through the numerous brothels in Basel, a town "which stands up most severely for the sanctity of marriage" (*SGT,* 290). Dinesen rejects the double standard which labels a woman with sexual experience a whore, while freeing her male suitors from any moral responsibility. No doubt, Dinesen also noticed the similarity of the name "Olalla" to the "Oh-la-la!" of the Parisian cancan girls, which is certainly worth a chuckle. Pellegrina is perfectly willing to play in a comedy whereby a prostitute marries into the highest social circles in England, until she becomes threatened by the exposure of her true identity. Pellegrina then resorts to the typical tragic ending for such a character and lets her die of a fever in the brothel.

Pilot's Madame Lola, a milliner in Lucerne, turns out to be a dangerous revolutionary. The female revolutionary was a figure who fired the imaginations of nineteenth-century women bound to their needlework and household duties. Charlotte Corday (1768–93), who slew Marat in his bath during the French Revolution, provided a role model of courage, rebellion, and self-sacrifice. The female revolutionary leads a life of action and makes a difference to history. This validation forms a stark contrast to the lives of most nineteenth-century women, who would cheerfully have traded in their crochet hooks for the opportunity to save a garrison. Although he is male, Pilot is similarly rescued from a purposeless life, in which his most important task is to procure ladies' hats, and made to feel useful and significant.

Hans Brix noticed that the nickname "Pilot" is borne by Rochester's dog in Charlotte Brontë's *Jane Eyre* (1847), making him a very minor Gothic character indeed. Pilot's limited spiritual abilities make him unreliable as a narrator. Not only is it possible that he has not committed the murder he is so proud of, but he may have been more of a pawn than he realized. Pilot learns that his uncle, the Baron de Watteville, has known all along of his whereabouts. Marcus says, "The Baron has much influence with the clergy of Lucerne, and it is doubtful whether we could have done without him" (*SGT,* 301–2). It is possible that Pilot has been held as a blissfully ignorant hostage, while his uncle has been forced to negotiate for concessions for the revolutionaries from the clergy.

Baron Guildenstern takes his name from a character out of *Hamlet,* one of Hamlet's old friends who betrays him by accepting Claudius's commission to kill him. Therefore, the name is not a particularly good character reference. The Baron Guildenstern is a self-styled Don Juan, who relates a tale of his greatest seductive triumph: the conquest of Rosalba. Rosalba is a saint, paradoxically a celibate with sexual experience, who has dedicated her life to the memory of General Zumala Carregui (correctly, Tomás Zumalacárregui [1788–1835], a general of the Carlists, which was a royalist faction opposed to women ascending to the throne of Spain). Rosalba lives on a Lenten diet and surrounds herself with ancient aristocrats who escaped the French Revolution. Rosalba has chosen her life of celibacy, not had it forced upon her by moral convention: "She uses in being a saint as much vigor as a commander in storming a citadel" (*SGT,* 305). Like Olalla, Rosalba does not seem victimized by her role. In the traditional Gothic, any sexual experience at all is unforgivable. Rosalba may have been named after the character, Rosalba la Pudica (Rosalba the Modest), in Barbey d'Aurevilly's *Les diaboliques* (1874). Despite her appellation and her ability to blush from head to toe, d'Aurevilly's Rosalba is described as a sexually depraved woman and camp follower. Thus she also possesses a double nature: sexual experience masked by a veil of innocence. D'Aurevilly's Rosalba is looked down upon and meets with a rather gruesome fate (her genitals are sealed with hot wax). Dinesen's Rosalba manages to achieve a high moral tone, despite her past, in the tradition of Mary Magdalene.

The irony of the Baron's pretensions to play Don Giovanni to Rosalba's helpless victim is that the Baron is unaware that he is the seduced and not the seducer. This is why Pellegrina cannot help laughing at him when they meet up on the mountainside. With her allusions to the sound of marble upon marble, Rosalba tries to dissuade the Baron from his purpose. In Mozart's opera, the stone statue of the Commendante comes to escort Don Giovanni to the pits of hell. Pellegrina is suggesting that the Baron's shallow lust for competition may result in dire consequences, but the Baron is too dense to get the message. The Baron imagines himself a great seducer but is unaware that the entire situation has been manipulated by a more skillful seducer than himself.

Pellegrina has tried on the roles of whore, saint, revolutionary, and even housewife as Frau Councilor Heerbrand of Altdorf, and pulled off each role with flair. Her true role in this Gothic tale is that of the dark romantic hero. This character type was spawned by the Romantic Movement and the Gothic and represents the rise of individualism. In the eras preceding romanticism, people saw themselves as subordinate to large social patterns, but in the words of Peter Thorslev, "The Romantic hero types, on the other hand—the Noble Outlaw, Faust, Cain or Ahasuerus, Satan or Prometheus—are invariably solitaries, and are fundamentally and heroically rebellious, at first against society only, and later against the natural universe or against God himself."[106] One may add to the gallery of romantic heroes Lord Byron, Peter Schlehmihl, and Don Juan/Don Giovanni. Although Don Juan was not esteemed by the English Gothic, he was a figure that interested both Kierkegaard and E. T. A. Hoffmann. Robert Langbaum notes Pellegrina's connections with all these figures, but without commenting upon how remarkable it is that a woman should cast herself as a dark romantic hero. These characters of romanticism all have rebellion in common, a rejection of society's moral claims upon them. They are wanderers and, occasionally, masters of disguise. The dark romantic hero, of course, exerts a compelling attraction upon the opposite sex. All of these things may be said to be true of Pellegrina.

In solving the puzzle of how to create a female romantic hero, Dinesen needed to find a woman who could move with ease geographically and socially. Most nineteenth-century women were literally confined to their homes and class. The solution may have been suggested in part by Georges Du Maurier's *Trilby* (1894).[107] Trilby is a young Parisian model who becomes a famous opera diva, tours Europe, and is celebrated by the nobility. She travels in the company of Svengali, her Jewish impresario. The similarities extend even to the scene in which Pellegrina's carriage is unhitched and drawn by her public. Beyond this rough outline and a few details, the similarities end. *Trilby* is a Victorian novel, with all the moralism, sexism, and anti-Semitism implied. Trilby is a hollow vessel made to sing under hypnosis by her unscrupulous impresario. Pellegrina is a much more independent and vigorous character. Svengali's sinister character reeks of anti-Semitism. Marcus Cocoza, his counterpart in "The Dreamers," lives in an anti-Semitic world, to judge from the Baron's remarks and Lincoln's dark suspicions. Marcus's great wealth makes him something of a literary stereotype. Nevertheless, as far as the attitude of the tale is concerned, he is the most honorable character in the story.

Pellegrina is said to sing like an angel, but receives the nickname "Lucifera," connecting her with the romantic Satan-type. Lucifer/Satan was an angel who rebelled against God, but who came to represent self-assertion and inventiveness in the romantic imagination. When Pellegrina loses her voice in the opera house fire, she is cast, like Satan in Milton's *Paradise Lost* (1667), in a cloud of flames from paradise. The role she is singing at the time is Donna Anna in *Don Giovanni.* Before the tragedy, we are told that Pellegrina was angry she could not play two roles in the same opera. Although one might assume Pellegrina wants to play Donna Elvira as well as Donna Anna, the role Pellegrina covets is that of Don Giovanni, just as Satan covets the role of God. Better to play the seducer than the rape victim. Better to reign in hell than serve in heaven. The scar that she receives in the fire, referred to as a witch's brand, is also a mark of Cain, confirming her exclusion from normal society. The figure of Cain in romanticism came to represent "that recurrent Romantic concern with the eternal and solitary wanderer, who had always an air about him of the mysterious and the supernatural and above all of destiny or tragic fate."[108]

After the loss of her voice, Pellegrina decides to sacrifice her identity to become many women. She erects a tombstone upon which is written "By the grace of God" (*SGT,* 344). Pellegrina has stopped living by the grace of God and has chosen the rebellious, demonic path. Marcus Cocoza with his enormous riches is a plausible literary device that enables Pellegrina to make this choice. Pellegrina claims to Lincoln that she has sold her shadow to the devil and that Marcus Cocoza is her unfortunate shadow. This joke invokes both the tales of Peter Schlehmihl and Faust. In one respect, Marcus plays Mephistopheles to Pellegrina's Faust. Lincoln tends to cast him in the role of demon and the fact that Marcus is able to get his heavy carriage up the hillside in a snowstorm hints at supernatural powers. On another level, Marcus is Ahasuerus, the Wandering Jew, who has found a soul mate in Pellegrina. Dinesen admired the figure of

Ahasuerus, as she wrote to Aage Henriksen, "The greatness of this figure lies in his isolation, his separation from the common humanity, and where the idea of pain is connected with it—as it is—it pertains to Ahasuerus himself, to the extent that his own pain at his separateness cannot be truly understood by others" (*KBD*, 2:334). When asked about his identity, Marcus claims only that he is the friend of Pellegrina Leoni.

Is Pellegrina Don Juan or Faust? Does she use her victims for her own gratification or is she in search of some higher purpose? Pellegrina seduces Lincoln, Pilot, and the Baron in turn by becoming the object of their adoration. There is more than a little demonism in her methods. She is a "holy witch and wanton saint" (*SGT*, 309); her atelier is a "witch's cauldron" (*SGT*, 293). Despite her demonic methods, Pellegrina's intentions appear to have been benign. Pellegrina tells Pilot: "I have tried to do you good" (*SGT*, 301). Similarly, she tells the Baron, "If I could help you, I would, but that is impossible to me" (*SGT*, 312). For each man, Pellegrina supplies a memory he will never forget. She saves Lincoln from the straitjacket of a conventional life. She draws Pilot into the world of action, where he can feel important for a time. For the Baron, she is the unassailable fortress to be conquered.

The fate of the romantic hero is either one of two things: salvation or damnation. Which fate awaits Pellegrina? When Lincoln, Pilot, and the Baron catch up with her on the mountainside, Pellegrina would rather die than admit her true identity. To do so would be to break the pact that she had made when she buried her true identity forever. Lincoln states, "She spread her wings and flew away" (*SGT*, 327). For one moment, the fantastic ambiguity of the story seems to be broken: the reader is in the presence of the supernatural. In the next moment, the tale is brought back into the realm of the plausible: Pellegrina has jumped off a cliff.

The topography of Pellegrina's final scenes has symbolic significance. At the end of his opera, Don Giovanni, who spends his life in pursuit of physical pleasures, is pulled down into the pit and damnation. At first, this seems to have been the fate of Pellegrina when she plunges down into the ravine. She is, significantly, rescued from the abyss by the three men she has seduced. They take Pellegrina up the mountain to a monastery, a more promising location for redemption. In fact, Lincoln has already remarked, "We might, for all I knew, be driving into heaven" (*SGT*, 317). In Goethe's *Faust*, Faust is redeemed, in part because of the intervention of Margarete, one of his victims. Further, Faust is saved because of the earnestness of his striving. He has been willing to sacrifice his soul to obtain ultimate knowledge: "Wer immer strebend sich bemüht, / Den können wir erlösen!" (Whoever strives with all his might, / Him we can redeem!)[109] Pellegrina is willing to sacrifice her life to protect her masquerades.

Pellegrina regains consciousness and imagines herself to be back on the stage of *Don Giovanni* at the point where she lost her voice, at the moment of her pact with demonic powers. Marcus reminds her of her place in the aria— *"Crudele?"*—which speaks of the pain of delaying the moment of consummation. Donna Anna wishes to delay her marriage to Don Ottavio. The last lines of the aria are: "One day, perhaps, heaven will again have pity on me"[110] (*SGT,* 351). Just before she dies, Pellegrina cries out, "It is Pellegrina Leoni—it is she, it is she herself again—she is back. Pellegrina, the greatest singer, poor Pellegrina, she is on the stage again. To the honor of God, as before" (*SGT,* 352). Like Faust, Pellegrina seems to be redeemed in her final act. She regains her identity by divine grace. Marcus looks on in a state of strain. As Mephistopheles, Ahasuerus, or even just her friend, he could not remain unmoved.

Although Marcus has understood the import of this scene, there is little sign that the other three male spectators have grasped the significance of what they have just witnessed. When Lincoln later imagines her as a jackal, she is "running about, playing with her own small graceful shadow, having a little ease of heart, a little fun" (*SGT,* 354). In other words, she has regained her shadow and kept the "little heart-ease, a little fun" that she sold it for (*SGT,* 287). Dinesen never breaks the fantastic uncertainty of this final scene. Pellegrina is either a woman delirious on her deathbed or a dark hero whose soul has been saved.

Susan Hardy Aiken, Grethe Rostbøll, and Kathryn Barnwell have all alluded to Pellegrina's fate as a feminine cooption of a masculine Faustian myth. Jørgensen and Juhl, together with Rostbøll, believe that revenge is part of Pellegrina's motivation. Pellegrina is seeking revenge against all the men who have sought to confine her to one existence, including Marcus. This vengefulness is an unsympathetic trait and such a reading seems contradicted by Pellegrina's expressed desire to help the men she encounters. Numerous undergraduates have been offended by Pellegrina's perceived insincerity while meddling in the lives of the men she encounters. Meddling in other people's existences is a dangerous undertaking even in Dinesen's fiction, as will be seen in "The Poet." Few have been as upset with Pellegrina's behavior as Kuno Poulsen, who disapproves of Pellegrina's inability to accept reality as it is and of the immoderate way she wishes to shape it to her liking. Poulsen goes so far as to call her a "nidding" (a villain).[111] Although it is likely that Dinesen thought of Pellegrina's behavior as heroic, the reader does not have to agree.

"The Poet"

In "The Poet," Dinesen takes up the familiar themes of puppets and the relationship of art to life, but this tale is dripping with more than her usual dose of irony. As part of her textual games, Dinesen has riddled the tale with poetic and artistic allusions. Some of these quotations are easier to catch in the Danish version, since many of the references are from Danish poets, like Emil Aarestrup and Sophus Claussen, and from the Danish ballads. In the Danish version, Dinesen expanded the story to include longer quotations of verse and additional literary allusions. Part of the point of this atmosphere of poetic and artistic allusion is that "the poet," Councilor Mathiesen, is not a particularly gifted poet and is occasionally blind to the art and poetry naturally springing up around him. One clear example of this is when Anders and Fransine's conversation is described in terms of tableaux from the artworks such as the Medici Venus and Michelangelo's Sistine Chapel. The narrator laconically remarks, "Such various reproductions of high classic art were moving about, in the evening, in the kitchen garden of *La Liberté*" (*SGT,* 403). The Councilor misses the spectacle because he has his nose in a book.

The tale may also be read in terms of Dinesen taking issue with the conventions of eighteenth- and nineteenth-century literature, particularly as they pertain to depictions of women. Although a number of poets are alluded to, the figure most clearly in the line of fire is Goethe. In a biographical sketch, Aage Henriksen described Dinesen's relationship to Goethe, "She always spoke of Goethe as a great and troublesome neighbour, with whom she was constantly involved in frontier disputes. . . . [Dinesen said:] 'But Goethe sat in his stuffy Weimar and allowed himself to be idolized. Actually, he was nothing but a *petit maitre,* and, what's more, a man. But where the supreme representatives of light and darkness enter into the awareness as males, there femininity itself admits the specially intimate relation and we get the Virgin Mary and the witch.'"[112] In this quote, Dinesen does not seem particularly pleased with Goethe's tendency to divide women into virgins or witches, each defined sexually with regard to a male incarnation of good or evil. Her reference to Goethe as a *petit maitre* (little fop/pedant) echoes the description of the Councilor as "a superman in miniature" (*SGT,* 361). Dinesen has made the Councilor into a caricature of all she dislikes about Goethe.

The Councilor lives on the memory of having once been of small service to Goethe and has ambitions to emulate the master in his own small way. As Ted Billy has commented, the Councilor's ideal is "not the *Sturm und Drang* Goethe of the *Werther* phase, but the Olympian poet and elder statesman of classical German literature."[113] The Councilor has "a talent for making life pleasant and comfortable" (*SGT,* 360). He opposes "uproars and rebellions against that law and order of which the Councilor was himself a staunch support" (*SGT,* 364). As an artist, the Councilor favors the Apollonian principle: structure, regulation, taste. He wants an absolute, sovereign control over his characters, even when they are not fictional, but actors in real life. He expects them to obey his dictates.

The reappearance of Augustus von Schimmelman in this story is a deliberate invocation of "The Roads Round Pisa." In that tale, Dinesen introduced the theme of the marionette play, in which human beings are marionettes who should try to enact their roles to the best of their ability while keeping the idea of the divine author clear. In "The Roads Round Pisa," despite several rebellious characters, the purposes of the divine author seem to be served in the end, although Augustus appears oblivious to all that has happened. The friendship between Augustus and the Councilor is a dubious character reference for them both. In "The Poet," Augustus is still a self-absorbed and passive character, living "upon the envy of the outside world, and [accepting] his happiness according to the quotation of the day" (*SGT,* 380). He still mirrors himself in others, in order to find if he is happy. Augustus and the Councilor both lack a creative spark and prefer to be comfortable men. While Augustus is passive, the Councilor imagines himself to be "a rearranger of existence" (*SGT,* 398). In "The Poet," the Councilor seeks to become a puppet master, rearranging the existences of Anders and Fransine. In doing so, he is usurping the role of the "divine author," and since he lacks poetic talent, the results will be catastrophic.

The Councilor is a tyrant with several character flaws. Perhaps the most serious of these in Dinesen's eyes is that he wants to "get off cheaply" from destiny (*KBD,* 1:391–92). He is not willing to risk his comfort but wants honor and art simply to come to him. Moreover, the Councilor has a pronounced cruel streak. Choosing to wear a yellow pansy on his visit to his mentally unstable wife appears calculated to drive her insane. When the Councilor delivers the news to Anders that he is about to marry, he is aware of the impact it will have. Count Schimmelman quotes Verner von Heidenstam's *Karolinerna* (1896–97, The Charles Men): "Das ist nur die Freude eines Helden den schönen Tod eines Helden zu sehen" (That is only the joy of a hero witnessing the beautiful death of a hero). The context is that Charles XII has set out a sentry who has frozen to death in the night and then smiles at the sight of the frozen soldier in the morning. The sadism of this parallel reflects back on the Councilor. A seemingly innocuous detail—the Councilor enjoys cross stitch—takes on a rather ominous significance when one realizes that the only other male Dinesen character who practices this hobby is the kindly Uncle Seneca, who turns out to be Jack the Ripper.

If the Councilor represents the Goethe of classical German literature and the Apollonian principle, his counterpart is Anders Kube who represents romanticism and the Dionysian principle. The stories Anders invents hearken to Old Norse literature, ballads, and folklore, as did the work of many romantic writers. Anders has "the playful mentality of those old mystics who populated [the world] with centaurs, fauns, and water deities who did not always behave properly" (*SGT,* 366). The Councilor notes he has in him "a very strong streak of primitive sensuality which would have to be watched if the tastefulness of his production were not to suffer" (*SGT,* 387). Like Dionysus, Anders enjoys drink and does not shrink from toasting the Councilor in confirmation wine. In that scene, Anders is also the romantic Lucifer rebelling. The unseemliness of this action is quietly smoothed away by the Councilor. Anders's alliance with the Dionysian, also associated with chaos and death, apparently makes suicide an easy thought.

The contrast between the Councilor and Anders is seen quite clearly in their separate reactions to the Easter sermon. Anders enters into a lengthy fantasy about whether Caiaphas would still act as he did if he understood that his crime would result in the salvation of mankind but doom the Jews to persecution for centuries. He imagines Caiaphas making a tragic/heroic choice: "If the world had really this one hope of salvation, they would have to fall in with the plan of God, however dreadful the deed" (*SGT,* 371–72). In the Danish version, there is an addition to the fantasy in which someone suggests they ask Christ himself what to do. The suggestion is turned down. Human beings must embrace their own tragic destinies and not look to divine powers to get them off easily. Anders's fantasy is reminiscent of the story of Barabbas in "The Deluge at Norderney" and the role of Judas in "Night Walk." For the Passion story to reach its completion these characters must be sacrificed. Anders is clearly ready to embrace whatever tragic destiny life has to offer him.

The Councilor's response to the Easter sermon is to reflect, "How strange it is that St. Peter, who was the only person who knew of it, and who must have been in a position to suppress it, should ever have allowed the story of the cock to get about" (*SGT,* 374). The Councilor is, of course, referring to the story in which Peter denies Christ three times, an archetypal account of cowardice and betrayal. Typical for the Councilor is that he would like to hush up anything unpleasant, rather than face the consequences. The Councilor seeks power, but no responsibility.

Fransine is caught between these two men and their two respective literary systems. Both want to cast her into literary roles of their own devising, but both have probably misread her. Susan Hardy Aiken has noted that the opening paragraphs of "The Poet" set the stage for a tale of feminine disruption.[114] Queen Sophie Magdalene kills a stag on the site of Hirschholm, giving the estate its name and invoking Diana, the goddess of the hunt. A later queen, Carolina Mathilda, also hunts deer in the area and becomes involved in a famous historical indiscretion by becoming the mistress of Dr. Struensee. This transgression is avenged by the representatives of virtue, the castle is dismantled, and a church is built on its site, "like a cross upon its grave" (*SGT,* 358).

The Councilor, whose perspective the narrative often takes, mistakes Fransine for a doll, a puppet he can manipulate, and assumes, "She was pretty sure to do, in life, as she was told" (*SGT,* 391). Growing up in a ghetto in Rome has taught Fransine respect for necessity and for power, hence her apparent submissiveness. But there are also signs of a disruptive force in her nature. The Councilor suspects her of harboring a secret joy, and after the Easter sermon, he wonders "whether she was really crying or laughing" (*SGT,* 371). Initially, Fransine is another Diana figure: "She was to the utmost shy of, or averse to, touch" (*SGT,* 368). Remembering the fate of Actaeon, the Councilor might have thought twice about spying on Fransine as she danced in her home. Fransine possesses the gift of *ballon,* a rare lightness. The ability to defy gravity is an ability she shares with Kasparson in "The Deluge at Norderney" and Berkeley Cole in *Out of Africa.* In English, defying gravity contains a double meaning. Fransine says that she can fly, thus defying one of the laws of physics. But gravity also means "seriousness." Such characters are usually able to take life lightly. When the Councilor discovers Fransine's abilities as a dancer, he realizes that she will not be a stabilizing influence upon Anders and changes his strategy towards them.

The Councilor has imagined Fransine to be a Christine Vulpius, Goethe's wife, and thus someone who would not trouble the poet Anders with questions about the meaning of life. The Councilor decides to ask Fransine to marry him instead of Anders, thus revising the plot to replicate Goethe's *The Sorrows of Young Werther* (1774). In that novel, the young romantic poet Werther falls in love with Lotte, who is already engaged to Albert. The story ends with Werther's suicide owing to his frustrated love, a fact that the Councilor is surely aware of despite his fantasy that an unrequited love will inspire Anders to great poetic feats. The Councilor is fully aware that one possible outcome of his machinations is that Anders and Fransine will make him a cuckold, a likelihood underlined by the scene in which Fransine gives Anders a horned medallion.

That Fransine accepts the Councilor can only be seen as the product of her ghetto background and her habit of bowing to necessity. But Fransine falls in love with Anders. The sight of Anders's features in his sister's child seems to melt Fransine's Diana resolve, and she becomes a blossom with the characteristic blush: "Waves of deep color washed over her face, but still she could not help smiling" (*SGT,* 394). Blossoms are erotically awakened women, who do not mind bending the rules to obtain the objects of their desire. Fransine would probably have no difficulty marrying the Councilor out of necessity and making him a cuckold with great rapidity. The result would be a comedy. The problem that Fransine will face, however, is that both Goethe's classicism and Anders's romanticism cast women into the roles of either saint or whore. Both of the men in her life can see her as only one or the other. The two men also have a taste for tragedy.

Lotte of *The Sorrows of Young Werther,* despite a genuine attachment to Werther, remains true to her betrothed and thus precipitates Werther's suicide. Her sainthood drives a man to his death. The Councilor may begin to doubt Fransine in the role of saint and substitutes instead the plot of Karl Gutzkow's *Wally die Zweiflerin* (1835, Wally the skeptic). Wally is also caught in a love triangle, having promised to marry a man she does not love. In a key scene, Wally reveals her nakedness to Cesare, the man she loves, on the night of her wedding in order to symbolize their spiritual marriage. The story does not turn out well for Wally, whose husband proves to be as Machiavellian in his cruelty as the Councilor, and whose lover, Cesare, deserts her. Since Wally is not a saint, she is by default a whore and ends up committing suicide in typical nineteenth-century fashion. The Councilor intentionally leaves Gutzkow's book behind where Fransine is sure to find it and drops a hint that her gazebo resembles the site of Wally's revelation. The night before her wedding, Fransine arranges to meet Anders, evidently with the intention of acting out the scene in the book.

Anders is drunk when he arrives for the rendezvous, and it takes Fransine a while to realize the import of what he is saying to her. Earlier, the narrator has commented, "Women, wanting to be happy, are up against a *force majeure.* Hence they may be justified in taking a short cut to happiness by declaring things to be, in fact, that which they want them to be" (*SGT,* 398). Fransine and Anders speak at cross purposes. In an earlier dream, Anders imagined that Fransine would cut off her left hand to prove her love for him. With his love of tragedy, he expects her to commit suicide and is disappointed that she has not reached this decision herself. In comparing her to the cook who kills a goose just to make giblet soup, Anders is charging Fransine with being a *femme fatale* and a man-eater. He refers to cocks crowing, an emblem of betrayal. In the Danish version, Fransine says, "It is not even the nightingale," turning the dialogue into a mangled version of act 2, scene 5 of *Romeo and Juliet* (*MU,* 2:255–56). Anders then makes his point clear by offering her money for her favors, in essence calling her a whore. When she asks if he wanted her to come to him tonight, he responds that he would rather be alone. His rejection of her is brutal. Anders is in love with his own tragic destiny and will not allow Fransine to make him happy. He shoots the Councilor, an act of not undeserved revenge, which will mean Anders's death by gallows or suicide.

The Councilor's carefully laid plans have begun to unravel. He did not imagine that his puppets would rebel so thoroughly, and he did not calculate any consequences for himself. Mortally wounded, the Councilor grows delirious and imagines himself "inside the magic circle of poetry" (*SGT,* 416). He imagines himself to be inside a work of Goethe. Dinesen commented on the Councilor's delusions in a letter to Bent Mohn, "The Councilor cannot in reality be said to feel he is in Goethe's hands. But Goethe has been for him the highest revelation of the divine, and he now feels secure in Goethe's hands, that is to say, God's. His words to the Moon, which are a repetition of his previous deferential comment to Goethe, are directed straight to God" (*KBD,* 1:500). Even though Dinesen seems willing to grant the Councilor an epiphany—the realization that he is not in control, but in the hands of forces greater than he is—the bloody finale of the tale indicates that his actions have not been excused.

The Councilor seems to savor Fransine's distress and compares her despair to that of Margarete in Goethe's *Faust,* who kills her child and ends up on the gallows. Fransine has been transformed by the experiences of the evening. She has lost her lightness: "Her despair kept her upright, like the lead in the little wooden figures which children play with, like the weight tied to dead seamen's feet, which keeps them standing up, swaying, at the bottom of the sea" (*SGT,* 418). She is no longer a Diana who shuns human touch, but she is compared to a maenad, a woman inspired with ecstatic frenzy by the god Dionysus. Injured by Anders, yet fearing for his safety, Fransine crushes the Councilor with a large rock. Both of them are now victims of the law of gravitation. It is as though the fictional Margarete has risen up against Goethe and avenged herself for the cruelties of the plot of *Faust.*

Susan Hardy Aiken interprets this final scene as follows: "The great stone Fransine dislodges in her frenzy figures both the founding walls of the phallic symbolic order and the monumental pride and obtuseness which the Councilor, as the representative of that order at its most extreme, has brutally exemplified in his casual objectifications of her. In this reading his own plots, in every sense, come crashing down upon him. But the stone also signifies the weight of women's collective creativity, ossified, blocked, and silenced by masculinist traditions, and now become the very weapon with which to strike them down."[115] The unusually brutal ending of this story seems to express a great deal of anger. Marianne Juhl and Bo Hakon Jørgensen have read *Seven Gothic Tales* as a vengeful book and at this moment, it certainly seems to be.

The future fate of Fransine and Anders does not look bright. Both have embraced their tragedies at great cost to themselves and will quite likely pay for it with their lives. According to the final lines of the story, the Councilor is hurled into an abyss, "He was thrown down in three or four great leaps from one cataract to the other" (*SGT,* 420). One suspects that Dinesen has consigned him to Dante's *Inferno,* where the third and fourth circles of hell are reserved for the greedy and gluttonous. Dinesen's alter ego, Pellegrina, was also a rearranger of existence and tried to turn life into art, but she was redeemed at the end of her story. The difference between Pellegrina and the Councilor appears to be talent and the willingness to make sacrifices for art. Trying to buy oneself off cheaply from Nemesis seems to be a mortal sin in Dinesen's fictional cosmos.

CHAPTER 3

Out of Africa

Isak Dinesen's second book, *Out of Africa,* seems at first glance to be a radical departure from the fantastic fiction of *Seven Gothic Tales.* Unlike her first book, *Out of Africa* deals with real people, places, and events. In 1934, a Danish interviewer asked Dinesen why her first book had not been about Africa. She responded that turning to that subject so soon would have been like writing "about a child the day one buried it. One must have things at a distance. In my tales I have put a whole century between me and the events."[1] Dinesen had written a poem titled "Ex Africa" in 1915, and she had completed a sketch about the Masai in 1926, but the two have only a slight connection with the finished *Out of Africa.* Work on the book began in 1935, when she published a version of "Kamante and Lulu" in a Swedish magazine and assured herself of her English publisher's interest in a complete book about Africa. Dinesen had difficulty finding the peace to work at Rungstedlund, the home she shared with her mother, so she checked into a hotel in Skagen on the northeast coast of Denmark's Jutland peninsula. There she wrote her book in an environment about as different from Africa as can be imagined. After almost six months she returned to Rungstedlund with most of the English manuscript completed.[2]

Dinesen had such a strong emotional link to her material that it seems to have taken her a while to find the right tone. When Dorothy Canfield Fisher asked Dinesen in 1933 why she did not write about Africa, Dinesen responded, "And if ever I write about Africa, it could not be helped that the book would contain much bitterness and complaint about the way in which the country and the people have been treated by the English, and in which they have let loose upon it our mechanical and mercenary civilization. It would not be meant as any sort of political propaganda, but would be just the cry of my heart, but it would come out as much as the bitterness against serfdom goes through Turgenev's 'Diary of a Sportsman'" (*KBD,* 1:100).

It is evident from Dinesen's letters from Africa that she had an aversion to what she calls "propaganda" and little faith in people's willingness to listen to sermons. She was also accustomed to having her views on the natives disapproved of by the English in Kenya. Constant Huntington, Dinesen's English publisher, wrote of his response to the first version of "Kamante and Lulu": "I am amused at the way your imagination conjures up and denounces those readers who will not like your book. Don't be afraid: there won't be any such readers!" (*KBD*, 1:206). Dinesen subsequently toned down this accusatory note in *Out of Africa*. Instead, she reverts to the distanced, ironic tone of her tales and leaves it to her readers to draw their own conclusions about the people and events she describes. This literary choice has resulted in a widely varying reception of *Out of Africa* over the years.

It was Isak Dinesen's intention that *Out of Africa* appear in Denmark, England, Sweden, and the United States simultaneously in 1937. Delays caused the American edition to be published in 1938. The initial reception of *Den afrikanske Farm* (The african farm) in Denmark was not overwhelmingly positive. Dinesen might have thought she stood a better chance among the Danish reviewers this time, since *Out of Africa* was at least closer to the social realism valued on the Danish literary scene. Marianne Juhl, who has studied the reception, is struck by the Danish reviewers' tendency to attack Dinesen personally, reviving the old accusation of snobbery brought against her in the case of *Seven Gothic Tales*. For example, Emil Frederiksen accuses Dinesen of enjoying the perception the natives have of her as "a higher being." Juhl speculates that these personal attacks may be the product of the Danish cultural tendency to want to cut people down to size.[3] The Danish public embraced the book despite the critics, and by 1984, *Out of Africa* had sold almost twice as many copies in Denmark as *Seven Gothic Tales*.

Swedish reviewers were, on the contrary, pleased with the tone of the book, as in the case of Torgny Segerstedt: "The natives are not viewed with condescending superiority."[4] Henning Kehler writes, "It is foreign to her to see them [the blacks] as people of a worse quality than the white race. . . . She confesses that the whites are not the only real people in the world, and that the world would be much more impoverished without the blacks."[5] By and large, the Swedish reviews focus more on the description of Africa and the Africans than on Dinesen's personal story. American reviewers were generally positive, but more interested in the autobiographical elements of the book: "This book is a revelation of a personality."[6] Some were appreciative of the relative simplicity of *Out of Africa* compared to her previous work: "Her prose runs clear as a mountain stream."[7]

The English reviews contain some special points of interest, particularly since Dinesen hoped to target English colonialism for criticism. The critique seems to have eluded David Garnett, who writes, "*Out of Africa* by Karen Blixen . . . is the first book to make me understand wanting to settle in the heart of Africa, and to have given me a picture of white people living a free and generous life there."[8] Sir John Squire seems to have better understood her meaning: "But what is new in this book . . . is the sympathy with the local population, who were there before we came and the oldest of whom cannot help feeling, when they are called 'squatters' on our farms, that we are squatters on theirs."[9] The reviewer from the *Journal of the Royal African Society* calls *Out of Africa* "restful," but even so, the book prompts a defensive reaction: "Eviction is frequently inevitable to make room for new developments, to provide space for expanding townships and for general public utilities. In the case of the Kikuyu who for generations have been in the habit of shifting their abode with comparative frequency, the hardship is not so severe as in the case of those who have had their roots in the same soil for centuries."[10] This defense of colonial practices may be a sign that *Out of Africa*'s subtle critiques in some cases did hit home. Dinesen was evidently told that "the great governing class" in England did not like *Out of Africa*—"they think there is a lion in the streets"—and this response pleased her.[11]

Over the years, *Out of Africa* has outsold all of Dinesen's other books. In its first year of release, the book sold 16,000 copies in Denmark and 99,000 copies in the United States. It is sobering to compare these figures with the 1938 sales numbers for *Facing Mt. Kenya* by the future Kenyan president Jomo Kenyatta. It sold a mere 517 copies. England was clearly not open to an African's version of Africa at that point in time. Dinesen reached such a large public not only because of her extraordinary literary talent, but also because she was a white European who sought to influence, but not offend.

Historical events and changing social views have affected the reception of *Out of Africa* over the years. In the wake of the Mau Mau rebellion (1952–56), some called into question the "romantic" view of Africa presented in the book. Tone Cederblad-Bengtsson writes in 1962, "One experiences the suggestive landscape depictions as immoral illusions, one defends oneself from the aestheticism of the descriptions of natives, and one reads difficult-to-solve problems into episodes that only possess the beautiful seriousness of a tale."[12] The political events in Kenya caused Dinesen herself to pronounce *Out of Africa* as dated as "a papyrus from a pyramid" (*OA,* 457).

Even if the book's usefulness as a depiction of Africa seemed limited after 1952, *Out of Africa* lived on in the hearts of many as a tale of personal freedom and loss. Carson McCullers thought of the book that way: "When I was ill or out of sorts with the world, I would turn to *Out of Africa,* which never failed to comfort and support me."[13] The author Janet Sternberg writes of how *Out of Africa* helped her through some difficult personal moments: "She was telling me not what life could be, but what it exacts. She was offering a sense of cost, in the way that one comes to understand it as one gets older: the experience of the consequences of one's actions. And she was offering something more—a stance, a self-fashioned set of personal, moral, and artistic imperatives that sustain in the teeth of pain."[14] Holden Caulfield in J. D. Salinger's *Catcher in the Rye* (1951) praises the author of *Out of Africa* for not being a phony.

Until the publication of Isak Dinesen's letters from Africa in 1978 in Denmark and 1981 in the United States, many considered the objectivity and truthfulness of *Out of Africa* to be one of the book's most attractive features. Eudora Welty took Robert Langbaum to task for treating *Out of Africa* as fiction in his 1964 study of Dinesen's works.[15] The letters demonstrate, however, that Dinesen has taken several creative liberties with the facts. For example, the bottle of Chambertin 1906 with which Dinesen sends Emmanuelson on his way to Tanganyika was really just a bottle of beer. Marianne Juhl feels that *Out of Africa* has thus been "liberated from biography" and critics are now free to treat the book as a novel.[16] Langbaum claimed in his review of the letters, "*Out of Africa* is no longer the same book now that the *Letters* have appeared. We will have to make a joint text of the two books, to the enhancement of both."[17]

The publication of the letters and Judith Thurman's acclaimed biography *Isak Dinesen: Life of a Storyteller* (1982) revived public interest in Dinesen's life and eclipsed *Out of Africa* as the main source of information. Sydney Pollack's 1985 film *Out of Africa* was based more on Thurman's biography than on Dinesen's novel. Pollack's Hollywood version of Dinesen's life in Africa was seen by a large audience and has shaped the public impression of her for a new generation of readers. This might be a source of concern. Brenda Cooper and David Descutner have carefully studied the film adaptation and concluded, "The film changes Blixen from the compassionate, culturally sensitive character found in her texts to a thoughtless colonialist through transference of her actual attitudes and values to Finch Hatton."[18]

Since the mid-1980s, scholars have approached *Out of Africa* from two main directions. As the theoretical discourse about colonialism has grown in sophistication, *Out of Africa* has become an obvious object of interest. The scholarly debate about Dinesen's status as a colonial writer is lively and will be discussed at length in this chapter. The second focus of scholarly attention has been the nature of *Out of Africa* as female autobiography, a topic that will also be treated below.

The Historical Context

"*Out of Africa* is one of the most dangerous books ever written about Africa," claims Kenyan author Ngugi wa Thiong'o.[19] One of the reasons that *Out of Africa* is held to be dangerous is that for many readers, it is the only source of knowledge they have about Africa.

Some critics are concerned that without a knowledge of the historical context of Kenya, readers might be persuaded by the "rosy" picture of colonialism presented in the book. Therefore, a consideration of the history behind *Out of Africa* and the extent to which it accurately reflects historical conditions seems an important starting point for an evaluation of the text. Because the narrative posture of the novel refrains from comment on some of the episodes, some readers have attributed to Dinesen racist attitudes that they assume would be typical for a white European aristocrat. Regardless of the current critical practice not to concern oneself with authorial intention, readers are intensely interested in what Dinesen's "real" opinions regarding the Africans were to the extent they can be reconstructed. The following segment will examine Kenya's history as it relates to *Out of Africa* and explore Dinesen's opinions and actions regarding Kenya's politics as they emerge in her letters and interviews and the testimony of those who knew her.

The development of British East Africa was initiated in 1887 by a private firm called the British East Africa Company, who had leased a strip of land along the coast from the Omani sultan, Seyyid Said, and intended to open up the land west of Mombasa. In 1895, the British government officially took over the company's interests. The British built a railway from Mombasa to Lake Victoria at great expense, prompted in part by a competition with German development nearby. In order to help pay for this costly venture, Sir Charles Eliot, the commissioner for East Africa, came up with the idea in 1901 to recruit settlers to farm land: "In turn, the settlers would need the railway to transport their goods; both the land and the railway would be productive and profitable."[20] Because of extant treaties with local tribes, it was not clear that Britain had a right to the land it needed to allocate to the farmers. The Lands Ordinance Act of 1902 solved the problem. Land which was "vacant" could be appropriated by the government. The Kikuyu were a nomadic, agricultural people who moved about to farm the most fertile land. The government interpreted these moves as permanent, and thus it was able to take over vast tracts of "vacant" land. The Baron Bror von Blixen-Finecke and his fiancée, Karen Dinesen, were among those recruited to British East Africa under these conditions in 1914.

Expansion of the British colonial presence in British East Africa led to a rapid decline in the living conditions of the Africans. The natives were relocated to "reserves," which were overcrowded and established on the poorest land. Thus, the natives were subject to inadequate housing, nutrition, and sanitation. From 1902 to 1921, the native population declined from 4 million to 2.5 million. In order to relieve some of the pressure on the reserves, the "squatter" system developed.

The Blixens, financed by Dinesen's family, took possession of a farm of six thousand acres. Although the original intention was to make a great deal of money, the farm never did particularly well. By 1921, Dinesen was appointed manager of the farm and Bror Blixen was forbidden to have anything to do with it. Six hundred acres of the farm were planted with coffee and approximately one thousand acres were settled by "squatters." As Dinesen explains in *Out of Africa*, "The squatters knew that in order to stay on the land they had got to work for me one hundred and eighty days out of each year, for which they were paid twelve shillings for every thirty days" (*OA*, 358). This feudal arrangement was somewhat to Dinesen's taste, but there are limits to the extent she exploited the squatters for her own gain. When Dinesen calls herself a "superior squatter" it is an acknowledgment that she inhabits land that belongs to the Kikuyu, but the colonial government has given Dinesen power over the natives on the farm. Dinesen was highly conscientious about using that power. The developer who bought the farm in 1931 attributed the farm's financial collapse to Dinesen's "stubborn devotion to the Africans. No one . . . made a success of coffee in Karen at six thousand feet. . . . But it would have made an ideal mixed farm—she could have well grown maize on a commercial scale and bred cattle at the same time; it was ideal for cattle. But to do so profitably she would have had to take back her squatters' land, and she wouldn't touch it. Her servants had the run of her place just because they were her servants, and she couldn't bear to interfere with them. Instead she ran the coffee at a dead loss, and the Africans made the profit. There were three thousand head of squatter cattle on the farm when I took it over."[21] What Remy Martin notes with disapproval, Kamante later recalled with pleasure: "She wouldn't prevent us from keeping cows or sheep in our camps. So nobody took the shamba to be of Europeans. We took it to be ours. We found this garden belonging to all of us."[22]

The expanding colony found that it had a labor shortage. Given enough land, the natives were self-sufficient with no inducements to work for the white settlers. The government began imposing taxes on the natives which could only be paid in cash, thus compelling the natives to work for a wage. Dinesen allows her disapproval of this practice to surface in *Out of Africa*: "They must pay the hut-tax to the Government, of twelve shillings to a hut, a heavy burden on a man, who with very little else in the world would own two or three grass-huts" (*OA*, 373). Moreover, the natives were prohibited from growing cash crops such as coffee, tobacco, and cotton, effectively curbing any chance they might have for financial independence. When the new governor visited her farm in 1922, Dinesen lobbied against this restriction: "We talked a lot about the natives and discovered we had very similar ideas, in that we consider the future of the country must depend far more than is now the case on native production. In Uganda the natives produce,—and export,—very great quantities of cotton, sim-sim [sesame] and also coffee, and in all probability these tribes could be taught to do many things" (*LA,* 135). Many readers have assumed that Dinesen wished to keep the natives in a state of Rousseauian innocence, and even if the idea might have appealed to her at times, she was aware that it was both impossible and undesirable. Dinesen was clear that the future of Kenya as a country lay in the hands of the natives, not the white settlers.

The high native mortality rate was in part due to a lack of medical care. In *Out of Africa,* Dinesen describes her own efforts to provide medical care to the natives on her farm, the most memorable case being that of Kamante. She paid for his stay at the Scotch Mission Hospital when she realized that his disease was beyond her skills. Dinesen lets us know that such concern for the physical welfare of the natives was not typical in the anecdote titled "The Elite of Bournemouth." Dinesen describes a physician who considers it beneath his dignity to treat natives, although he has made one exception for a medical emergency. Another source of native mortality was the Carrier Corps during the First World War. Natives were press-ganged into the Carrier Corps where they were essentially forced to perform as beasts of burden. Forty-seven thousand black Kenyans died.[23] In *Out of Africa,* Dinesen tells of "a small lady with a sharp face" who threatens her cook, Esa, with the Carrier Corps if he does not come to work for her (*OA,* 243). Given the above statistics, we understand why Esa is "beside himself with fear and despair" and responds to the threat immediately (*OA,* 243).

Dinesen describes how the Masai were willing to side with the English at the beginning of the First World War, "But the English Government did not think it wise to organize the Masai to make war on white men, be they even Germans" (*OA,* 211). Dinesen is pointing to the nervousness the British felt about the possibility of armed revolt against colonial power. Africans were not allowed to possess firearms, so Dinesen takes over the shooting of animals for food or ridding the farm of nuisance animals such as snakes, lions, or serval cats. Natives on the farm had to be registered with the government and carry an identity card, the *kipanda.* In *Shadows on the Grass,* Dinesen compares the *kipanda* system to the one imposed by the Nazis on the occupied Danish citizenry during the Second World War (*OA,* 451).

Whenever possible, Dinesen tried to act as a buffer between the natives on the farm and official government agencies, including the police. Kamante recalled, "In reality, Mrs. Barance was all good because even police couldn't enter into her shamba to trouble people. She used to tell them *her shamba* is hers and she knows how to regulate her people" (original emphasis).[24] Also according to Kamante, Dinesen sheltered natives who had gotten into trouble on other farms: "That means if somebody was chased away by his master she would employ him in her garden and give him places to build his house, together with a piece of land where he could grow some crops."[25] In a letter to her mother from 1923, Dinesen describes her efforts to get the district commissioner to allow the people on the farm to establish their own *kyama,* a native court, which would not be under the jurisdiction of Kinanjui (*LA,* 167). Kinanjui was appointed chief by the colonial government and so Dinesen's efforts seem to be an attempt to gain the natives more local autonomy. Dinesen describes the kyama called to settle the incident of the shooting accident in *Out of Africa,* but the case proves too difficult to solve locally, and Kinanjui is called in at the end.

It is clear that Dinesen did not arrive in British East Africa with an instant understanding of the political conditions or the natives. One can see how her attitudes evolve with regard to the issue of education. Soon after her arrival in 1914, Dinesen wrote to her mother about Farah's desire to go to school and learn to read: "I would not help him to do that because I think that leads to their becoming unhappy and useless" (*LA,* 23). This is the sort of attitude that many readers expect from Dinesen. By 1923, Dinesen writes, "I think that every large farm ought to have a school; there is no point in saying that natives are more happy in their primitive state; besides that being very questionable in itself, it is impossible to keep them there and by making no attempt to educate them all that results is that they get hold of all the worst aspects of civilization" (*LA,* 177). In a speech from 1938, Dinesen described a conversation she had had with a Father Bernhard from the Scotch mission about the school she established on her farm. According to Dinesen, Father Bernhard admonished Dinesen to "teach the natives something that we will have a use for." She replied, "I have a use for people who can think." The Father's response to this was, "My, but you are foolish, Madame."[26] An even more extreme version of this attitude is presented in *Out of Africa* in the episode of the Belgian who claims in French, "One must teach the Negroes to be honest and to work. Nothing else. Nothing. Nothing. Nothing" (*OA,* 293).

Dinesen was highly interested in Kenyan politics, but was doubly disenfranchised because she was not a man and not a British citizen. Dinesen described her position and her political strategy in a letter to her brother, Thomas: "I dare not talk to any of the English, [and] I think my influence here as a woman and a foreigner must be strictly confined to being an example; if I start to preach I will lose my power, which must be won through being a hostess and friend; even my glasses and my big cupboard must work in my mission for my 'black brothers,' but the 'example' takes effect so slowly, and sometimes one feels like firing off a broadside right in their silly faces, when that typical English stupidity starts braying too loudly!" (*LA*, 241). In her letters and interviews, Dinesen describes her efforts to speak on the natives' behalf to several important figures, including Lord Islington and the Prince of Wales. With this quote, one can begin to see why Dinesen eventually chose to adopt a nonaccusatory tone in *Out of Africa*. Dinesen correspondingly invites the reader into her beautiful text and by the end of the novel hopes to have won the reader's sympathy for the natives.

Carolyn Martin Shaw has advanced the following theory about the social dynamics in colonial Kenya: "An imperative for the British middle class was to maintain the prestige and standing of the white race, to protect white privilege through control of morality and control of the means of production. But such a neat moral order could not be maintained in the face of aristocratic dissoluteness, Afrikaner degeneracy, middle-class downward mobility, and the demands of Africans for more land and cultural autonomy. White prestige was built on middle-class morality and discipline, and on the maintenance of distinct boundaries between the colonizer and the colonized."[27] If what Shaw claims is true, then Dinesen's farm would have been the site of multiple transgressions. Not only did she host the dissolute aristocrats, but downwardly mobile figures such as Emmanuelson (Casparson) and Old Knudsen (Aarup). Her pro-native stance would have constituted an even greater threat to the English middle class, which she despised. The Ngomas of the Kikuyu were often forbidden by the government because they were morally suspect. Dinesen's support of these rituals was yet another act of transgression. In *Out of Africa*, Dinesen describes how the wife of Belknap has twenty-five of her laborers arrested for dancing in a forbidden Ngoma even though the dance was held four or five miles from her home (*OA*, 157). The incident provides an example of the nervousness and prudery of the middle class.

Many European visitors to Kenya were attracted by the prospect of big game hunting, and Dinesen herself was no exception. During one safari in the first year of her residence in Kenya, Dinesen boasts of shooting forty-four head of game with one hundred cartridges (*LA*, 18). Although Dinesen remained entranced by the romanticism of the hunt, by the time she wrote *Out of Africa*, it is clear that she had become concerned about the effects such continued exploitation of the wildlife would have. She writes disapprovingly of how "many young Nairobi shop-people ran out into the hills on Sundays, on their motorcycles, and shot at anything they saw" (*OA*, 6). The anecdote of "The Naturalist and the Monkeys," in which a Swedish professor applies to shoot fifteen hundred monkeys for his research and is allowed to shoot only six, provides another example of European arrogance in the face of the natural world.

Perhaps the most significant indicator of Dinesen's attitudes and actions towards the Africans is the testimony of those who lived on the farm under her jurisdiction. In *Africa's Song of Karen Blixen,* Tove Hussein has tracked down and interviewed surviving members of Dinesen's household, and none of them accuse her of racism. Kamante was particularly outspoken in his defense of Dinesen in 1991: "Mrs. Karen was not a racist. She was Mzungu, but that didn't matter. Mrs. Karen had a very kind heart. She did not discriminate against African or Mzungu, child or grownup. There were very few quarrels because Mrs. Karen showed no tribalism."[28] Farah's brother, Abdullahi Ahmed Weid, who later became a judge, wrote, "The Baroness felt that all were equal and that justice and fairness was everyone's right. In those days, racial discrimination in that multiracial country was similar to a war in which there was no actual field combat. The Baroness always pretended that racial discrimination was non-existent. She knew it existed, but at the same time she knew she could do nothing to remedy the situation."[29] These comments illustrate how politically difficult acting in such a racist society was.

Dinesen has been accused of practicing "noblesse oblige" towards the natives. "Noblesse oblige" is defined in Webster's New World Dictionary as "the inferred obligation of people of high rank or social position to behave nobly or kindly towards others." The critics who use the term with reference to Dinesen do so disapprovingly because of the class snobbery it implies. Dinesen did not see the term as negative and was clear that the political realities of Kenya made the concept necessary: "The only really reliable principle in the relationship between parties, where one is technologically and economically superior to such a fantastic degree must be 'Noblesse oblige.' . . . Yes, if society was so democratic that white people could recognize the blacks as equals, a modus vivendi might possibly be found. But it is my experience, that the longer one comes in socially into a white democratic society, the stronger the whites feel and insist upon their race's superiority. . . . Noblesse: It is nothing else or less than this: to keep one's word. It is to take responsibility for what one says and does."[30] Some notes dating to 1938 characterize Dinesen's feelings towards the Africans on her farm: "I loved the natives. In a way the strongest and the most incalculable emotion I have known in my life. Did they love me? No. But they relied on me in a strange, incomprehensible, mysterious way. A stupendous obligation. One would die for them. They took that quite for granted."[31]

When the farm had to declare bankruptcy, it is clear from Dinesen's letters that the issue that weighed the most on her mind was the fate of the Africans living on the farm. The new owners felt no responsibility toward them and simply planned to evict the squatters without thought as to where they might go. In *Out of Africa,* Dinesen comes as close to preaching a sermon on this topic as she does anywhere in the novel: "It is more than their land that you take away from the people, whose Native land you take. It is their past as well, their roots and their identity" (*OA,* 359). When she lost her farm, Dinesen seriously contemplated suicide, but found strength in the midst of her personal despair to plead the case of the natives: "I stood against all of Kenya's Civil Service with the Governor in the lead; I was bankrupt, which in England really means outcast, but I was more in my patched shoes than the gentlemen in their uniforms, and I made them give my squatters land around Dagoretti and around Limura and around Mbagathi" (*KBD,* 2:280). The Africans on Dinesen's farm may have gained some land, but they lost a passionate advocate when Dinesen was forced to return to Denmark. In 1937, Jomo Kenyatta, who was then a student, sent Dinesen the following greeting: "Dear Friend, I send you many greetings. Whatever you do, remember the country you love and the natives in the country."[32] Dinesen did not forget them.

The Mau Mau rebellion (1952–58) was a revolt that originated among the Kikuyu against colonial conditions. To a great extent, it was a civil war with the rebels pitting themselves against black loyalists. Atrocities were committed on both sides, but the violence escalated after the government declared a state of emergency in 1952 and imprisoned rebel leaders, including Jomo Kenyatta, in 1953. During the rebellion, Dinesen let the media know that she placed the responsibility for the conflict on the white settlers. At a time when the BBC broadcast news of white settlers being slaughtered, and British soldiers were instructed to shoot on sight any black man walking though the forest, Dinesen stressed the honesty and the decency of the Kikuyu she knew. *Berlingske Tidende* asked Dinesen to go to Kenya to report on the revolt. Despite her extremely frail health, Dinesen was prepared to go and considered it "a kind of duty that I should not disregard" (*KBD,* 2:182). A change of heart by the newspaper and Dinesen's health concerns caused the project to be abandoned. Accurate figures are difficult to come by, but out of the approximately 13,000 who died in the rebellion, 11,503 were rebels killed by security forces, and 1,819 were loyalists killed by rebels. White casualties were slight by comparison: 32 white civilians and 63 white soldiers.[33]

In a newspaper interview, Dinesen remarked about the Mau Mau revolt, "You understand it is a great sorrow to me when whites and blacks fight each other, and Africa is for me always the blacks' own country."[34] On another occasion, Dinesen explained, "And to me it seems to the highest degree to be our own fault. We were responsible for how things went, and we behaved very badly. We lacked understanding to such a great degree. We lacked respect for the natives' traditions. We counted them as a people without culture, but they *had* a high culture. And if we succeed in making them despise their traditions, then it will be very sad. They will become a rootless and, in some ways, even a worthless people."[35] Dinesen's opinions on what should be done for Kenya's future go beyond the political realities of today: "Personally, I think the whites should leave Africa, also South Africa, even if it will take several years."[36]

Out of Africa and Colonial Literature

Out of Africa is a work of colonial literature, a genre that in recent decades has fallen into disrepute. The major criticisms of *Out of Africa* as a work of colonial literature fall into two categories: sins of omission and sins of commission. A number of critics have castigated Dinesen for what she left out of her book—her sins of omission.[37] These critics feel that the picture of native life in *Out of Africa* is too pleasant, since as a rule it was anything but pleasant. One omission of concern regards an event about which Dinesen must surely have known. In 1922, British soldiers fired on men, women, and children outside the Hotel Norfolk in Nairobi, killing 150 of them. Dinesen does not mention this incident in either her letters or *Out of Africa*. Lord Delamere, whom Dinesen thought so highly of and calls a friend of the Masai, hoarded one million acres of land while urging that the Kikuyu reserves be cut back even more. Although Dinesen does make reference to the Carrier Corps and other negative aspects of native life, the references are too subtle and have eluded a number of readers. The overall impression from the farm is one of harmony. Conditions on the farm appear to have been idyllic and—according to JanMohamed—"a major exception to the . . . pattern of conquest and irresponsible exploitation."[38]

With regard to these omissions, Dinesen's defenders point out that, in *Out of Africa,* the author has apparently chosen to exclude "all painful or unseemly experiences."[39] For example, Dinesen does not mention her own bouts with syphilis or her husband's womanizing. Bror Blixen is mentioned only once and not by name. Dane Kennedy interprets Dinesen's omissions as a sign of contempt, particularly with regard to the white laborers on the farm: "As many as six white employees oversaw its [the farm's] operations, yet *Out of Africa* offers only fleeting references to the single pseudonymous manager Belknap."[40] Evidently, Dinesen consciously exercised restraint in *Out of Africa* when it came to addressing the political injustices suffered by the natives, avoiding any urge to editorialize or admonish. She hoped that conditions would speak for themselves, but she overestimated her average reader's knowledge of the circumstances to which she alludes. Dinesen writes in her story "The Blank Page" that "silence will speak," but it appears that readers will not always read the same message into the silence. Where one reader sees an attempt to paint a rosy picture of colonialism, another sees an indictment of colonialism. The distant irony of her narrative has opened up both interpretive possibilities.

Among the foremost of Dinesen's sins of commission is the use of animal metaphors to describe the natives. A host of critics have disapproved of Dinesen's incessant comparison of the natives to animals, and they interpret this as a sign that Dinesen felt the natives to be less than human.[41] Else Brundbjerg has rebutted this point by claiming that such comparisons were "a part of her way of expressing herself."[42] Certainly, Dinesen's animal metaphors are legion throughout all her works and are used in reference to both white and black characters. In "The Supper at Elsinore," for example, Elsinore is described as a poultry yard populated by swans, birds of prey, and chickens.

Even though Rashna B. Singh does not care for Dinesen's animal metaphors, she nonetheless acknowledges that there is a significant difference between Dinesen's comparisons and those in other colonial literature. When Dinesen describes members of the Nyeri Kikuyu tribe as "shaggy old Hyenas," it is because they have come to exploit the death of a child for their own gain, even though they took no interest in him when he was alive. The metaphor is meant to be descriptive. Singh compares Dinesen favorably to Maud Diver who, in her novel *Far to Seek* (1921), describes a struggle between the English hero, Roy, and Chandranath, an Indian freedom fighter: "Suddenly, blessedly, the thing stumbled and dropped to its knees. With the spring of a panther, he was on it, his fingers at its throat, pinning it to earth."[43] As Singh herself remarks, one is hard-pressed to tell by this passage that Chandranath is human.

Chinua Achebe has pointed out that Joseph Conrad in *Heart of Darkness* (1902) was capable of equally offensive and dehumanizing references, as in the following: "And between whiles I had to look after the savage who was fireman. He was an improved specimen; he could fire up a vertical boiler. He was there below me, and, upon my word, to look at him was as edifying as seeing a dog in a parody of breeches and a feather hat, walking on his hind legs."[44] Clearly this animal comparison is insulting and more than implies that the African in question is not fully human. Carolyn Martin Shaw has posited a central fear among colonialists: "That Africans were capable of only a thin veneer of civilization which, with just a little pressure, would give way to violence and depravity."[45] Drawing a thin line metaphorically between Africans and animals is a way of reinforcing the potentials of this fear and the threat the Africans pose to civilization, that is to say, the colonial enterprise. Viewing Africans as barely improved animals also justifies treating them in a less humane manner.

The notion of a "thin veneer of civilization" is made even more manifest in a passage from Joyce Cary's *The African Witch* (1936), singled out by Raoul Granqvist in his work *Stereotypes in Western Fiction on Africa* (1984). In Cary's novel, an African named Tom affects European manners and speech. When his hat, the symbol of his civilized veneer falls off, Tom undergoes a curious transformation: "He fell suddenly on all fours. He began to creep along the yard, still muttering. But his arms seemed to grow shorter; his head and blue shirt became lower, flatter . . . until he was creeping like a lizard [and later] . . . his legs spread out like a frog's, trailed behind him . . . he had acquired a snake's power to move without limbs [and in the end] . . . he seemed to have lost shape; to be spreading like a flattened, bone-less mass—a black jelly, protoplasm."[46] Tom appears to have undergone a process of reverse evolution.

Dinesen's animal metaphors do not sink to these dehumanizing depths. Nonetheless, no matter how benign Dinesen's intentions when using animal metaphors, the racially charged context in which she utters them renders them easily misunderstood. Sidonie Smith eloquently states her objection: "It is one thing for a white woman . . . to identify herself and other white settlers with animals. It is quite another for the black Africans, no matter how regal and untamed the animals with which they are identified, to be positioned metaphorically where they are already positioned literally and discursively. The material realities of racial politics disrupt the largess of metaphorical politics."[47] Thus, no matter how frequently Dinesen calls Kamante a genius or professes her admiration for him, she does him no service when she describes him as follows: "Here even his intelligence sometimes failed him, and he came and offered me a Kikuyu delicacy,—a roasted sweet potato or a lump of sheep's fat,—as even a civilized dog, that has lived for a long time with people, will place a bone on the floor before you, as a present" (*OA,* 37). Dinesen's usual perspicacity fails her. It is as though she reasoned that since she was fond of both dogs and Kamante it would be no disgrace to compare them to each other. The previously mentioned quote from Joseph Conrad demonstrates that comparisons between dogs and natives were not uncommon and could be used to ridicule the domestic role of blacks and deny their essential humanity. Dinesen's use of animal metaphors has generated more outrage among critics than any other single feature of the novel. Given the frequent abuse of this device in colonial literature, it is easy to understand why.

Dinesen has a tendency to depict the natives in *Out of Africa* as Rousseauian children of nature. Like Jean-Jacques Rousseau (1712–78), Dinesen uses nature as a tool with which to criticize the dangers of civilization. Europe is a "rushed and noisy" place, whereas, Africa is "a still country" (*OA,* 94). Even though Dinesen's valuation of nature is positive, the choice of this rhetorical strategy entails some risks. Colonialists typically feared the "uncivilized," and hence their valuation of nature is negatively charged, opening up the possibilities for interpreting the native's closeness to nature as negative. Carolyn Martin Shaw is offended by Dinesen's attitude towards the natives: "Blixen's romanticism never removed Europeans from their pinnacle. She delights in nature, and her belief that Africans had not quite severed the umbilical cord with nature results in both admiration and disdain for them. This is paternalism (maternalism), and it is racist."[48] In Shaw's view, Dinesen does not sufficiently undermine the power hierarchy of civilization/nature, and, thus, the Africans are pushed into a subordinate position, since they are associated with nature.

Influenced by the Rousseauian linear view of history, Dinesen has a tendency to describe the Africans as "primitive" and at an earlier stage of historical development than the Europeans: "We took these nations over not quite forty years ago; if we compare that moment to the moment of the birth of the Lord, and allow them to catch up with us, three years to our hundred, it will now be time to send them out Saint Francis of Assisi, and in a few years Rabelais" (*OA*, 282). Tone Selboe, along with anthropologist Johannes Fabian, calls this a "denial of coevalness," which is "a persistent and systematic tendency to place the referent(s) of anthropology in a time other than the present of the producer of anthropological discourse."[49] This narrative stance, relegating the natives to a lower rung of the temporal ladder, is another means of placing the Africans in a subordinate position.

Ngugi wa Thiong'o phrases yet another objection to *Out of Africa*, "The racism is catching, because it is persuasively put forward as love."[50] Wa Thiong'o clearly does not believe that the affection Dinesen felt for the natives in her household was sincere, although Tove Hussein's interviews indicate otherwise. Rob Nixon makes a related objection, "But the problem with Blixen's relatively benevolent attentions, and with her regard for Africans in general, is that she perceived her relation to them as a species of philanthropic feudalism, with her at the center exercising noblesse oblige and anticipating a deferential loyalty in return."[51] Dinesen herself noted the similarity between colonial Kenya and eighteenth-century Denmark and rather enjoyed the parallels. The power structure in Kenya gave her the power of a feudal lord over the Africans on the farm. Dinesen would be the first to admit that she exercised noblesse oblige, but, as discussed in the previous section, Nixon's assumption that she expected deferential loyalty in return may not be justified. Nonetheless, it is an irritant to some readers that Dinesen makes frequent use of the possessive pronoun ("my farm," "my boys") which underscores her power role.[52]

Abdul JanMohamed describes the relationship between Dinesen and the natives in the novel somewhat differently: "Dinesen is perfectly aware that her self-image as an omnipotent master and philanthropist is a reciprocal function of the Africans' willingness to act as her servants and of their receptivity to her benefaction: her role as Lord of the Manor is entirely dependent upon their role as serfs."[53] Dinesen's ironic consciousness that she is acting a role thus sets her apart from those who felt their power over the natives was justified and self-evident. JanMohamed points to the scene in *Out of Africa* where she is asked to act as judge on the farm. Dinesen describes her role as that of "a Prima Donna who does not remember a word of her part and has to be prompted through it by the rest of the cast" (*OA*, 96). She acknowledges the validity of the native laws, even if she does not understand them. The natives need her to validate the proceedings should the English authorities question the outcome. Therefore, each side enacts the role expected of them. In JanMohamed's view: "The narcissistic pleasure she derives from her own importance is mitigated by her realization that she is deliberately being indulged by the natives. This combination disarms the reader's potential criticism of her colonialist narcissism."[54]

Some critics have praised *Out of Africa* for its unique focus—that is, unique for 1934. On the eve of the Second World War, Europe was about to slide into one of the worst chapters of racial violence in its history. Dane Kennedy observes, "Kamante and Farah, rather than Denys and Berkeley, occupy center stage in the book, a racial focus unique among settler memoirs."[55] After having read through European depictions of Africa from 1860 to 1960, Per Wästberg seconds this observation, also calling *Out of Africa* unique.[56] Brenda Cooper and David Descutner weigh up the positive references to the Kenyans against the negative remarks made about Europeans and conclude that these two elements "work in combination to fracture the imperialist hierarchy on which rests the justification for colonialism."[57]

At times, Dinesen makes sweeping generalizations about "the Natives," such as "the tempo of life of the colored races is everywhere the same" (*OA*, 177). In one critic's view, however, the sweeping generalizations "become insignificant in comparison with the knowledge of the way of life of individuals which the author shows elsewhere."[58] In *Manichean Aesthetics,* Abdul JanMohamed ranks Dinesen highly among colonial authors particularly for her sincere interest in the natives and their culture. As a stranger, she does not always interpret her facts correctly, but she makes an effort to understand the ways of tribes and individuals. The experience changes her. JanMohamed claims, "Dinesen's more substantial interactions with the Africans gradually, but profoundly, alter some aspects of her personality and values and eventually influence her art."[59]

This is seen in positive contrast to the attitudes of other colonial authors, what JanMohamed calls Joseph Conrad's and E. M. Forster's desire to "exterminate the brutes" and Joyce Cary's threatened paranoia.

One particular episode in *Out of Africa* has garnered considerable attention regarding colonial issues in the novel: the Kitosch episode. It is the story of an African boy who is severely beaten by an English settler and then chained to a stove where he dies by morning. The subsequent legal inquiry tried to establish a "wish to die" defense for the settler, claiming that Kitosch had died because he wished to, not from his injuries. The controversy over this episode illustrates a number of the difficulties associated with interpreting the colonial views of the novel. In *Detained: A Writer's Prison Diary* (1981), Ngugi wa Thiong'o singles out the episode involving Kitosch for his wrath. What annoys Ngugi is that there is "Not a single word of condemnation for this practice of colonial justice. No evidence of any discomfiture."[60] Further, because of this episode, he accuses Isak Dinesen of the "literary glorification of the settler culture of murder and torture."[61] Ngugi is not satisfied with the distanced narrative of the episode and reads approval where he cannot find any sign of outright condemnation. The Kenyan author is not alone in this reading of the story. Danish critic Harald Nielsen is every bit as outraged by the same elements as Ngugi wa Thiong'o.[62] Both Nielsen and Ngugi assume that Dinesen approves of what has happened to Kitosch.

The opposite is the case. Dinesen was deeply upset by the matter and asked her friend Gustav Mohr to obtain for her the documents of the case without telling anyone who wanted them (*KBD*, 1:217). The implication of her concern for anonymity is that the officials would not surrender them if they knew for whom and for what purpose the papers were intended. In an undated manuscript among her papers, Dinesen expresses her thoughts upon the Kitosch case, evidently provoked by early misunderstandings of this passage: "It was my deepest hope that my race, by handing down a just verdict in the case, would make up for the shame that a single individual—who certainly might have been upset—had brought upon us. But it did not happen that way, and the verdict itself, but particularly the testimony of the two doctors, which to me was so obviously meant to save his skin, was not only a source of sorrow, but filled me with a feeling of deep disgrace. . . . I do not understand how the description of these shocking details could fail to give the reader an impression of my indignation over them."[63]

In interviews with the Danish press, Dinesen said that her English publisher had tried to convince her to leave out the passage about Kitosch. In one version of the tale, the publisher claimed it would "break down the English prestige," and in another, he claimed that one should remain silent about some things and "it would pay." In both cases, Dinesen ends her account by proudly announcing that she refused: "Either that chapter is included or the book will not come out at all."[64] Referring to such disturbing incidents at all in 1934 would be considered subversive and threatening by the procolonial segments of the British and Kenyan readership. In relating the story of Kitosch, Dinesen felt that she was making one of her strongest political statements against colonial practices.

Out of Africa's purpose in the 1930s was not just to provide a nostalgic look at "Paradise Lost," but also to elicit in Dinesen's white readership a sense of sympathy and respect for the indigenous cultures of Africa, so that the bad practices of the colonial government would be exposed as unjust. The story of Kitosch contains a revealing reference as to whom Dinesen imagined her audience to be: "It seems to you, as you read the case through, a strange, a humiliating fact that the European should not, in Africa, have power to throw the African out of existence" (*OA*, 271). Dinesen's implied reader is a white racist, most likely a British settler, and this line comes as a jolt to the modern reader who does not think in these terms. Dinesen takes the opportunity to lecture this reader in "The Iguana": "In a foreign country and with foreign species of life one should take measures to find out whether things will be keeping their value when dead. To the settlers of East Africa I give the advice: 'For the sake of your own eyes and heart, shoot not the Iguana'" (*OA*, 248). This is an admonishment to learn from Dinesen's own experiences. She regrets shooting the iguana. She regrets buying the native girl's bracelet. Both retained their value only as long as they remained in their native context. The urge to possess and exploit leads to damage.

Dinesen wrote *Out of Africa*, it seems, for a rather narrow readership, but its audience has been both vast and diverse. One of the major premises of this present book is that, in Dinesen's ambiguous and enigmatic texts, meaning is generated by the individual reader's confrontation with the work. *Out of Africa* is no different. The reading experience of a modern black Kenyan will almost certainly be different than that of a white American who is not directly threatened by the continued legacy of colonialism.

Out of Africa and Autobiography

"I do not want to be in any way the heroine of the book, it should be a book of Africa, but at the same time it might make some things in it clearer to know that it had been lived by a young person, not by an elderly woman" (*KBD*, 1:234). These words to Dinesen's American publisher were prompted by the question of whether to publish a photograph of the author along with *Out of Africa*. Dinesen proposes a photograph from her years in Kenya, not a contemporary picture. This hints at the fact that Dinesen perceived the person she was in Kenya to be different from the author writing in Denmark. Despite Dinesen's protestations that attention should be focused on Africa, many readers have enjoyed *Out of Africa* as a personal tale. As mentioned previously, both Carson McCullers and Janet Sternberg turned to the book for comfort and strength. What these readers find inspiring is the strength the narrator shows in the face of disaster and loss. Dinesen's narrator is a strong female protagonist who does not position herself as a victim even in the midst of adversity. Instead, the reader is presented with multiple examples of positive action and courage.

Out of Africa is a fragmented episodic narrative, presenting snippets of events recalled long after the fact. Unlike so many other autobiographies that use a more traditional linear narrative, it is difficult to trace a developmental "plot," especially since the narrator's attention is so often focused on other people. Moreover, *Out of Africa* is relatively devoid of chronology and concrete historical references, a quality which gives the work a sense of timelessness. Robert Langbaum was the first to suggest that the structure of *Out of Africa* is mythic: "It is because she assimilated her African memories to the myth of the Fall that Isak Dinesen made a unified book of what started out to be a series of disconnected anecdotes."[65] Langbaum sees Dinesen's Africa as a sort of "Paradise Lost." Several other critics have followed Langbaum's lead and identified mythic elements in *Out of Africa.*

Judith Lee sees the narrator of *Out of Africa* as a mask, a fictional projection of the self, and has sought to examine the contours of the mask by comparing Dinesen's accounts in *Out of Africa* with those in her letters from Africa. Lee finds in *Out of Africa* a story of Luciferian rebellion: "to believe that she can, as a woman, be sovereign and autonomous in a world she has not created is a Luciferian act of hubris."[66] Lucifer is, of course, cast out of paradise, just as Dinesen is forced to leave Africa. Dinesen establishes her relationship to Africa through the native, the wild animal, and the immigrant: Kamante, Lulu, and Old Knudsen. At the beginning of the book, references to the gender of the narrator are few, and the American reader who might not know that Isak Dinesen is female could be surprised to run across them when they occur. The narrator is master of her farm, living a life of masculine independence and autonomy. In fact, when Dinesen gets into a bureaucratic tangle over Old Knudsen's funeral arrangements, she claims: "Thus I was no longer Madam Knudsen, but a brother" (*OA,* 188). Lee sees the shooting accident on the farm as an important turning point in the novel. Lee notes that, in the letters, Dinesen heard the shot in the afternoon and did not think much of it. In *Out of Africa,* the shot rings ominously in the night just as the narrator has been enjoying a sense of freedom. This is the moment when necessity is introduced, and the dream turns to a nightmare. Because the case becomes so difficult to resolve, Dinesen must call upon chief Kinanjui: "She must awaken from the dream of her own autonomy to her actual and necessary dependence on another, specifically an African man."[67]

Dinesen enacts the role of a Diana figure, as she hints in the Nietzschean epigraph to the novel given in Latin: "To ride, to shoot a bow, to tell the truth." As discussed in chapter 1, Diana figures adopt a male role, guard their independence, and violently reject the gaze that would reduce them to sexual objects. Brenda Cooper and David Descutner suggest that Dinesen's desire to emphasize her own independence lies behind the choice to downplay her relationship with Denys Finch Hatton: "Proud of the self-reliance she exhibited in Kenya, she also could avoid portraying herself as emotionally dependent on any man, even Finch Hatton, by omitting references to the intimacy they shared."[68] Instead, the prominent episodes in which the two act together involve hunting as a team in Diana-fashion. Dinesen presents their relationship as symbolically reciprocal in the story of how they each shoot a lion on the giraffe carcass: Denys shoots the female and Dinesen the male (*OA*, 221–22). In the letters, Denys shot both lions and they were both male.

In the final section of the book, "Farewell to the Farm," Dinesen experiences a series of failures and losses that shatter her dream of autonomy. These events coincide with more frequent references to the narrator as female. Dinesen fails Kinanjui when he asks for the favor of dying on her farm. She has lost her Diana-like courage. When Denys dies, she assumes the role of bereaved widow, the chief mourner, who selects his grave site. She identifies with the Kikuyu woman carrying her hut on her back, a woman forced to leave the place she felt was her home. As Dinesen takes leave of her farm, Ingrid Lindström visits to comfort her in her loss. Dinesen strongly stresses that they are women, friends, who behave differently than men: "We were in reality a pair of mythical women, shrouded respectively in white and black, a unity, the Genii of the farmer's life in Africa" (*OA*, 357). Dinesen and her friend walk about the farm naming the things to be lost. Susan Hardy Aiken interprets this act through a mythic lense and sees it as a reversal of Adam's naming the things of creation in order to take possession of them.[69] Thus, the mythic plot of *Out of Africa* identified by Lee and supported by the observations of these other critics might be described as follows: The narrator, a woman, imagines herself to be master of her domain and able to act with the independence of a male. This act of hubris is punished: Lucifer is expelled from paradise. The narrator is relegated to her female role, which is one of loss and dispossession.

Sirkka Heiskanen-Mäkelä has found another mythic plot in *Out of Africa,* which she sees as "a *rite de passage,* a symbolic recreation of the author's life in Africa as an initiation, consisting of certain instructions and ordeals and ending in a symbolic death, which finally transforms the initiated into a new being, with a new status in life. The very name of the book tells the message it wants to convey: Isak Dinesen, the author, was born out of Africa."[70] Heiskanen-Mäkelä uses the mythic model of shamanism to inform her reading of the novel, which enables her to interpret the end of the novel not as a moment of defeat but as a moment of rebirth. The shaman/author, Isak Dinesen, demonstrates by writing *Out of Africa* that she is able to revisit her paradise at will.

Isak Dinesen's *Out of Africa* has been compared in recent years with other frontier memoirs penned by women. Most frequently, Dinesen has been linked with Olive Schreiner, Elspeth Huxley, and Beryl Markham. Dinesen admired Schreiner, knew Beryl Markham, and moved in overlapping circles with the younger Elspeth Huxley. The link between these writers, however, seems to be more profound than simply Africa and mutual acquaintance. The frontier conditions that these women lived in, together with the experience of cultural diversity, seem to have released them from traditional gender expectations, leaving them free range in which to construct their own identities. This experience appears common to many women writers, regardless of whether they are writing of Africa, Australia, or frontier Canada. Thus, Sandra Hutchinson, speaking of Canadian writer Dorothy Livesay, claims, "Blixen in Kenya and Livesay in Zambia found a place of psychic and spiritual liberation where they could escape from the imaginative constraints of their northern cultures and discover a point of identification for their vision as women writers."[71] Susan Horton characterizes Dinesen's frontier experience as "living on the slash" between masculine/feminine, white/black, European/African.[72] White women living in Africa could, to a certain extent, act as honorary males, which appears to have been the case with Dinesen. She was charged with managing the farm and entrusted with power that would not have come her way in Denmark. Frontier conditions bring with them greater mobility with regard to traditional constructions of gender, race, and nationality.

Sarah Gilead has noted yet another "slash" represented by Dinesen's African farm, that of nature/culture. Bringing civilization to the wilderness is an issue that has interested fiction since *Robinson Crusoe* (1719). However, this process possesses a special complexity for the woman writer, since, historically, culture has imposed great limitations on women. Gilead sees "the transformation of nature into culture as a model for socialization of the self—socialization at once necessary and unimaginable or intolerable."[73] Culture accords to the self social significance—tells you who you are—but at the same time threatens the self with traditional limits. The farm awards Dinesen her social status as an independent farmer, but during the First World War she is threatened with a concentration camp for women because it is not deemed appropriate for a white woman to be alone with so many natives. Dinesen clings to culture but yearns for the freedom of the wild. On her farm, Dinesen tries to create a place where the wild and the domestic coexist. The "covenant" between the farm and the bushbuck Lulu becomes an example of just such cooperation.

Throughout all her work, Dinesen is interested in dualisms and the interaction of opposites. As mentioned in the first chapter, Dinesen often seeks to undermine the implied hierarchy of the dualism, thus rejecting, for example, the notion that Europe is better than Africa or male is better than female. The difficulties of disrupting such dualistic hierarchies is represented in the figure of the hybrid. In *Out of Africa,* Dinesen tells the story of a half-wild ox that the farm manager tries to break by leaving it in the paddock with all four of his legs tied together. In the night, a leopard comes and eats off one of the ox's legs. This desperate story falls under the rubric, "The Wild Comes to the Aid of the Wild," thus implying that the leopard has done the ox a favor in killing it before its wildness could come under the yoke of domesticity. A vengeful society punishes those who do not conform. The greater danger to the ox comes not from the leopard, but from the farm manager.

Hybridism, the ability to experience both sides of the slash, is fraught with peril. This theme is further developed in "In the Menagerie," where the hyena is presented as a hermaphrodite, a hybrid of both male and female qualities. The showman asks whether it would be harder for a hyena to be shut up alone in a cage: "Would he feel a double want, or is he, because he unites in himself the complementary qualities of creation, satisfied in himself, and in harmony?" (*OA,* 290). The question is not answered directly, but it seems that experiencing both sides of the slash is an asset and a liability. *Out of Africa*'s narrator is also a hybrid, uniting the qualities of male/female, domestic/wild, north/south, European/African. The implication is that, although her world is immeasurably enriched, discontent is always near, and she fears confinement in a world where only one set of values prevail. Thus, she identifies with the hybrid ox and the lions, giraffes, and flamingos that are being sent off to zoos. Dinesen is literally threatened with confinement during the First World War: "If I am to go into a ladies' Concentration Camp in this country for months,—and who knows how long the war is going to last?—I shall die" (*OA,* 255). Dinesen found the narrowminded sameness of views she experienced among the British settlers and her fellow Danes to be an anathema. Dinesen once wrote to her brother, "I believe that life demands of us that we love it, not merely certain sides of it and not only one's own ideas and ideals, but life itself in all its forms, before it will give us anything in return, and when you mention my philosophy of life, I have no other than that" (*LA,* 61).

Although frontier living brings women a greater freedom to construct their own identities, this freedom comes at a cost. On the one hand, there is the anxiety of losing that freedom, but there is a further complication in the case of colonial women writers. As Hariclea Zengos points out, "In a sense, this is the irony of the situation of colonial women: their own freedom is the consequence of the subjugation of others."[74] Dinesen's unconventional life on her farm in Africa is enabled by the colonial subjugation of the Kikuyu. This paradox, in Horton's opinion, creates a psychic economy "in which identification with Africa and Africans was alternately an identification with mastery over Africans and the masculinity implied by that mastery, and an identification with those who had been mastered."[75] As a member of the oppressed feminine gender, Dinesen can relate to, and sympathize with, the powerlessness of the natives. At the same time, this powerlessness enables her own empowerment as "Lord of the Manor," an attractive role for Dinesen.

Sidonie Smith, with some reservations, explores the parallels between the colonial ideologies of race and the patriarchal ideologies of gender: "As a result of in/corporation, woman and African remain other-than-fully human, on the one hand childlike and on the other monstrous. And always, they require some kind of 'parental' oversight. . . . [White women] shared a marginal positionality in relation to white men, caught as they were in their embodiment; and this embodiment they shared with the Africans, who vis-a-vis Europeans were cast in the essentialism of race as surely as the women were cast in an essentialism of gender. (I do not mean to imply here that they experienced the same degree of marginalization as the Africans. They did not.)"[76] Both women and Africans are defined in terms of characteristics of their bodies and biology, and since it is difficult to escape the body, it is equally difficult to escape the attendant social constructions of gender and race. Smith's reservation is significant, because even if white women were marginalized in colonial society, they still outranked the Africans. This paradox of Dinesen's existence—that she can be characterized as both oppressor and oppressed—accounts for some of the lack of consensus among readers about how to assess *Out of Africa.* Dinesen gains the sympathy of some for her achievements as a woman but loses that of others because she is a member of colonial society.

The concept of "the social construction of the self" is a notion that has become current in recent decades along with postmodern ways of thinking. In other words, our sense of identity is built up of multiple layers of socially deter-mined norms, such as what a woman is or what a Dane is. Abdul JanMohamed writes that Dinesen's confrontation with Africa led to a "disintegration of the self," which "allows her to experience the transcendent qualities of that self which lay buried under the encrustations of the social personality."[77] Dinesen saw encountering cultural difference as an essential tool for discovering one's self-identity. She explained the process in a speech delivered to students at Lund University in 1938:

It may happen to some of you . . . that you will travel to distant lands, unknown to you. I can tell you that this will be a strange experience for you. You will find that not only will your surroundings change and be strange and unknown wherever you turn, but that you yourselves will change in your own eyes so that you will eventually ask the question, "Who am I? What do I look like?"

As long as you are a child at home, this question does not arise, all your surroundings can answer it; they are in agreement and their common judgement usually affords the basis of the evaluation we make of our-selves. And as long as you remain in your native country, you are in a sense at home, all the people you meet there have approximately the same background . . .

But one day you come to a people who see us with different eyes. Even if you learn their language, they won't have the same kind of ear you are used to addressing. If you tell them that you come from Lund, it will mean nothing at all to them. . . . If you tell them that your father is a man-aging director or a bishop or a general, it won't mean anything to them because they don't know what a director or a bishop or a general is. . . . They won't even know that you are polite when you raise your hat, and well-dressed when you are in tails.

And while you are divesting yourselves, in a way, of your social and intellectual attitudes one by one, it will slowly dawn upon you that, after all, these may not have constituted your true being, and that something remains behind when they disappear. Who am I then, since I am no longer the same person I have previously been taken for? Then the truest answer must be: a human being. Simply and solely as a human being you meet the black, primitive people.[78]

It may be that in *Out of Africa,* Dinesen is trying to create a similar cultural striptease in the minds of her implied white European readers. Dinesen presents several moments when an African calls into question what the European would take for granted. In interpreting "The Merchant of Venice," Farah sides with Shylock instead of wishing for the happy outcome for the young lovers. Kamante feels that the value of Dinesen's book lies not in its content, but in its color and hardness. Dinesen relishes the thought, though it turns out not to be true, that the Swahili numeral system does not possess the number nine: "Here, I thought, was a people who have got originality of mind, and courage to break with the pedantry of the numeral series" (*OA, 262*). These episodes are not introduced to ridicule the Africans for their ignorance, but instead to open up in the reader's mind other possibilities than the familiar cultural understanding of these things. So, in a sense, *Out of Africa* is about both constructing the identity of the narrator and deconstructing the identity of the reader.

Thematic Resonances

Although *Out of Africa* seems at first glance to be a radical departure from Dinesen's fantastic tales, there are a number of themes and references that intimately connect the book to the rest of Dinesen's fiction. The interaction of opposites and animal metaphors are two such themes which have already been discussed. Judith Lee's suggestion that the narrator of *Out of Africa* is a mask also links the novel thematically to the rest of Dinesen's work, as does the entire discussion about the truthfulness of the book. Dinesen's creative disregard for facts is in keeping with the style of her fictional characters. As she explained once to her mother, "To 'be true' is something positive and by no means merely to refrain from lying,—indeed, it has nothing whatsoever to do with that, in fact" (*LA, 375*).

Despite her many assurances to the press that *Out of Africa* was a "true" book, Dinesen has intentionally integrated fiction and fact. "In the Menagerie" is an inset fictional tale in this otherwise "truthful" book, featuring Augustus von Schimmelman, a character we know from "Roads Round Pisa" and "The Poet" in *Seven Gothic Tales*. Schimmelman is his familiar self-absorbed self, unwilling to acknowledge the existence of giraffes until he himself has seen them. In some respects, he is a caricature of the Eurocentric perspective that Dinesen is trying to dislodge in her readers. Another fictional anecdote includes "Of the Millennium," which fits with Dinesen's thematic interest in Christ's passion throughout her work. Although the reception committee wants Christ's return to be as pleasant as possible, he is most interested in revisiting the site of his crucifixion. The darkest moment of his earthly existence was also the most significant. The story of the parrot who quotes Sappho is another fictional moment, which introduces a note of isolation and loneliness as Dinesen moves into the chapter about the loss of the farm.

There are several more concrete intertextual references to Dinesen's fiction in *Out of Africa*. The description of Hugh Martin and his resemblance to a Chinese idol recalls the description of Prince Pozentiani in "Roads Round Pisa." Mr. Bulpett, the English gentleman from the Victorian Age, speaks the words of the bishop in "The Supper at Elsinore" when he suggests that it might not be appropriate for a lady to fly. The imaginary Madam Knudsen loathes the sea, and both "The Monkey" and "The Deluge at Norderney" refer to woman's natural antipathy for the sea. Dinesen's fear of confinement echoes Athena's in "The Monkey." Berkeley Cole is not subject to the law of gravity, as is the case with many of Dinesen's fictional characters. Emmanuelson bears a strong resemblance to Kasparson in "The Deluge at Norderney" down to the ironic bow they give as they go to meet their respective fates.

When Dinesen describes the Somali women, she does so with an eye to the parallels that exist between them and the European women she describes in her tales: "On these occasions they so strongly reminded me of the ladies of a former generation in my own country, that in my mind I saw them in bustles and long narrow trains. Not otherwise did the Scandinavian women of the days of my Mothers, and Grandmothers,—the civilized slaves of good-natured barbarians, —do the honours at those tremendous sacred masculine festivals" (*OA*, 176–77). The Somali women are conscious of their price, in this case a literal bride price, in a fashion similar to the way in which Malin Nat-og-Dag kept her price incredibly high. The old maids of Closter Seven in "The Monkey" are also conscious of a sexual economy in which women are the highest prize in life. The vast skirts of the Somali women recall the praise of the Old Chevalier for the mysteries concealed by women's clothing. The little Somali girl moves through the transition stage from adolescent tomboy to Woman, from individual to symbol as described in "The Old Chevalier."

Despite the fact that the Somali women are utterly dependent upon their men for everything, they tell stories to each other in which women are always getting the better of men, so there is a taste for subversion even though it does not take the shape of actual rebellion. Dinesen speculates that they live for "the ideal of a Millennium when women were to reign supreme in the world" (*OA*, 175). Although, in *Out of Africa*, Dinesen describes the Somali women with the utmost cultural respect, in her letters she expressed some reservations about the Muhammadan view of women: "I cannot resist trying to get my Muhammadan women a little way out of their cage . . . not even if in the eyes of the world I could become as lovely as the Virgin Mary herself would I give up the freedom of my relationship with nature and people and be confined to four walls and get the whole of life at second hand through one man" (*LA,* 399). This contrast provides some insight into the choices Dinesen made as a narrator. She refrains completely from criticizing the Somali attitude towards women and instead presents it to her readers for their sympathy and understanding. The parallels Dinesen draws between the Somali women and European women of a previous age establish a link between the culture of Africa and the culture of her implied readers.

The episode in which Dinesen writes down for Jogona the story of his adoption of Wamai echoes the theme of the story as a source of identity prevalent in a number of her tales. It is possible to answer the question "Who are you?" with a name or a profession, but a story places a person's identity into a context and crafts disparate details into a coherent, artistic whole. In "The Cardinal's First Tale," the Cardinal answers the question "Who are you?" in what he calls "the classic manner," by telling a story (*LT,* 5). Pellegrina has given up being any one single person and flees from the question "Who are you?" She receives her identity back when Marcus tells her story to the three who have chased her up the mountain demanding to know who she is. Jonathan Mærsk in "The Deluge at Norderney" answers the same question by putting together a tale of his experiences, thinking he might understand them for the first time if he does. Malin Nat-og-Dag performs a similar service for Calypso, who is just beginning to understand who she is. Calypso acknowledges the tale with "a clear deep glance" (*SGT,* 46). Similarly the writing of Jogona's story is described as a laborious process: "Once he went and leaned his face against the wall, as the Kikuyu women do when they are giving birth to their children" (*OA,* 113). When Dinesen reads the story back to him he responds with "a great fierce flaming glance" (*OA,* 115). Dinesen elaborates, "Such a glance did Adam give the Lord when He formed him out of the dust, and breathed into his nostrils the breath of life, and man became a living soul. I had created him and shown him himself" (*OA,* 115).

"The Roads of Life" is a short, but significant, anecdote. Tone Selboe considers it a crucial moment in *Out of Africa* that also reverberates throughout Dinesen's entire fictional oeuvre.[79] The story is told with the help of visual aids. A man who lives in a small round house with a triangular yard and a fish pond some distance away lives through a terrible night in which he rushes from place to place seeking the source of a noise. He falls into ditches and finally discovers that the water is rushing out of the pond. Visually, the house and yard are the head and the beak of the stork, and the fish pond is the wing. The path the man runs during the night traces the shape of the rest of the stork, and the ditches have been a necessity in drawing the talons of the bird. In the morning, the man can see the stork: "He must have laughed out loud then" (*OA,* 242). The completed picture provides the man with an epiphany so that he can see the sense in his apparently aimless wandering.

Dinesen goes on to draw a parallel between this tale and her own life: "The tight place, the dark pit in which I am now lying, of what bird is it the talon? When the design of my life is completed, shall I, shall other people see a stork?" (*OA*, 242). This story contains the primary message of consolation in *Out of Africa*. It suggests a strategy for coping with misfortune: Have faith that there is a design even if it is not evident at the moment. Dinesen mentioned this story in a letter to her mother: "Just when one feels one is floundering in the deepest despair,—'fall into a ditch, get out again,'—is when one is perfecting the work of art of one's life, as microcosm. I have experienced this in my own life, and the greatest moments have been those when I have been able to glimpse the stork" (*LA*, 49). Life is a work of art and the good and bad may be aesthetically necessary. This existential advice echoes throughout Dinesen's fiction.

This anecdote also describes a sudden shift of perspective, when disparate or dissonant elements suddenly fall into place. Dinesen experiences similar shifts in perspective elsewhere in *Out of Africa,* as when she suddenly understands why Molly the Mule is called "the spoon" when viewed from the vantage point of the driver's seat (*OA*, 285). The experience of flying with Denys also provides a sense of godlike overview, but the glimpse is temporary. It may be argued that Dinesen precipitates similar shifts in perspective in certain of her tales. In "The Deluge at Norderney," when the Cardinal is revealed as an imposter, everything that has gone before in the tale must be reevaluated. The same shift occurs in "The Monkey" when the Prioress undergoes her metamorphosis and in "The Dreamers" when Pellegrina's identity is finally revealed. Agnese's revelation at the duel in "The Roads Round Pisa" causes many pieces of the narrative puzzle to fall into place. It is not until the end of the tale or the end of a life that the design of the artwork becomes clear.

At the end of *Out of Africa,* Dinesen is looking for the "central principle" in her "run of bad luck:" "If I looked in the right place, I reflected, the coherence of things might become clear to me. I must, I thought, get up and look for a sign" (*OA*, 353). The sign she receives is witnessing a rooster pluck the tongue out of a chameleon. Although Dinesen appears to understand the import of this sign immediately, a number of readers have been baffled by its significance. In order to draw a parallel between the chameleon and Dinesen the artist, Else Brundbjerg points to the fact that Shelley compares the poet to a chameleon, and that Jens in "The Dreaming Child" dreams of chameleon art.[80] Brundbjerg goes on to suggest that the rooster symbolizes betrayal. This would imply that the scene describes some sort of betrayal of Dinesen, the artist.

Another interpretation of the rooster is suggested by a domestic accident described by Dinesen in one of her letters: "That brass rooster, you know, that I brought back with me. It was on top of a cupboard, and as I was trying to shut a drawer that had got stuck, underneath the cupboard, it fell down on my head. I collapsed completely and woke up in a pool of blood; Farah came in and raised his arms to the skies at the sight of me. If I had died it would have been roman-tic; because it was of course, an old West African idol, and I think it would have looked rather grand, if anyone had been there to see when it fell and hit me with its beak" (*LA,* 126). If this association is correct, then it is the gods of Africa themselves who have answered Dinesen with a sign. Africa has rejected Dinesen and taken away her livelihood: "Great powers had laughed to me, with an echo from the hills to follow the laughter, they had said among the trumpets, among the cocks and Chameleons, Ha ha!" (*OA,* 354). A chameleon tries to blend in with its environment, as Dinesen thought to become one with Africa. Failure to blend in, for the chameleon, results in death. Dinesen also mentions elsewhere the sensation that Africa was withdrawing itself from her. Dinesen no longer belongs in Africa and it is time to depart.

CHAPTER 4

Winter's Tales

The German occupation of Denmark began on April 9, 1940, and the bulk of *Winter's Tales* was written and polished under that influence. Dinesen's mother had died in 1939, so Dinesen lived alone at Rungstedlund under very difficult circumstances. She alluded briefly to her sense of confinement in a way that made it past the censors in a 1942 interview with Hans Brix: "Winter is here and we cannot go out anymore. It is as in Shakespeare's day. Now we sit indoors and tell stories, all the while longing to be outside again."[1] As had been the case with *Seven Gothic Tales,* Dinesen wrote her stories first in English and then recast them into Danish. Dinesen secured a special visa to allow her to travel to Stockholm on April 24, 1942, where she was able to send her English manuscript to London and New York via diplomatic channels. Dinesen could gain no news of the fate of her English manuscripts until after the occupation ended in 1945. She was then pleased to learn that *Winter's Tales* had come out in an Armed Forces edition and had been carried by American soldiers in the field.

Her American publisher, Robert Haas, once again took the liberty of changing the order of the tales from the one proposed by Dinesen, so the American edition varies from the English and Danish editions:

USA	England
The Young Man with the Carnation	The Sailor-boy's Tale
Sorrow-Acre	The Young Man with the Carnation
The Heroine	The Pearls
The Sailor-boy's Tale	The Invincible Slave-owners
The Pearls	The Heroine
The Invincible Slave-owners	The Dreaming Child
The Dreaming Child	The Fish
Alkmene	Alkmene
The Fish	Peter and Rosa
Peter and Rosa	Sorrow-Acre
A Consolatory Tale	A Consolatory Tale

Haas favored an order that framed the collection with two stories featuring the character Charlie Despard. Robert Langbaum reports that Dinesen was not happy with this arrangement. When Langbaum tried to argue for the logic of it, "she grew angry and said that for some instinctive reason which she could not explain she had wanted 'Sailor-boy' first."[2] "The Sailor-boy's Tale" relates the adventures of a young sailor in a coming-of-age story. According to Dinesen's plan, this tale would have been followed by one in which an author goes to a sailor's bar and listens to sailors' stories to gain inspiration. This shift from one tale to the other would have described a progression from actual experience to the artistic reworking of vicarious experience. Perhaps there was something in this move towards aesthetic distance that appealed to Dinesen.

Various critics have looked for the mark they feel the German occupation must have left upon *Winter's Tales*. The title is a slight variation on the title of Shakespeare's *The Winter's Tale*. Dinesen readily pointed out the connection herself and told one interviewer: "'A sad tale is best for winter,' says the little prince in Shakespeare and perhaps there is a somewhat melancholy tone in my tales."[3] The winter of the title becomes a metaphor for a state of siege and confinement, clearly pointing to the occupation. Vibeke Schröder has suggested that the title might also refer to Heinrich Heine's *Germany: A Winter's Tale* (1844), a long satirical poem critiquing Germany's political life from the perspective of an exile.[4] Political tyranny made Heine an exile and Dinesen a prisoner. Judith Thurman notes that *Winter's Tales* is the most Danish of Dinesen's books and interprets this a show of national solidarity.[5] Else Brunbjerg observes that even though confinement is a theme that runs throughout Dinesen's work, references to imprisonment and captivity are especially numerous in *Winter's Tales*.[6] Shirley Clouse De Simone claims that three of the tales, "The Heroine," "The Fish," and "Sorrow-Acre," "comprise a programme for dealing with power: ethical resistance, violent opposition, and in circumstances where those solutions do not apply, affirmative acceptance."[7]

In *Winter's Tales,* Dinesen returned to the tale genre of her first collection, but made a few changes. She characterized the relationship between the two volumes as follows: "[*Winter's Tales*] consists of eleven short stories, somewhat shorter than my seven fantastic tales, and more concise in form—this time, they stick more to what actually happened. I feel myself that the author of *Seven Gothic Tales* was too talkative. These stories are also not quite as fantastic in their subject matter as the others."[8] Under the circumstances, Dinesen might have expected a better reception in Denmark for *Winter's Tales,* but was once again to be disappointed. Danish critic Henning Kehler wrote a particularly scathing review in which he regrets that Dinesen has reverted to the style of her first book. In the end, he dismisses Dinesen as a good writer of pastische: "She has that truly feminine capacity to be able to copy superbly."[9] Lack of originality is a charge that has been leveled at women writers since they first put pen to paper, but in Dinesen's case it is palpably unfair. Hans Brix commented unfavorably on her complexity: "She cannot seriously expect to be, on the average, more than half or three-quarters understood."[10]

Dinesen only had to go as far as Sweden for a kinder view of her new book. One Swedish reviewer wrote: "War books and proletarian books can be very good—bad too, heaven only knows—but one must be forgiven if one feels grateful to be able to get away from both the dramas of the world and the tenant farmers."[11] Dinesen meant for her collection to be entertaining in hard times. America received *Winter's Tales* with enthusiasm. William Maxwell wrote in the *New York Times Book Review:* "Many people, I feel sure, will read all eleven *Winter's Tales* as I did—as fast as possible in order to have as soon as possible the pleasure of reading them for the second, the third, and inevitably the fourth time."[12]

"The Young Man with the Carnation"

"The Young Man with the Carnation" is a story about an author in crisis and some have drawn the conclusion that the crisis must have been Dinesen's own. Hans Brix has gone so far as to claim that Charlie Despard's initials point to Dinesen's own name: Karen *C*hristenze *D*inesen.[13] Robert Langbaum, on the other hand, warns against making this easy identification, noting that Charlie as an author of social realism is not at all the same type as Dinesen.[14] Moreover, Charlie is a young man who has not yet reached thirty, whereas, Dinesen was almost fifty-eight when the story was published. It might be well to heed Langbaum's caution.

Charlie Despard is in despair, as his name suggests, because he does not know how he will follow the success of his first book. Charlie's first book was about the lot of poor children, written from his own experiences. Now that he has been transformed into a famous author he wonders how he will ever have any authentic experiences again that can serve as an inspiration to his art. He worries that "he had, from his own free will, exchanged the things of the Lord—the moon, the sea, friendship, fights—for the words that describe them" (*WT,* 10). Charlie is afraid that because of this, his work will become superficial and carry no weight. To begin with, "superficial" is a negative term to Charlie, but during the course of the evening he comes to reevaluate the merits of superficiality. The ships in the harbor help him to change his understanding of superficial: "The ships were superficial, and kept to the surface. Therein lay their power; to ships the danger is to get to the bottom of things, to run aground. They were even hollow, and hollowness was the secret of their being; the great depths slaved for them as long as they remained hollow" (*WT,* 11). The ships suggest that there may yet be hope for Charlie as an artist.

Charlie follows a ship's captain to a tavern called Le Croix du Midi (The Southern Cross) after a constellation that sailors use to navigate. Charlie is looking for his own sense of direction and begins to find it in his vicarious experiences of the sailors' adventures: "Here, in the inn of La Croix du Midi he had already lived through much. He had seen a ship burn down, a snowstorm in the North Sea, and the sailor's homecoming to his wife and children" (*WT,* 17). As an artist of imagination, Charlie is able to experience vicariously the sailors' adventures as his own. In repayment of the sailors' tales, Charlie invents a story, a blue story. After her ship catches fire, Lady Helena sails alone for nine days with a young English sailor in a life raft. Once they are rescued, the sailor is sent away and Lady Helena spends the rest of her life looking for a particular shade of blue porcelain "from the time when all the world was blue" (*WT,* 19). In other words, the blue porcelain becomes a symbolic representation of the nine days in which Lady Helena was able to live her real life with the sailor surrounded by the blue of the sea and the sky. Since a reunion with the sailor is impossible, Lady Helena must content herself with symbols, not the real thing, and requests to have her heart buried in the blue jar. This tale echoes the plight of Charlie who will also learn to content himself with symbols and vicarious experience, rather than with the adventures of real life. It will be Charlie's fate to write love stories while being content with only "a shilling's worth" of love (*WT,* 25).

Dinesen wrote of the significance of the blue story to her friend Johannes Rosendahl: "It [the blue story] is part of the longer tale of 'The Young Man with the Carnation' in order to illuminate or confirm Charlie's inevitable fate: that for him everything, including his enthusiasm for the eventful life of action and his aversion to poetry, takes shape as a 'story,' so that he, in order to create it, appropriates and uses the images from the life of action which have gripped him most strongly and forced him into enthusiasm,—and aversion. That the story he tells to the sailors in the tavern, after they have told him about their experiences at sea, also mirrors his own isolation and eternal seeking, serves—within the tale—the same purpose" (*KBD,* 1:471).

It is Charlie's fate that he will be torn between enthusiasm and aversion, but both moods will inspire his creative processes. In the same letter, Dinesen goes on to say that she had originally planned to have Charlie tell two stories, one "burlesque and grotesque" and the other, the blue story, "romantic," but the first story did not get by the censors, though it is difficult to say why (*KBD,* 1:471). Charlie appears to be learning a new literary style, inspired by the oral tradition of the sailors. The blue story is not social realism, but a romantic imaginative tale, for which he can use borrowed images and experiences. The superficiality will not harm it.

In addition to Charlie's vacillation between the life of deeds and the life of words, another source of his discontent may be that he has been drawn into the world of the bourgeois, as described in the first chapter of this book. Art and the bourgeois are incompatible, which may be at the root of Charlie's fear and discontent regarding his wife who is a solid representative of bourgeois values. She is the lighthouse, both the guide and the antithesis of the ships Charlie has claimed as his sisters and doubles. Charlie's background is from the proletariat and his mother even had a few drops of gypsy blood in her. As an artist, Charlie wants to skim the waves and remain in contact with the depths: "For where the lighthouse stands, there is shoal water, or rocks. To all floating objects the approach means death" (*WT*, 22). The lighthouse, his wife, is rooted in the shallows. She represents an existence of comfort and stability, an anathema to the artistic temperament.

The Queen's Hotel is a locus of bourgeois values: "It was a neat, respectable place, where sea captains stayed with their wives" (*WT*, 3). Charlie feels ill at ease there and seeks refuge in the disreputable harbor where prostitutes greet the sailors. One of Charlie's doubles in this story is the tame monkey named Charlie, whom he describes to the sailors. The monkey came originally from a brothel where it thrived: "But when I came home the English food did not agree with him, nor did the English Sunday. So he grew sick, and he grew worse, and one Sabbath evening he died on me" (*WT*, 14). The English Sunday represents bourgeois rectitude that makes Charlie Despard feel "sick, even to death" (*WT*, 3). When Charlie returns to the hotel, his wife is waiting for him in the restaurant which "took on a sabbath-morning look" (*WT*, 22). The setting makes Charlie begin to feel uneasy again. No matter how sweet and loving Charlie's wife may be, their relationship is doomed. In the sequel to this tale, "A Consolatory Tale," Charlie has left his wife.

When Charlie realizes what actually happened the previous evening when he believed he was in bed with his wife, he experiences an epiphany that leads into a conversation with God. At first, Charlie reacts with delight and his face mirrors the expression of the young man with the carnation when he first opened the door: "an expression of rapture, laughter and delight" (*WT*, 23). Upon their first meeting, Charlie is envious of this expression of "infinite happiness" and mourns that he has lost his way to it (*WT*, 9). Charlie has therefore regained what he thought he had lost. Next, he savors the details of the scene as an artist "like honey on his tongue" (*WT*, 23). In fact, in the Danish version of the tale, Charlie savors the moment for an additional paragraph, fleshing out the feelings of the young woman in the bed: "Would she have thanked them [Eros and his mother] later, when she understood that she had saved her life at the cost of the hour that was worth more to her than life itself, and which would never come again?" (*MU,* 4:51). Charlie's vicarious experience of the lovers' feelings will inspire him to write a love story. The creative block that plagued Charlie at the outset of the tale is broken, because now he is assured that he stands in God's favor.

A covenant is established during Charlie's talk with God: "I will not measure you out any more distress than you need to write your books" (*WT,* 25). Dinesen wrote of this exchange: "Charlie's 'Conversation with God' is a discussion of this issue [Nemesis], his anxious cry: 'Can't I get off more easily?' and his resignation and at last understanding of God's answer: 'You cannot, and you do not want to either'" (*KBD,* 1:392). Artists in Dinesen's tales most often must make a sacrifice. In Charlie's case, he must sacrifice his life of action and content himself with the words that describe it. Moreover, he will probably sacrifice the stability and comfort of his life with his wife. Dinesen wrote of the ending of the tale, "Charlie himself feels his pact with God to be a reparation and an ennoblement,—he can even declare himself satisfied with the previous experience, yes, look upon with pity the person he has previously envied" (*KBD,* 1:575). Dinesen alludes to the last line of the story which says in French: "Oh, the poor young man with the carnation" (*WT,* 26). This line echoes a previous line, also in French, in which Charlie imagines what the young man thinks of him: "Oh, the poor little man in the green robe" (*WT,* 10). Charlie has covered considerable emotional ground: from self-pity to sympathy, from sadness to joy, from resentment to reconciliation, from writer's block to creative inspiration.

"Sorrow-Acre"

"Sorrow-Acre" has gained more attention than any other tale in *Winter's Tales.* In 1954, Swedish director Alf Sjöberg considered filming the story, though the project did not come to fruition. In 1987, Danish TV produced a film version that was directed by Morten Henriksen. The tale has also been anthologized more than any other of Dinesen's stories. According to Dinesen, the impetus for the tale arose from a conversation with her neighbor Hartvig Frisch about proletarian culture. Frisch challenged Dinesen to describe a distinctly manorial culture. Dinesen evidently wrote this answer to the challenge while she was staying at just such a manor house in the late 1930s.

The events of "Sorrow-Acre" take place at a pivotal point in history.[15] The date is 1775, the year in which Johannes Ewald's *The Death of Balder* was published. Major historical changes are on the horizon. America will begin its revolution in 1775, the serfs will be liberated in Denmark in 1787, the French Revolution will start in 1789, and King Gustaf III of Sweden will be assassinated in 1792. The ancient feudal order will soon be replaced by the values of bourgeois humanism. Oddly enough, this ideological shift expresses itself in a taste in gardening. The manor house of "Sorrow-Acre" possesses a French rose garden laid out to please the new lady of the manor. Such gardens are characterized by geometrical forms and neatly pruned order, as in the gardens of the Palace at Versailles. In the feudal world, the individual is subordinated to the social order, in the same way that the individual plants of the French garden are made to serve a larger design. In England, Adam, the young nephew of the manor, "had acquired a freer taste in gardening, and he wondered if he could liberate these blushing captives, and make them thrive outside their cut hedges" (*WT,* 36). The romantic garden popular with the era of bourgeois humanism respected the natural characteristics of the plants and allowed them to flourish in an idealized imitation of nature. Similarly, bourgeois humanism places value on individual self-realization, instead of subordinating the individual to the social order. At the moment the story takes place, these two worldviews exist at the same time, represented by the figures of the old lord and Adam. Adam's ideological world is easier for most readers to understand, since it is still the dominant view of the modern world.

In the feudal world, identity was determined by one's place in society. The old lord is designated throughout the story by his station in life, not by an individual name like Adam: "To the King and the country, to his family and to the individual lord of the manor himself it was a matter of minor consequence which particular Rosenkrantz, Juel or Skeel, out of a long row of fathers and sons, at the moment in his person incarnated the fields and woods, the peasants, cattle and game of the estate" (*WT,* 31). In feudal society, the individual gains significance only by assuming his role in the social order. The opening paragraphs of "Sorrow-Acre" give a detailed description of the landscape which the reader is invited to "read . . . like a book" (*WT,* 29).[16] The landscape is dominated by the manor house at the apex of "the lordly, pyramidal silhouette of the cut lime avenues" (*WT,* 30). Thus, the landscape itself reproduces the figure of the feudal pyramid. The lord of the manor, God's representative on earth, sits at the apex of the pyramid and exercises power over those below him.

Ritual and ceremony possess great power in the feudal world, since ritual enactment reinforces the social order that endows significance and identity to every person within it. At one point when Adam is looking at the old lord standing in the field with Anne-Marie, he is reminded of "the meeting between Esau and Jacob in Edom" (*WT,* 53). Jens Aage Doctor has described how the biblical tale of Esau and Jacob (Genesis 27) helps to illustrate the attitude the old lord adopts in his behavior towards Anne-Marie. By assuming a disguise, Jacob is able to trick his father Isaac into giving him the paternal blessing meant for his older brother Esau. It is an important ritual and once the blessing is given, it cannot be taken back. In the modern world, such a contract would be declared null and void because the blessing was obtained under false pretenses. In the Old Testament, once the word is given it cannot be taken back, regardless of the consequences or the circumstances under which it was given. Esau is simply out of luck. The blessing would not have the value it possesses if it could be given or rescinded at a whim. Similarly, when Adam begs the old lord to call off the agreement he has made with Anne-Marie, the old lord says simply: "I gave Anne-Marie my word" (*WT,* 56). From Adam's modern viewpoint, he cannot understand his uncle's position: "A life is a greater thing even than a word" (*WT,* 56). The feudal order values the ritual above the individual and bourgeois humanism values the individual above all. The old lord recognizes that his young nephew does not understand him and comments, "I have been quoting to you texts a thousand years old" (*WT,* 57).

In England, Adam has learned of "the great new ideas of the age: of nature, of the right and freedom of man, of justice and beauty" (*WT,* 34). He is convinced "his success in life depended on his personal ability," not on the ancient name he has inherited (*WT,* 34). Adam wears his hair naturally and dresses plainly, whereas, his uncle dons the powdered wig and regalia of his station to witness Anne-Marie's toils. Adam says he will return at the end of the day to see the completion of Anne-Marie's task, but he does not keep his word. Instead of texts a thousand years old, Adam is enthralled by Johannes Ewald's latest drama, *The Death of Balder.* In fact, Adam is named after a character from an earlier Ewald play, *Adam and Eve* (1769). The story is the familiar tale of the Fall, but at this point in history Ewald and other European writers began to interpret the Fall, not as original sin, but as a fortunate event. Eating from the tree of knowledge bestows free will and the power to strive for one's own redemption. According to Jens Aage Doctor, *Adam and Eve* is the first text in Danish literature to advance the idea that it might be right to disobey the law and does not consider it beneficial to man to conform to given limits. Rebellion and revolution are in the air, even if they have not yet broken forth.

The different worldviews of the uncle and the nephew come to a head over the fate of Anne-Marie. The issue is complicated because it is not clear whether or not Anne-Marie's son, Goske Pil is guilty of arson. The old lord has lost a son, whose only playmate as a child was this same Goske Pil. There may be murky personal motivations at play. The old lord makes Anne-Marie an offer: If she mows a certain field, the work of three men, between sunrise and sunset, then she can save her son from prison and execution. The old lord views this as an act of mercy. One might infer that he would have embraced the chance to save his own son through some heroic act. From the old lord's point of view, he is offering Anne-Marie a chance at immortality, to become part of a tragic story that will be long remembered. The old lord explains himself more fully in a passage not included in the American edition, but present in some later British editions.[17] The old lord compares himself proudly to the pharaohs who built the pyramids. He reasons that even if the pharaoh had used his resources to feed his people instead of building a monument, his subjects would still be dead today, but the pyramids live on and have become a source of pride and consolation to future generations. Because the common man thinks only of his daily bread, the old lord argues, the aristocrat must be the one who looks to the future for the common good. Anne-Marie's heroic example and the monument raised to her is the old lord's answer to the pyramids. The old lord accepts full responsibility for his choices.

Adam views Anne-Marie's ordeal as an act of tyranny and oppression and demands that the deal be called off. When his uncle refuses, Adam is on the brink of total rebellion and threatens to leave forever. Many reviewers have felt themselves kindred spirits with Adam. Jørgen Sandved called "Sorrow-Acre" "the world's most disgusting novella" because of his outrage over the old lord's treatment of Anne-Marie.[18] Danish author Tom Kristensen told Dinesen to her face that "she ought to be shot" for having written "Sorrow-Acre."[19] Dinesen was evidently only pleased to have evoked such a strong reaction. Kristensen, like many other readers, felt that the views of the old lord were Dinesen's own—after all, she was a Baroness. As usual, it might be wise to exercise caution when making such easy identifications between Dinesen and her fictional characters. In "Sorrow-Acre," Dinesen attempts to recreate the feudal order's understanding of itself, and, of course, the old lord does not perceive himself to be a tyrant. The new world order judges him differently, but even that is incorporated into Dinesen's tale.

Instead of a violent break between uncle and nephew, a revolution, there is a subversive compromise involving the young aunt Sophie Magdalena. Several critics have noted that "Sorrow-Acre" presents an Oedipal drama.[20] Although the Oedipus complex is most often used to explain the behavior of individuals, it has also been applied to generations. The young generation must symbolically kill the older generation (or its ideas) before striking off in a new direction. Adam, the new generation, must symbolically overthrow the old lord. In Greek, "Oedipus" means "the swollen-footed" and Adam walks with a limp. He perceives the old lord to be his second father. The overthrow of the old lord will take the form of Adam having an affair with Sophie.

Critics are generally united in their assumption that Adam will sleep with his uncle's wife. After all, a gypsy has foretold that Adam's son is to sit in the seat of his fathers. Moreover, the old lord has given Adam permission to eat freely from every tree in his Garden of Eden, and Sophie Magdalena is ripe for the picking to judge from the scene in which she examines her naked body in the mirror. What has not always been certain is whether or not the old lord has orchestrated the infidelity himself in order to secure a healthy heir to his name of his own blood, although some have suspected as much.[21] Dinesen herself was clear that the old lord knows what is going on, as she explained in a letter to Aage Henriksen: "the story of Adam's conversion bottoms out in this: Instead of traveling to America, he will stay where he is and put a pair of horns on the old lord's head. In this way, his 'abhorrence of the tyrant [can] die out of him, and his pity for all creation extend even to the sombre form before him.' The old lord understands him to the extent that, when Adam predicts Anne-Marie's death and the consequences that will come over his own head, he takes his hat off and lets his hand run over his powdered forehead and asks: 'Upon my head? In what shape will it come upon my head, my nephew?'" (*KBD*, 2:275). Dinesen reminds her reader to pay careful attention to the body language of her characters. The horns that the old lord seeks upon his head are the ancient symbol of the cuckold.

When "Sorrow-Acre" is read as a tale of generational strife, it is easy to focus on Adam and the old lord and lose sight of the significant roles played by the women in the tale. Anne-Marie's name is a composite of the two highest female saints in the Christian canon. The monument raised for the comfort of future generations is purchased at the cost of her heroic sacrifice. She is the source and the inspiration for the name "Sorrow-Acre," even if she herself will be forgotten, as many women have been forgotten in history. Sophie Magdalene has been groomed to be a caryatid, but as she blushes before the mirror, she shows signs of becoming a transgressive blossom figure, akin to the roses Adam wants to liberate from their pruned hedges. Sophie is Eve who will convince Adam to taste the apple and experience the fortunate Fall. Women are the weak link in the unbroken chain from father to son in this patriarchal feudal order. Susan Hardy Aiken points out an ironic inversion of the feudal pyramid described in the initial paragraphs of the tale: "The whole structural force of the introduction culminates as all its 'lines' converge—not in the apices of the phallic 'pyramids' of paternal authority . . . , but in their precise inversion: the small triangulated 'laps' of the women, signs at once of maternity and of female sexuality." Sophie's affair with Adam will be a subversion of the feudal order. In a way, the end result of Sophie's affair with Adam may constitute something of an allegory for the history of Denmark. Denmark is a monarchy, in fact it has one of the oldest unbroken royal lines in Europe, but it is also a Social Democracy. This compromise was reached without a violent revolution. The old forms were retained, but the substance was changed. The heir to the manor in "Sorrow-acre" will to all appearances be part of an unbroken line, but through his veins will flow the blood of the new age.

There is little unity among critics about what will happen after the close of "Sorrow-Acre." David H. Richter is convinced that "Adam's fate will be to die, at the hands of his uncle or his minions, sacrificing himself to save the woman and their son."[22] Richter points to Sophie's murder of the flea as a portent of Adam's fate to come, as well as other details that support a bleak ending for Adam. Poul Behrendt argues, "Not for nothing is there a thunderclap after Adam's words to his uncle, the thunder that sounds in Ewald's *Adam and Eve* when they eat the apple. . . . The next morning Adam will be forced to leave the manor, separated from both the new and the old world."[23] Robert Langbaum foresees a milder future for Adam: "It is the destiny of Adam to inherit the lord's estate and marry his young wife—to serve the lord's idea of continuity."[24] Clearly, it is up to the reader to imagine his or her own continuation of events. Judith Thurman's speculations along these lines are detailed and raise an interesting point: "The sequel to 'Sorrow Acre,' which will be the story of young Adam's romantic wanderings, his philanthropy to the peasants, his struggles of conscience, his love for his uncle's wife, is the realm of the novel."[25]

The historical shift described in "Sorrow-Acre" is not only ideological, but aesthetic.[26] In "The Cardinal's First Tale" from *Last Tales,* the Cardinal describes the difference between the story, a divine art, and the novel, "the literature of individuals" (*LT,* 24). The story values plot over character, and as such, the storyteller must sometimes be cruel to the characters in order to remain true to the story. The novel allows characters to remain in the foreground and will sacrifice the plot for their sake. The old lord and Anne-Marie belong to the age of the story, and see the plot through regardless of its cruelty. The original germ of this part of "Sorrow-Acre" was a folktale collected by Frederik Ohrt and published in 1919. Donald Hannah has translated the folktale and even assures us that such a memorial stone can still be found in the village of Ballum on the west coast of Jutland.[27] The original tale took place in 1634, so Dinesen has moved up the date in order to emphasize the particular historical shift she wants to illuminate. Even so, the tale had lived on in oral tradition for over three hundred years, thus vindicating the old lord's sense of the enduring power of this heroic story.

The new age with its emphasis on the individual will not be suitable for generating such enduring stories. Instead, as Thurman suggests, the novel will be the more appropriate mode for telling Adam's life. Instead of witnessing the end of

Anne-Marie's story, Adam chooses to remain in the manor accompanying his young aunt as she sings an air from Christoph Willibald von Gluck's opera, *Alceste* (1767). The French lines of the song have echoed throughout the tale: "To die for the one you love / Is an effort too sweet for words" (*WT,* 60). The lines appear to have an obvious resonance with the events out in the field. In the opera, Apollo's oracle has decreed that Admetus's life can be saved if someone will die in his place. Admetus's wife Alceste agrees to make this supreme sacrifice. Up to this point, we have an almost perfect parallel to Anne-Marie's tragic story. However, Gluck's 1767 opera belongs to this new age which cannot bear such cruelty. At the last minute, Apollo descends to take back the word of his oracle and allows both husband and wife to live. The result is a happy ending, but a mediocre tragedy. Unlike Gluck's Apollo, the old lord refuses retract his word and sees the tragedy through to its sublime end. In a sense, the old lord's world is also meeting its tragic end. Adam and Sophie as the representatives of the new age will live happily ever after. The humanistic age has gained freedom for the individual at the cost of aesthetic values.

"The Heroine"

"'The Heroine' has a sort of interest for theologians, as a sort of commentary to the doctrine of atonement, and is perhaps somewhat specific," commented Dinesen in a letter to a friend (*KBD,* 1:169). At first glance, the story of a nude dancer who repulses the advances of a German soldier may not seem to have much to do with theological issues. Hans Holmberg has performed a detailed reading of "The Heroine" in which the parallels between Christ and Heloise are clear, but where Heloise is a lion, instead of a Lamb of God.[28] At the onset of the Franco-Prussian war, a group of travelers is arrested because the Bible verse Isaiah 53:6 is thought to be a coded message announcing details of the German advance. This verse is a prophecy of the coming Messiah. Heloise appears on the scene and calms the nervous travelers, "as if she realized that they must needs have been looking forward in suspense to her arrival" (*WT,* 73). Heloise's flock consists of solid, decent people, but with perhaps a potential for weakness, implied by the priest's treatise on the denial of Peter. Heloise faces the demands of the German officer with her hands held behind her waist, and "it gave her the look of having her hands tied upon her back" (*WT,* 79). Similarly, Christ is bound during his interrogation. The party awaits the German officer's decision in the courtyard, just as the disciples wait with Christ in Gethsemane, but Heloise's followers do not betray her. She is handed a bouquet of roses, instead of a crown of thorns. The party celebrates with a communion supper, "a hurried, spare meal of bread and wine" (*WT,* 81). Holmberg characterizes the central difference between Heloise and Christ as follows: "Heloise's fate will remind them for all time of their moral victory, whereas Christ, from a certain point of view, always reminds us of our guilt and our moral defeat, when we sacrificed an innocent person."[29]

Dinesen had difficulty accepting the Christian doctrine of atonement, the belief that Christ died for our sins and we are therefore "saved" without any particular effort on our part. Dinesen once wrote to her sister: "For two thousand years human beings have felt gratitude to Christ because he 'sacrificed himself' for them; but I really think there would be very few who would not, if they were offered the chance of having the crucifixion carried out for their own personal salvation, this very afternoon—even if they were directly confronted with flaming Hell and eternal damnation,—rush up and say: for Heaven's sake do not take that upon yourself" (*LA,* 347). Dinesen has staged in her story a situation in which it is more important for each individual to share in the sacrifice.

Heloise's heroism lies in the fact that she could easily have appeared naked before the German officer without any offense to her sensibilities, since she is by profession a nude dancer, but she refuses to take the easy way out, because she realizes in time what a devastating effect it would have on her staid traveling companions: "They would have repented it all their lives, and have held themselves to be great sinners" (*WT,* 86). Dinesen wrote about Heloise's heroism to Johannes Rosendahl:

> She could really have "gotten off easily," considering the circumstances, especially easily. When her hand "for a moment went up to the collar of her mantilla, as if, choking under the wave of her disdain, she must free herself of it," her impulse is to tear it off, as well as all her beautiful clothes, and she regrets later that Frederick did not get to see her without them at that time. She could really regret it because her unveiled beauty was her life's asset, and the basis for her existence,—"such as it was,"— and she knows that the moment, in this sense, which lay nearest to her own limited mentality, would have been a triumph for her. But she had a sort of sound sense, an instinct, that told her that one, in that situation, and when dealing with values such as those that were at stake, *could* not "get off easily." Rather, for her friends, it was precisely a matter, by all means, of paying as high a price as possible. . . . Heloise's heroism, as Frederick comes to understand, consists of the fact that she, for the sake of her friends, personally makes a sacrifice in that she lets them be saved by the conviction that they have sacrificed themselves, yes, that she is willing to risk her life for it. (*KBD,* 1:391–92)

Dinesen once again reminds us that a gesture can speak volumes in one of her tales. The narrative itself interprets Heloise's clutching at her collar "incorrectly" as horror, so the attentive reader must stay alert.

In addition to engaging in a challenge to the doctrine of atonement, "The Heroine" also provides an ironic commentary on the issue of women and sexual morality. This story is a reworking of Guy de Maupassant's "Ball-of-Fat" in which a good-hearted prostitute saves a group of people by giving herself to a Prussian officer, but is later despised by them. Maupassant's story provides us with the likely outcome if Heloise had given in to her first impulse. Her companions, instead of celebrating her, would have condemned her. Once again, Dinesen has rewritten a nineteenth-century female role, so that the prostitute/victim becomes a heroine. Heloise is not a prostitute, even if she does perform in the nude, "her private life is quite respectable" (*WT,* 83). Heloise's traveling companions, who include a priest, two nuns, a theologian, and two businessmen, feel that Heloise's womanly modesty is a value worth all their lives to protect. Heloise clearly does not feel the same way, and she remarks later, "If Madam Bellot had not had stomach-ache with fear, she would have had everything off me in no time, I can promise you" (*WT,* 87). Heloise is like the woman sitting with a torch on the empty powder keg in "The Old Chevalier." Another woman of experience who knows that the keg is empty, that the naked female form is nothing special, would have called the bluff.

In a letter to her sister, Dinesen shows us that the ultimatum issued in "The Heroine" is more common in literature than one might imagine: "In one of Blicher's stories the heroine is given the choice between her young brother's life and the sacrifice of her (womanly) honor to the enemy commander, and neither she nor her brother entertain a moment's doubt:—it is his life that must be sacrificed. In a modern story,—by Jakob Wassermann,—a Bolshevik officer gives a young lady the promise of sparing a company of refugees if she will come to his quarters at night; she hesitates no longer than Blicher's brother and sister, but replies: 'Yes, of course,—here I am.' I think there are very few young women whose conscience and moral sense would not bid them give the same answer" (*LA,* 336). The context of this comment is a discussion of modern sexual morality. Dinesen evidently does not feel that the "ultimate female sacrifice" is much of a sacrifice at all. Regardless of Dinesen's own views on the matter, she acknowledges the power of the strongly held cultural belief in feminine virtue. Those who believe in it will die to protect it.

Frederick Lamond's role in "The Heroine" is a source of some critical dispute. The reader perceives events from his point of view, so the "misinterpretations" of the narrative might be attributed to him. Frederick is writing a book on the doctrine of atonement, a clear pointer to the main theme of the story. Hans

Brix asserts that Frederick will learn more from Heloise than he will from his studies.[30] Because of his relationship to Heloise, Frederick can be associated with the medieval theologian Abelard, who argued that we must take up our own cross and accept responsibility for our own salvation.

Frederick's relationship to Heloise is ambiguous: Is it romantic or platonic? Is Heloise Venus or Diana? Marianne Juhl and Bo Hakon Jørgensen feel that "What Heloise really wanted was for Frederick to love her as a woman and a human being, instead of like Aktaeon, simply looking at her."[31] Juhl and Jørgensen interpret this scenario out of Heloise's choice of final tableau, "Diana's Revenge," but they seem to be describing the attitude of Venus rather than the chaste Diana. Grethe Rostbøll, on the other hand, suggests that Heloise has chosen the role of Diana: "If she married or let herself be seduced, her free and independent life would be over. Chastity is the prerequisite for her continuing to be the Diana men admire on the stage."[32]

Heloise and Abelard are famous lovers from the French Middle Ages. When Heloise's guardian discovered the illicit affair, he had Abelard castrated. Abelard became a monk and Heloise a nun. Frederick seems cast in the role of the castrated Abelard. He enjoys his fantasies of seeing Heloise as Venus, but his glance is not tinged with desire, unlike the German officer's. Frederick is, in fact, offended by the sexual desire of the German officer, describing it as "blasphemy" and "a nauseating baseness" (*WT*, 78). The officer is described as having "the appearance of a young god," perhaps Adonis the lover of Aphrodite (Venus) (*WT*, 77). The German officer and Heloise seem evenly matched, and if Heloise was to become Venus, he would play Adonis. Circumstances do not allow it. Curiously, Frederick Lamond later writes a book on the Egyptian Adonis. Aage Henriksen explains that in this cult, "through ritual castration, the priests arrive at a vision of the celestial Venus."[33] Once again, the motif of castration is associated with Frederick Lamond. If Heloise is Diana and Frederick is symbolically castrated, then the two enjoy a platonic affection that suits them both. Frederick's aesthetic appreciation of Heloise's beauty, untinged by desire, is what pleases Heloise about Frederick. If Heloise is Venus and Frederick is a castrated Adonis, then their relationship is an unhappy one for Heloise. The Heloise of history was also tormented by the desire that could not be slaked by her castrated Abelard. Both arguments have a basis in the story, so the reader must be the final arbiter.

"The Sailor-Boy's Tale"

Dinesen intended that "The Sailor-Boy's Tale" should be the first story in *Winter's Tales*. The tale is closer to an actual folktale than many of her more elaborate narratives. Ulla Albreck has compared it to a fable, like "Androcles and the Lion," in which a favor performed for an animal repays the helper on a later occasion.[34] Both Albreck and Lionel Trilling liken "The Sailor-Boy's Tale" to folktales in which the hero gains the aid of a magical helper by passing a test.[35] Like many such folktales, "The Sailor-Boy's Tale" seems to be a coming-of-age story, about a boy's passage into manhood.

Simon's good deed is to release a falcon that has become entangled in the rigging of his ship. He saves the beleaguered bird because he feels a kinship with it. This act becomes a reversal of an episode narrated in Wilhelm Dinesen's *Hunting Letters* (no. 19), in which such a falcon is shot and the ship later goes to the bottom. The crime of shooting a bird at sea recalls Coleridge's "Rime of the Ancient Mariner" (1798), one of Denys Finch Hatton's favorite poems. Instead of an evil deed bringing about doom, Simon's good deed brings him good fortune. The falcon turns out to have been a Lappish witch named Sunniva who travels between Northern Norway and Takaunga in Africa. Sunniva is a figure who represents freedom and imagination. She is a traveler, at home in both the north and the south, and a witch who does not abide by rules. Simon sees himself in her. The sailors in Dinesen's tales live lives of masculine adventure. Morten De Coninck in "The Supper at Elsinore" becomes a pirate; Skipper Mærsk in "The Deluge at Norderney" digs up pirate treasure for exercise; Peter in "Peter and Rosa" dreams of such a sailor's life; and even Old Knudsen in *Out of Africa* is the remnant of such an irrepressible adventurer. Although he is still a young boy, this is the sort of life that awaits Simon.

Simon's difficulties begin when he leaves the sea and goes ashore, the realm of women. Simon buys an orange, rejecting the flawed watches. This may well be another of Simon's folkloric tests, which he passes with flying colors. Sara Stambaugh associates the watches with "a masculine mercantile system," whereas the orange is a reflection of a "feminine system of values," presumably because of its association with the earth and growing things.[36] The orange also recalls the round shape of the moon which figures prominently in this meeting with Nora. Simon is able to exchange the orange for a kiss, but he cannot collect it right away. Nora is the female opposite of Sunniva. Nora is always described as being behind a fence. Her father is a pastor. She is as confined by convention as any princess locked in a tower.

On his way to collect his kiss, Simon runs into Ivan who gives him a watch chain, a masculine symbol, and smothers him with affection. Rather than be late for his meeting with Nora, Simon stabs and kills Ivan. This slaying of a sort of dragon wins Simon his princess, if only symbolically. Nora gives him his kiss, but he must keep his bloodied hands behind his back and she remains on the other side of the fence. She cannot leave her enclosure to flee with him, and she cannot invite him in to give him safe haven. Nora promises to not marry anyone as long as she lives, thereby becoming for Simon the dream of the faithful woman awaiting in the harbor that he will no doubt relish to the end of his days. The experience makes him feel that his life has been fulfilled.

Simon is saved by Sunniva the witch who intercepts him, takes him back to her hut, and misdirects the Russians who are hunting for the murderer of their friend Ivan. Sunniva cuts her hand, in order to account for the blood on Simon's. The falcon had slashed Simon's hand as he freed her from the rigging. She sends him out into the world with a knock on the head that corresponds to the blow Simon gave the bird after it cut him. The blood, the closed womb-like nature of Sunniva's hut, and the parting slap all evoke the image of birth. Simon, after his ordeals of the evening, is reborn as a new man.

Critics are fairly united in their opinion that Simon has undergone a *rite of passage,* but the exact nature of his transformation is open to discussion. Because of the homosexual overtones in Ivan's advances towards Simon, Sara Stambaugh has concluded, "'The Sailor-Boy's Tale,' then, is about natural and proper sexual relations between male and female."[37] As a reward for his choices, Sunniva places a mark on Simon's forehead, so that women will like him. Antonine M. L. Marquart Scholtz feels that the story is not so much about Simon's birth into manhood, as about his birth as an artist.[38] She points to the final line of the tale in which it is said that Simon "lived to tell the story" (*WT,* 103). Perhaps the tale is simply about a process of maturation. Sunniva tells Simon to put his knife away, so perhaps he will learn to temper his boyish wildness. He has obtained the blessings of the woman's realm, the shore, which he will carry with him in spirit during his adventures on the sea. Simon has attained a sort of balance, a harmony of opposites.

"The Pearls"

Dinesen said that she wrote "The Pearls" as a response to Sigrid Undset's *Kristin Lavransdatter* (1920–22). In her letters from Africa, one can read how Dinesen was put off by the dreary mood in Undset's work: "I don't think reality is like this; there is most probably always a certain amount of jollity even during an outbreak of plague and among people who are to go the the guillotine the next day" (*LA,* 274). Kristin, a serious and religious girl, falls in love with the dark, romantic figure of Erland, sleeps with him before their wedding, and spends much of the trilogy riddled with guilt for her actions. Dinesen told an interviewer: "The heavy view of life in Kristin Lavransdatter made me want to write a marital story from the opposite point of view, in order to show how it goes, if the light-hearted partner is right. That became the novella, 'The Pearls.'" In "The Pearls," Jensine is a serious bourgeois girl who marries Alexander, a carefree aristocrat. The above comment by Dinesen illustrates which side the author favors.

Dinesen considered the bourgeois view to be the dominant view of her culture, so she spends most of her time in her stories defining the nature of the aristocrat. "The Pearls" is one of a handful of stories in which she specifically explores the bourgeois worldview. Jensine comes from "people capable of making a fortune by their wits" (*WT*, 111). They prefer a world that is flat and unchanging, giving them a sense of security. Fear of losing what they have earned infiltrates every aspect of their lives: "Her father was an honest tradesman, afraid both to lose his own money, and to let down his customers" (*WT*, 109–10). Material goods are a mark of success, but the bourgeois also pride themselves on their strict morality, which assures them they are better than others. The bourgeois are deepwater fish who feel "at home only under the pressure of existence" (*WT*, 116).

Alexander's aristocratic world is diametrically opposed to Jensine's. Alexander has inherited his fortune, not earned it. He enjoys the vertical landscapes of Norway, since he does not fear rising and falling. Alexander gambles, is at home with risk, and trusts to luck to pay his bills. Jensine thinks of her husband as "a person totally ignorant of the law of gravitation" (*WT*, 110). Gravity is a charged word in Dinesen's vocabulary, meaning both seriousness and the natural force that prevents us from flying. Jensine's world is thoroughly marked by gravity in both senses of the word. Alexander has debts and avoids his tailor, so as not to have to pay them, something which Jensine feels is immoral. He is described as a salmon or a flyingfish, who is not held down by the pressures of existence.

Jensine wants to convert Alexander to her view of the world, and thus decides to teach him to fear. Her daring actions make him believe that she has come over to his way of thinking. Once when she is playing with the string of pearls that Alexander has given her, he cautions her to be careful or she will break it. Jensine hopes that this foretelling of disaster is a sign of weakening on Alexander's part. Alexander is not afraid for the pearls because of their monetary value, but because they are a family heirloom. Tradition means more to him than money. One day, the pearls do break and Jensine is mortified: "She had broken the one thing in the world that she had been afraid of breaking. What omen did that have for them?" (*WT*, 115). The breaking of the pearls is a turning point in the story. The feared disaster becomes the moment that causes a chain of events that will result in Jensine's change and the addition of the most valuable pearl to the string. Through this, Jensine can learn not to fear, since a momentary setback might bring unexpected rewards.

Jensine takes her pearls to the shoemaker with no feet, Peiter Viken. She feels at home in his workshop: "An honest man, hard tried by destiny, had passed his long years in this little room. It was a place where people worked, and bore troubles patiently, in anxiety for their daily bread" (*WT,* 116). Jensine's bourgeois sensibilities feel at home in a place of hard work and anxiety, but she is mistaken. Peiter Viken turns out to be a poet, an artist. No less a personage than Henrik Ibsen comes to him to collect "pearls," folktales. He is also whimsical enough to play a joke on Jensine, adding the valuable pearl to her string. The material value of the pearl means nothing to him, but the story it will inspire is priceless. When Jensine emerges from the workshop, Ibsen asks her "You have not lost your sole in the mountains?" (*WT,* 117). This homonymic pun (which only works in English, not Danish) points to a dual function for Peiter Viken in the tale. He is a shoemaker who can mend Jensine's sole, but more importantly, he is an artist who will mend Jensine's soul.

Jensine's accidental meeting with Henrik Ibsen is also something of a textual joke. Henrik Ibsen is, of course, acknowledged to be Norway's greatest writer and is a real person appearing in an otherwise fictional space. Ibsen is in the early years of his career, and Jensine gives him the advice to go back to his trade as an apothecary, agreeing that greatness and the applause of the masses are nothing to build a life upon. Ibsen chuckles and makes a self-deprecating remark, but the reader should know that if Ibsen had followed this bourgeois advice, the world would have lost one of its greatest playwrights. Ibsen has observed Alexander and Jensine together and says that he thought: "That he might be the bird, which upward soars, and you the breeze, which carries him along. Do you know the quotation? Does it tell you anything?" (*WT,* 117). Ibsen is quoting his own play, *Love's Comedy* (1862), and comparing Jensine to the character Svanhild. Svanhild loves the high-flying, romantic poet Falk, but agrees to marry the businessman Guldstad, because he is a steadier prospect. Svanhild turns down the offer to be the wind beneath Falk's wings. Jensine, on the contrary, has made the more adventurous choice in marrying Alexander instead of Peter Skov.

When Jensine gets her pearls back, she refuses to count them, a truly aristocratic gesture (the English lady evidently did not count her pearls either). When her bourgeois sensibilities can bear it no longer, Jensine counts the pearls and learns that there is one more pearl on the string than there was before. The letter that Peiter Viken sends to explain the presence of the pearl initiates a cascade of changes in Jensine's psyche. Earlier in the tale, when she contemplated

Alexander's gambling, Jensine thought, "He is really a thief, or if not that, a receiver of stolen goods, and no better than a thief" (*WT,* 111). Now, Jensine looks in the mirror and thinks: "You are really a thief, or if not that, a receiver of stolen goods, and no better than a thief" (*WT,* 123). Jensine is becoming like Alexander. Previously, Alexander had expressed his disregard for danger with the line: "In a hundred years it will all be one" (*WT,* 110). Jensine thinks of Alexander as "a very small figure in the background of life" and repeats his line word for word (*WT,* 123). Shirley Clouse De Simone interprets this repetition: "Now she too is fearless; she too begins to think in centuries, in generations. From this point of view even Alexander seems small; she no longer feels that everything depends on winning her contest with him."[39] She had earlier made a vow not to cry quarter (*WT,* 112). Now Jensine thinks: "Why not? Yes, I shall cry as high as I can. I cannot, now, remember the reason why I would not cry" (*WT,* 124). The deliberate repetition of these lines in the final scene of the tale are clear signposts of Jensine's transformation from bourgeois into aristocrat.

What is the insight that causes this profound reaction? In part, Peiter Viken's joking response to a domestic catastrophe helps Jensine to overcome her fear, because the incident has only enriched her both spiritually and materially. The letter also contains the wish that something pleasant should happen to Jensine that day. Hans Holmberg and Aage Henriksen have argued convincingly that part of the epiphany Jensine experiences as she looks into the mirror is the realization that she is pregnant.[40] Jensine has not felt well since her return from Norway, which both scholars interpret as the early signs of pregnancy. Jensine's eyes widen as she looks into the mirror and thinks of the moon, a symbol of female fertility. Holmberg further agues that the moment of conception likely occurred after she refused to count the pearls, stopped straining against Alexander and his way of life, and opened herself up to his influences. Holmberg goes so far as to state that the pearl of the title is first and foremost the child that Jensine is bearing. Henriksen writes, "Two things happen in the story: Jensine gets a pearl and Jensine gets pregnant, both by accident."[41] The fact that these two gifts have not cost her anything, but have been given to her as an act of grace is what helps to cause Jensine to tear up her bourgeois balance sheet. Dinesen herself endorsed Henriksen's reading of "The Pearls" in a letter to Aage Kabell (*KBD,* 2:393–94).

The Danish title of "The Pearls" is "The Story of the Pearls," and the vision that comes to Jensine as she looks in the mirror is described as follows: "Something, she decided, was of great importance, which had come into the world now, and in a hundred years would still remain. The pearls. In a hundred years, she saw, a young man would hand them over to his wife and tell the young woman her own story about them, just as Alexander had given them to her, and had told her of his grandmother" (*WT*, 124). Jensine has learned to think not just of her individual woes, but of the generations to come and of family traditions. The additional pearl on the string is also the story of how it came to be there. Toby Foshay argues that the ability to see herself as part of a story told in the future helps Jensine to transcend time and overcome whatever resentments she may hold against her circumstances in the present.[42] The story endures and lends a type of immortality.

Although Alexander's worldview "wins" the battle, it will not win the war. In 1864, the war over Schlesvig/Holstein is approaching and will result in a devastating defeat for Denmark, which is described, like Alexander, as "without fear" (*WT*, 120). Although the defeat will sound a death knell for the aristocratic worldview, it is a defeat for the entire country. Even Jensine's bourgeois family is reconciled to having a soldier among them because of their patriotism. Alexander may fall in battle and make Jensine a widow, but in the aristocratic world the women are in charge of continuance. A new convert, Jensine will ensure that the family traditions are carried on even after Alexander is gone.

Critical opinion is divided as to how to interpret the final scene of "The Pearls." The bourgeois aunt approaches the house with a bouquet as the young couple looks upon her from their house. The opinions are divided fairly neatly between the Danish and the English critics, because of a slight difference in the final line of the Danish versus the English edition. In the English version, "From the window the husband and wife looked down into the street" (*WT*, 124). Jensine and Alexander stand at the same window showing a united front to the bourgeois aunt who approaches. This image underscores the fact that Jensine and Alexander are now on the same side. Thus, Toby Foshay writes that Jensine can "take up a stance alongside her husband, as they look from a window down into the street."[43] In the Danish version: "Fra hver sit Vindue saa Mand og Kone ned paa Gaden" (From each their own window husband and wife looked down into the street. *MU* 4:79). Jensine and Alexander are at two different windows in two different rooms. This detail caused Marianne Juhl and Bo Hakon Jørgensen to conclude: "The tale's last image of Jensine and Alexander at each their own window and Alexander as a very small man indicate that they are finally separated from each other."[44] Juhl and Jørgensen's interpretation posits a continuing hostility on Jensine's part towards Alexander. It is impossible to know why Dinesen changed this small detail in the Danish version, but it brings into relief the issue that the Danish and English versions of Dinesen's tales are not always interchangeable, even if they are often treated as such. Depending upon which version is held to be primary, a reader's interpretation of the end of the story could change dramatically.

"The Invincible Slave-Owners"

Like "Sorrow-Acre," "The Invincible Slave-Owners" focuses on a transitional moment in time. In the year 1875 Hans Christian Andersen dies and Rainer Maria Rilke is born. European letters have entered a "decadent" phase, in which the old aristocratic world is perceived as moribund and threatened by the increasing vigor of the masses. The story takes place at the resort in Baden-Baden, a watering place for the doomed aristocracy. The English lady sets the tone for the group when she praises King Ludwig of Bavaria (1845–86), quoting the decadent French poet Paul Verlaine: "The only true king of the century, I salute you!" (*WT*, 128).[45] For several poets at the end of the nineteenth century, Ludwig became the emblem of the decadent monarch, building fantastic castles, shunning human contact, and commissioning opera performances with himself as sole spectator. Ludwig was eventually deemed insane and deposed. He drowned under mysterious circumstances together with his psychiatrist.

Axel Leth, a young Danish nobleman, does not really fit into this company. Axel is not an aging aristocrat dependent on slaves. A passage in the Danish version of the tale, absent in the English, makes it clear that Axel is rather like Adam in "Sorrow-Acre:" "Axel himself was filled with ideas of freedom, progress, and justice. He was deeply opposed to one person slaving for another and would have put an end to the whole system if it had been within his power" (*MU*, 4:93). The other guests at the resort cannot exist without their servants, or the belief that their servants would die for them. Axel Leth's name may indicate that he is a portal figure into the new age. Although "Leth" is an actual Danish family name, it resembles "Lethe" the name of the river of forgetfulness on the way to the underworld in classical mythology. Axel looks on as an entire way of life passes into oblivion.

Into this world walk two women, a young girl and her governess. Mizzi, the young girl, appears to be the epitome of all this world venerates in women. She is compared to a rose, a swan, and "a big, beautiful doll," all familiar images from Dinesen's other fiction (*WT*, 150, 129). Mizzi seems helpless, unable to complete the simplest task without the aid of her exemplary governess. She stands on a pedestal, out of reach of sexual desire like the stars in the poem by Goethe, quoted by Axel: "One does not desire the stars / One rejoices in their glory" (*WT*, 144). Mizzi is, however, not what she seems to be and one indication of this is her tendency to blush for no apparent reason. Axel senses something "dangerous" and "alarming" about this phenomenon, since it hints at deep emotional turmoil beneath the surface (*WT,* 135). When Axel first sees Mizzi, he is reminded of a ship, another Dinesen image, yet this time the image is passed through the filter of Charles Baudelaire and his poem "The Beautiful Ship" from *The Flowers of Evil* (1857): "With air triumphant and yet mild, / You go along your way, majestic child."[46] Despite these placid lines, the woman of Baudelaire's poem also broadcasts an aura of danger. She has arms like boa constrictors, strong enough to crush her lover to her. Mizzi is described as having red hair "averse to the law of gravitation" (*WT,* 130). Although this might be a reference to a Dinesenian lightness-of-being, in this context it seems more likely to be a reference to the snakes on the head of the Medusa. One of Mizzi's most frequently described physical characteristics is her "thick, sullen, flaming mouth," a feature at odds with the innocence she seeks to project (*WT,* 130). Mizzi is like a double-exposure of the innocent woman/child and the *femme fatale.*

Axel accidentally learns the truth about the two women. They are not master/servant, but two aristocratic, but impoverished sisters enacting roles that enable them to appear where aristocrats seasonally gather. Mizzi and Lotti are true aristocrats, for whom the half is more than the whole (*WT,* 137). As a dance becomes a substitute for love-making to the true aristocrat, the symbols and rituals of Mizzi and Lotti's aristocratic world are more important to them than any full-fledged reality. Among these symbols are the clothing and the jewels that women of their station should wear. Mizzi is in despair because she is growing out of her little-girl costume, and her sister tries to comfort her with the thought that she is growing lovelier each year. Mizzi replies: "You might as well say I should be lovelier without any clothes at all" (*WT,* 141). Many would indeed think so, but for Mizzi, the symbols, the mystery, the mask of femininity are more important than unveiled beauty. Because Mizzi cannot act differently than her upbringing dictates, she is caught in an unsolvable paradox: She cannot love a man who can be so easily fooled by her role-playing, but if a man perceives the truth, he will no longer love her.

Isak Dinesen said about this story that "the sisters are certainly people alienated from reality, but this like my other tales has a meaning behind the action, and this should show how closely tied a person is to his environment, his upbringing. For the two young women, it is the only reasonable and natural thing to have slaves, and that, which for others appears to be a lie and a comedy, is truth for them."[47] After he has overheard the sisters' revelations, Axel puts his head down on his arms: "Later he did not know whether, within his own arms, he had laughed or wept" (*WT,* 142). Dinesen points to two possible responses to the sisters' plight: One can perceive them as ridiculous in their faithfulness to a way of life beyond their means or one can feel sympathy for them and see their situation as tragic. Axel does not share the sisters' views on the necessity of servants, but his subsequent behavior towards them indicates that he will try, for a moment, to understand their world and become a part of it through his own role-playing.

Axel has himself costumed to play the role of Frantz, the faithful retainer of the two women. At first, the women are terrified, because they fear that he will reveal all. When it becomes clear that he is merely paying homage to their world and their actions, Mizzi and Lotti are relieved and perhaps even grateful. Mizzi sends Axel, via Frantz, a fading rose as an apparent gesture of thanks, although the wilting symbol also has a certain fatalism about it. Axel has enacted the role of the servant in the master/servant dichotomy, a dualism popular in both Dinesen's fiction and in world literature in general. Don Quixote and Sancho Panza, Don Juan and Leoporello, Dinesen and Farah, are all prime examples of the topos. Because of changing historical and sociological conditions, the realm of art will soon be the only acceptable place for this relationship.

Axel's role-playing creates a unity of opposites, wherein each part endows the other with its identity, and this brings the women a sense of harmony and happiness. This reaction is emphasized much more strongly in the Danish version than in the English. In the English edition, as Axel takes a last look at them, the women "were looking strangely, pathetically happy and at ease, in harmony with life" (*WT,* 149). The Danish version reads: "They were transfigured by happiness and by a harmony with life. They felt Frantz's consideration all around them, they were in Frantz's hands. . . . All of existence was friendly and secure, because Frantz was there, the faithful Frantz" (*MU,* 4:109). It is much clearer in the Danish version that it is Axel's actions which have brought Mizzi and Lotti to this state of harmony. Nevertheless, Axel walks away from the two sisters. His role-playing is a temporary gift, as is the happiness it brings. Although Axel appreciates and understands the power that the master/servant relationship has for the two women, he chooses not to remain in their world.

In the final scene of the story, Axel is gazing at a waterfall, and "each second, new particles of water hurled over the edge, rushing into a precipice and disappearing. It was a flight, a whirl, an incessant catastrophe" (*WT,* 151). Axel's final thought in the tale is to recall the lines from Baudelaire's "The Beautiful Ship," evoking an image of the sisters as a ship hurtling to its destruction over the precipice. A similar image exists in Hans Christian Andersen's "Den standhaftige Tinsoldat" ("The Steadfast Tin Soldier") from 1838, where the tin soldier proudly remains at attention as he is swept over a waterfall in a paper boat. The Danish title, "De standhaftige Slaveejere" (The Steadfast Slave-owners), contains a reference to Andersen's tale. The sisters proudly maintain their style as they rush towards their destruction. Like the tin soldier, they can do nothing else because of the way they are made. Axel also thinks of the Fuga, the musical fugue, whose name is etymologically related to fugitive, implying both fleeting and a state of flight, words which describe the situation of the sisters. The fugue also relies on counterpoint: the central theme announced by one voice or instrument is developed contrapuntally in strict order by each of the other voices or instruments. The sisters are losing their answering voices, the slaves, so soon their music will fade.

Critical opinion is divided in its judgment of Axel's actions. Marianne Juhl is disappointed in Axel and considers him weak, passive, and a coward without the courage to rescue Mizzi from her charade.[48] Juhl does not believe that the half is more than the whole and is not willing to valorize an artistic substitute over a flesh-and-blood reality: Axel ought to have married Mizzi. Grethe Rostbøll compares Axel to other weak and passive men in Dinesen's fiction: Baron von Brackel in "The Old Chevalier," Vilhelm in "Alkmene," Frederick Lamond in "The Heroine," and Boris in "The Monkey."[49] Although Brackel and Vilhelm are failures because of their inability to act, Frederick and Boris are also implied to be failures because of their inability to desire a woman sexually. Axel similarly thinks of Mizzi aesthetically, comparing her to works of art, and "he wished that he were her brother, or an old friend, with a right to help her" (*WT,* 133). Although both Juhl and Rostbøll imply that a lack of sexual desire is a flaw in a relationship between a man and a woman, Sara Stambaugh feels that "Some of the most sympathetic male characters in Dinesen's fiction are those who are capable of treating women as sisters."[50] Depending upon one's point of view, this capacity or incapacity is either a flaw or an asset. Robert Langbaum sees Axel's masquerade as "a charming, creative jest," which brings "the great lady in Mizzi into full flower."[51] Hans Holmberg endorses Axel's actions and suggests that his aestheticizing of his relationship to the sisters is viewed positively in the story.[52] Holmberg feels that the message that life is an artwork is central to Dinesen's writing, therefore the individual who perceives the art in life is an initiate to the secrets of life.

"The Dreaming Child"

An interviewer once asked Dinesen which story was her favorite. She replied: "One can never say. But from a certain point of view 'The Dreaming Child' in *Winter's Tales.*"[53] The power of imagination to transform reality is a theme close to Dinesen's heart: She preferred Lamarck's theory of evolution to Darwin's. The dreaming child of the title is a character who is able to transform his world through the force of his creative imagination. Dinesen confided in Aage Henriksen that "her plan for the tale arose after reading an old sentimental story from an almanac. It dealt with an orphaned child who lived under terrible and sad conditions; then chance intervened and the poor thing was adopted into a rich family, and his fortune was made. The crux of Jens's story became the question of whether such a social promotion is always and without question identical with greater happiness."[54] This comment suggests that one of the story's themes is the value of spiritual riches over material riches. Jens's affluent environment does not nourish him spiritually, and so he fades away and dies. From another thematic point of view, "The Dreaming Child" can in some ways be compared to "The Pearls": The values of bourgeois society are turned topsy turvy through the imaginative play of the artist, who in this case is the dreaming child.

Jakob and Emilie Vandamm are paragons of nineteenth-century bourgeois values. They belong to a family that has earned its fortune, "a long row of competent and honest tradesmen" (*WT,* 160). They are prosperous and therefore, according to the views of their time, they should be happy. There is something wrong between the couple that can trace its roots to Victorian attitudes toward sexuality. Jakob learns of sex through prostitutes: "To him, as to the other young men out of the strictly moral Copenhagen bourgeoisie, his first experience of love had been extremely gross" (*WT,* 163). Victorian men were allowed sexual experience, but their wives had to be pure and innocent "like a doll or an icon" (*WT,* 164). Jakob places his wife on a pedestal and although he would like to protect and shelter her, he remains a little afraid of her. He seeks solace in an extramarital affair, but does not find it. He is placed in the paradoxical position of "the young lover who passionately adores virginity" (*WT,* 174).

Emilie has been raised on ideas of romantic love that do not admit any sexual realities. As a young girl, she becomes enamored of a sailor, Charlie Dreyer, whom others describe as a Don Juan. She refuses to believe it, since such ideas are not commensurate with her ideas of romantic love. The night Charlie is about to depart, Emilie offers him a white rose, a symbol of chaste love. Charlie asks to spend the night and Emilie is terrified. Victorian women were taught to fear the animal lusts of men and submit to them only as part of the duties of marriage. Emilie runs from Charlie's passion and bolts the gate against him as if he were an angry lion. The story poses the rhetorical question: "On which side of the gate was the lion?" (*WT,* 162). Emilie's Victorian upbringing has not prepared her to discover sexual desire within herself. In locking the gate, Emilie is symbolically locking herself away from sexual desire.

Having successfully evaded this Victorian peril, Emilie throws herself into the moral order of the bourgeoisie. She is characterized by "the suppleness of her body and the rigidity of her mind," indicating the ongoing conflict in Emilie's character (*WT*, 161). Although Emily practices charity, she distinguishes carefully between the "deserving and undeserving poor" (*WT*, 160). Emilie divides life into simple categories: good and bad, right and wrong, happiness and unhappiness. She holds tightly to what is "true:" "Once a thing is not true . . . it matters little to me whatever else it may be" (*WT*, 164). When Jakob introduces the idea of adopting a child, she is at first opposed. An adopted child would not be her true child. Emilie eventually relents because adopting a child will mean that "there would be no more obligation to her of producing an heir to the firm" (*WT*, 165). In other words, Emilie will not be obligated to have sex with her husband and she can shut herself off completely from sexual desire.

Jens, the child they take into their home, turns out to be a poet, a dreamer, and a humorist. He threatens all of Emilie's neat categories as "one, who welcomed light and darkness, pleasure and pain, in the same spirit of gallant, debonair approval and fellowship" (*WT*, 178). It is a theme that runs throughout Dinesen's fiction that dark and light are both aesthetically necessary, so the true artist must embrace both tragedy and comedy. Emilie has tried to keep the dark and the tragic from her life, and as such has experienced an imbalance. Jens, as he is living in the Copenhagen slum, longs for the beautiful house of his dreams. When his dreams come true, he comes to long for the rats of the slums. Part of Jens's artistic nature is longing, so he cannot be truly happy in an environment that satisfies his every whim, and eventually fades away. Before this, he will teach Emilie to appreciate the dark side of her nature which she has pushed away. Jens is described several times as a cupid, and his very existence will enable Jakob and Emilie to bridge that gap between them through imagination.

Both Aage Henriksen and Robert Langbaum have identified Jens with the Jungian archetype of the Divine Child.[55] The Divine Child is often born into lowly circumstances and works miraculous changes in the world about him. Jens's powers of imagination seem almost magical. He dies at the end of March, suggesting a parallel between Jens and Christ and the possibility that Jens's death will in some way redeem Jakob and Emilie. Jens is explicitly connected to the biblical dreamer, Joseph (*WT*, 172). Like Joseph, Jens's father is also named Jakob and is married to his cousin. When Emilie quotes scripture without knowing it, she characterizes Jens with the words Pharaoh used for Joseph when he was raised to overseer of Egypt: "Can we find such a man as this, in whom is the Spirit of God? . . . Since God has shown you all this, there is none so discreet and wise as you are; you shall be over my house" (Genesis 41:38–39). Robert

Langbaum sees in these echoes the influence of Thomas Mann's *Joseph and His Brothers* (1933–42), and the idea that in fulfilling desire, one unconsciously repeats the patterns of myth.[56]

After Jens's death, Emilie and Jacob take a walk in a green wood, a place of regeneration. Emilie asks Jakob to believe that Jens was her illegitimate child with Charlie Dreyer. This statement is in some sense mad, untrue, a figment of Emilie's imagination, but Emilie has learned from Jens about the power of imagination. In her imagination, Emilie can unlock the gate that she closed many years ago and embrace her own sexuality. This fabrication also serves the purpose of taking Emilie down from her pedestal, so that Jakob might be able to love her on a more even footing. Dinesen wrote of the ending of the story: "By the way, in 'The Dreaming Child' it is not the point that Emilie is enchanted by imagination. The problem in the story is the very old one: 'What is Truth?' Was not Charlie's child the only child that Emilie could have,—or which she had, and through which she reached a sort of, from her point of view, delayed and confused maternal joy?" (*KBD*, 1:391–92). Emilie's lie enables her to regain what she has lost and to get back in touch with her true self: "I have got back my sight, and my sense of smell. . . . And I, I am Emilie. Nothing can alter that either" (*WT*, 187). Emilie's tale will in fact make it easier for both Jakob and Emilie, which Jakob acknowledges in his ambiguous final line: "Yes, my dear, . . . that is true" (*WT*, 187).

The honest Emilie's surprising lie has caused some Dinesen critics to look for a grain of truth behind it. Both Hans Brix and Aage Henriksen thought that Jens might actually have been the child of Charlie Dreyer conceived with a prostitute the night Emilie rejected him.[57] Dinesen denied this unequivocally (*KBD*, 1:570–71). Evidently, it was important to Dinesen that Emilie's relationship to Jens should be one of pure imagination, but "true" for all that. The final confession scene inspired Sara Stambaugh to predict a happy future for both Jakob and Emilie: "a happy and harmonious future in which husband and wife live together in mental and sexual harmony, very likely having the children previously denied them in their nineteenth century marriage."[58] Indeed, Jensine in "The Pearls" was not able to conceive as long as she fought against her husband, so perhaps this new state of marital harmony will have a beneficial effect on Emilie and Jakob's fertility. Even if "The Dreaming Child" was Dinesen's personal favorite, the tale does not find favor with Johan Christian Jørgensen, who condemns the tale from a sociopolitical point of view. He feels that the story propagates the notion that there will always be poor and it does no good to change the material circumstances of people. Jørgensen feels that society has an obligation to raise the material conditions of the poor, hence, Dinesen's tale is damaging.[59]

"Alkmene"

"Alkmene" takes up some familiar themes from other stories in *Winter's Tales*. Like "The Dreaming Child," it is a story of an orphan with extraordinary powers. As in the case of Jens, Alkmene is indirectly associated with Joseph, the dreamer, when the pastor quotes Rachel's desperate plea: "Give me children or else I die" (*WT,* 193). Like "The Pearls," "Alkmene" describes a struggle between two conflicting worldviews. To a certain extent, the familiar categories of aristocrat and bourgeois fight for hegemony over Alkmene's soul, but most commentators have seen the struggle as a battle between the values of pagan antiquity and Christianity.[60] The story is unusual in that it is narrated by a first-person narrator, Vilhelm. Several of Dinesen's characters tell their own stories, but usually from within a narrative frame. Vilhelm's account is unmediated and the reader must decide whether or not Vilhelm fully understands the implications of what he sees.

Alkmene is an orphan of mysterious origins who arrives in a parsonage in the Danish countryside like "a brand to be snatched from the fire" (*WT,* 195). This reference together with Alkmene's hair that rose "like a flame above her head" and the gold that later appears as if from some "demonic source" causes Pil Dahlerup to speculate that Alkmene is something of a child of Lucifer (*WT,* 199, 213).[61] Her name links her clearly to Greek antiquity. Alkmene was the wife of Amphitryon, for whom Zeus developed a fancy while her husband was away at war. Zeus came to Alkmene in the shape of Amphytrion and later the same night the real Amphytrion arrived home. Alkmene later gave birth to twins. Amphytrion's son was a normal child, but Zeus's son become the great hero Hercules. Several critics have thought to analyze how Dinesen's "Alkmene" relates to the myth. Aage Henriksen and Pil Dahlerup feel that the pastor is Zeus and Vilhelm is Amphitryon.[62] If the pastor is Zeus, however, he is so in a highly ironic manner. Far from being a pagan god, the pastor is a purveyor of Christian values. Langbaum sees the relationship of "Alkmene" to the myth as this: "In Isak Dinesen's story, no god comes to make up for the failure of the mortal men; and her Alkmene, who ought to have been the mother of a hero, remains barren."[63]

Alkmene naturally possesses the qualities of pagan antiquity and her Christian parsonage environment works hard to eradicate them. Alkmene moves gracefully, but is forbidden to dance, since dancing is sinful. She learns Greek easily, but is forbidden to read the stories of antiquity, which are thought to be of dubious moral value to a young girl. She is good at the hunt, like Diana, but is afraid of death. For the ancient Greeks, death was the end of all things, whereas for Christians it marks the entrance to the Christian afterlife. Alkmene is not afraid of the gander or the bull, forms that Zeus might adopt for one of his unorthodox courtships. Alkmene admires Gertrud's Venus-like beauty, which the modest parson's-wife clothing does its best to conceal. Some of Alkmene's attributes are familiar from descriptions of aristocrats in other Dinesen tales. "She seemed to be altogether without fear" like Alexander in "The Pearls" and, like Jensine, Gertrud resolves to teach her to fear. Alkmene does not seem to "know truth from untruth" and "she would often lose or even give away what Gertrud with great trouble had got together for her" (*WT,* 200). Around the time of her Christian confirmation, Alkmene borrows a gown that belonged to Vilhelm's mother and they walk through the forest and share a loaf of bread. Marianne Juhl and Bo Hakon Jørgensen have pointed to this as a type of pagan confirmation.[64] Both Gertrud and the pastor have had their own connections with pagan antiquity, which have been subdued and subordinated to Christian values: Gertrud's beauty and the pastor's ambition to be a great poet. They wish to work a similar metamorphosis upon Alkmene. As a symbol of the effect Alkmene's upbringing has upon her, her name is shortened from the Greek Alkmene to Mene, part of a biblical prophecy of doom (Daniel 5:25–28).

Despite being dearly loved by her adoptive parents, Alkmene tries to run away twice, once to join the gypsies. In Dinesen's tales, gypsies tend to represent a type of lawlessness and magic that is admired. Alkmene's parents and even her confederate Vilhelm do not understand why Alkmene should want to run away. Alkmene compares herself to the children "who do not want to be loved" (*WT,* 205). This is perhaps a reference to Rilke's *Malte Laurids Brigge* (1910), which ends with a free adaptation of the parable of the Prodigal Son, in which being loved is compared to being consumed. Dinesen once wrote in a letter to her brother of her own feelings about her upbringing which echo Alkmene's sentiments: "And their great unlimited goodness and love for me, all the kindnesses they showered upon me were only so many misfortunes the more. They made it impossible for me to show any opposition" (*LA,* 245). Alkmene's environment wears her down slowly. After her pagan ritual in the forest with Vilhelm, Alkmene returns to find her mother darning a pile of socks: "Alkmene stood behind her and looked at her and at the stockings, and it seemed to me that she was growing very white" (*WT,* 209). Gertrud's selfless labor on her behalf is impossible to defend against. Hans Holmberg points to this pile of socks as a counterpart to the pile of gold that suddenly appears from some marvelous source.[65] The sudden wealth which proves Alkmene's noble origins might have had the power to free her, but it is too late. The pile of socks has more power.

Vilhelm might have been able to "save" Alkmene from her fate, but seems to be possessed by an inability to act characteristic of other Dinesen characters, such as Augustus von Schimmelman, Baron von Brackel, Frederik Lamond, among others. Vilhelm might have seduced Alkmene and cast her in the role of the tragic heroine. Or, he should have been the suitor who asked for her hand in time. The professor who places Alkmene with the pastor and his wife suggests that Alkmene might be renamed "Perdita after the heroine of Shakespeare's tragedy" (*WT,* 194). The reference is to *The Winter's Tale* and although a great many sad things happen in the play, it is traditionally described as a romance. Perdita's fate is not tragic in the end. She is rejected by her father, the king, and placed on a desolate shore where she is found and raised by a shepherd. Later, Florizel, a prince, falls in love with her, but his father the king disapproves. The lovers are able to be together when Perdita proves her royal parentage. Vilhelm had an inclination to play the part of Florizel, thinking to propose to Alkmene despite his father's disapproval. Unlike in Shakespeare's play, the gold, proof of Alkmene's noble origins, prevents the groom from proposing to the royal bride. Alkmene's life forms an ironic answer to Shakespeare's play. Instead of being raised by a shepherd from an Arcadian idyll, Alkmene is put in the hands of a Christian shepherd, and her fate becomes something quite different.

An irrevocable turning point in Alkmene's life takes place after the death of her father, the pastor. Alkmene asks Vilhelm to take her to Copenhagen to witness the execution of Ole Sjælsmark. The lines Alkmene quotes to Vilhelm ("Now over each head has quivered / The blade that is quivering over mine") come from the scene in Goethe's *Faust* in which Margarete is being executed for having killed her mother and child (*WT,* 218). Hans Brix and Robert Langbaum interpret this to mean that Alkmene has considered murdering her mother, Gertrud, and views the execution in order to prevent herself from committing such a crime.[66] Hans Holmberg, Marianne Juhl and Bo Hakon Jørgensen argue that Alkmene is symbolically watching the death of her self.[67] Brix observed that this execution scene is based on the historical execution of a man named Ole Kollerød. Dinesen has changed the name to Sjælsmark, which is another of her talking names. "Sjælsmark" means "the field of the soul" with the additional nuance of "the borderland of the soul," implying a site of transition. In witnessing the execution, Alkmene's soul has been killed. She explains to Vilhelm: "They were the strongest. It could not be otherwise when they were so good, when they were always right. Alkmene was alone. . . . She could see no way out, but she must die, too" (*WT,* 220). Alkmene speaks of herself in the third person as someone who no longer exists.

Alkmene's fate is tragic. Instead of the mother of gods, she becomes a caricature of the values her parents tried to instill in her. She has become a shepherd, like her father the pastor, but instead of a Christian shepherd of souls, Alkmene's farming interest in her flock is monetary. When Alkmene was a child, Gertrud worried over Alkmene's generosity with things that had been hard to come by. Now Alkmene gives away nothing. Gertrud herself learned to fear as a young girl when her father lost everything in an economic crash and then her mother began to farm sheep to keep the family together. Alkmene is living a life equated with fear: "The world, surely, is a dangerous place, Vilhelm . . . and what better thing will we find in it than that hard, honest work which the Lord has set us here to do? We should not question" (*WT,* 223). This line, spoken by Gertrud at the end of the tale, echoes a line she used earlier to sum up her childhood experiences (*WT,* 198). Gertrud's values have prevailed, and the gold remains in the bank as a bulwark against fear. The body of Venus has become square. In other tales, Dinesen has used the device of repeating lines, either to indicate the adoption of a view of life (for example, Jensine in "The Pearls": "In a hundred years it will all be one," *WT* 123) or to show that the context of the utterance has changed so drastically that the meaning has also changed (for example, "*Discite justitiam, et non temnere divos*" in "The Monkey," *SGT* 114, 163). The line, "Do you know? She has got no shift on!" (*WT,* 199, 224), appears to belong to the latter category. The first time it is uttered is when Alkmene is introduced into the house. Her nakedness is at once a sign of her innocence and her pagan sensuality. The last time the line is uttered, it is an example of her parsimony. Alkmene is too stingy to buy herself a shift.

Dinesen once referred to "Alkmene" as "a self-portrait in miniature."[68] Dinesen playfully reinforced her identification with Alkmene in a letter to Aage Henriksen from 1954:

"You, who are so at home in 'Alkmene,' must be able to understand my own lament: 'Africa mi fe,' disfecemi Danimarca' (Africa made me, Denmark undid me), Dante, Purgatorio, cant. 5. I really feel that Denmark has invested more energy in teaching me to fear than the pastor's wife ever did for Alkmene. . . . It is not far from it, that I must ask you to follow me to Copenhagen and Nørrefælled, so that I finally, by seeing for myself, can avoid deep moral pitfalls and missteps in the future. I can certainly be said to be ready for the sheep farm" (*KBD,* 2:238). It is clear from this quote which set of values—ancient Greek or Christian—has the author's sympathy.

"The Fish"

With regard to "The Fish," the reading experience of the American versus the Danish reader is likely to be quite different. The difference lies not so much in the texts as in the cultural information each reader is likely to possess. The historical/legendary material that "The Fish" plays upon is well known to Danish audiences through ballads and literary versions of the story. Dinesen herself tried her hand at composing a verse drama on the theme when she was quite young. As a concession to the American reader, the English version ends with a paragraph describing the future fate of King Erik Glipping, which was not deemed necessary for the Danish audience. The Danish title is "Fra det gamle Danmark" (From Old Denmark), which appeals to the Dane's sense of history, whereas "The Fish" focuses American attention upon the central symbol of fate in the tale. The story takes place about ten years before Erik Glipping's death at the hands of his vassals, but it focuses on a fateful turning point that will lead the king to his death further down the line. In a sense, it is rather like reading a story about Abraham Lincoln deciding to attend Ford's Theater. Dinesen builds suspense by not mentioning the name of the king, until towards the end of the story where it comes as a revelation for the Danish reader. This suspense effect is all but lost on American readers who cannot be expected to pick up the small clues that hint at the king's identity, and who will not know what to make of the fact that the ring belongs to Ingeborg, Mærsk Stig's wife. As a result, Danish commentators have taken a much greater interest in the tale than American critics.

At the beginning of the tale, King Erik is experiencing a restless night and lies between waking and dreams. Although he may not realize it, King Erik is at a crossroads of fate. He has been a success in life up to this point, but he has lost his taste for women and wine, much like Barabbas in "The Wine of the Tetrarch" from "The Deluge at Norderney." Barabbas's unhappy state was brought on by having missed his opportunity to carry his own cross and experience his own martyrdom. King Erik identifies with the Wandering Jew, who according to legend did not take up Jesus's cross and was condemned to wander restlessly for eternity. "The great forces within him cried out for mightier undertakings, and for a fuller task," so it would seem that Erik is longing for some deed that will marry him to his destiny (*WT,* 229).

The king begins to contemplate the star that was mentioned in the first line of the tale, "Ave Stella Maris," which is a symbol of the Virgin Mary, high above the earth and untouchable by mortal man. He dreams of being the Virgin's knight and defender. The king thinks, "O Lord, it is time . . . that I should turn away from them, that I should throw off everybody that stands in the way of the happiness of my soul" (*WT,* 230). This line is important, apparently expressing a wish to do away with earthly cares, so that the King can focus on spiritual matters. This wish is clearer in the Danish version of the tale: "O Lord, it is time that I turn away from people. It is time that I throw away everything that stands in the way of my soul's welfare and happiness" (*MU,* 4:184). The phrase "throw away," *kaster fra mig,* becomes an echo of the story of Polycrates which is one of the main intertexts of the tale. Polycrates experienced great fortune and was advised to throw away something dear to him, so that the gods would not become envious. Polycrates threw a ring into the sea, which was later returned to him in the belly of a fish, a sign that the punishment of the gods was inevitable. Similarly, at this moment, the King becomes a Polycrates himself, throwing away his earthly concerns, but they will return to him in the shape of a ring in a fish that will lead him to Ingeborg, eroticism, and death. Immediately after this resolution, the king imagines that he hears a bell. Johan de Mylius associates this sound with Hans Christian Andersen's story "The Bell," in which the sound of a mysterious bell ringing in nature can be construed as a pantheistic symbol.[69] The king associates the sound with the sea, "Its waves of sound enclosed him as the sea a drowning man," which hints that the king has thrown something central into the sea (*WT,* 230). He will hear the sound again as he views the sea from the top of the downs before he rides down to the coast and Granze's hut (*WT,* 238). The King falls asleep, but his first thought upon waking is that he must visit Granze.

Commentators on "The Fish" are generally agreed that King Erik is torn between two forces represented by Sune Pedersen and Granze: "The memories that he had in common with Sune, he reflected, were all bright, as if clearly illuminated; those connected with the Wend belonged to earlier days, when he had hardly been conscious of himself or the world. They stirred dully in the dark, and smelled of seaweeds and mussels" (*WT,* 233). Most critics suggest that the conflict is between Christian and pagan forces, but Vibeke Schröder puts forward another familiar dualism: the Apollonian and the Dionysian.[70] Sune Pedersen is a member of the Hvide clan which will be responsible for King Erik's death ten years later. He has studied in Paris and is compelled by the life of the mind and great cathedrals. He is a priest who has renounced sexuality, something which has caused him some difficulty. When Granze first meets him, his clairvoyant powers tell him that Sune was near death by poisoning seven months ago: "If the rats would go into the holes that God made for them, people would not poison them" (*WT,* 239). Hans Holmberg interprets this to mean that Sune had been poisoned by a woman scorned and angered by his oath of celibacy.[71] Granze, on the other hand, is a pagan who lives in an earthy, pantheistic world where even the stones copulate.

Holmberg has noted a significant symbolic topography in this tale. King Erik undergoes a journey from high to low, from the spiritual to the material/erotic. His thoughts begin with the star in the heavens, and end with the ring plucked from the depths of the sea. Holmberg sees the star and the stone in the ring as corresponding images. The sky is spirit and the sea is desire. On his way to Granze, the King pauses at the top of the downs and takes in the view: "All round the horizon the sea and the sky played together, unsteadily and beguilingly. . . . But to the north the sea and the sky joined without the faintest line of division, and became but the universe, unfathomable space" (*WT,* 238). Later the King wonders if "Paradise, which Sune had spoken of, perhaps began where the sea and the sky met in front of him" (*WT,* 243). The King is looking for a balance between the sky and the sea, between the spiritual and the physical. Whether or not he achieves this remains to be seen. The King then rides downward to Granze's hut, the site of the pagan/Dionysian. Granze tells him that while he was at the top of the downs "you had a shining ring round your head, such as your holy pictures have" (*WT,* 243). Holmberg suggests that this spiritual ring becomes transmuted into the erotic ring in the fish as the King moves downward towards Granze. King Erik is, of course, not a saint, but saints have often earned their halos through martyrdom.

Holmberg has also noted that Granze invites Sune and King Erik to join him in something of a pagan communion. He offers his guests a strong-tasting beer, and announces: "Now what we dream and scheme may differ, but the water that we make will be the same" (*WT,* 240). They have been united by their animal need to urinate. Granze finds the ring in the fish's belly and Sune identifies it as belonging to Ingeborg. Granze offers the fish to the King, not to Sune, as a ritual meal. Holmberg writes, "When the King eats the fish, he is united with the external sign of his fate. From now on it is as inevitable as the effects of poison upon the one who has consumed it."[72] The King will go on to meet his destiny in ten years and will die a martyr, not to spiritual causes but to his own eroticism.

Critics are divided about whether this is a punishment or a reward. Is the King being punished for hubris or has he been rewarded by embracing his fate? At least twice, the King has compared himself to Christ. Erik thinks of himself, "Yes, he was himself the way, the truth and the life," which is a paraphrase of John 14:6 (*WT,* 231). The King contemplates the story of King Canute, who in order to fend off the praise and flattery of his subjects, ordered the waves not to touch his chair. The waves did not obey. Adam Oehlenschlæger presents this story as a lesson in Christian piety. Only Christ could still the waves (Mark 4:41), so a mortal king is his inferior. But King Erik replies, "But if the sea had obeyed him?" (*WT,* 245). Both Johan de Mylius and Grethe Rostbøll feel that King Erik is punished for the hubris of competing with Christ.[73] Vibeke Schröder and Svend Bjerg feel that in embracing his fate, King Erik has achieved a unity of the forces competing within him. Svend Bjerg expresses it as follows: "During the short day that the story lasts, the King acquires a Christ-prefiguration which is complemented by a heathen life that makes the divided King whole."[74] Vibeke

Schröder explains: "The change that occurs in the King during the course of the tale is that he accepts his fate—even if he is establishing the prerequisites to his own fall. . . . The person who is created by this has the nature of an artist, who has a pact with both the Dionysian and the Apollonian powers."[75] The perfect union of sky and sea, which the King imagines to be Paradise, is located in the north, the traditional location of the underworld in pagan Scandinavia. Perhaps meeting his death, carrying his own cross—albeit pagan—will satisfy the restlessness of the King's soul. As in so many other cases, the reader is the final arbiter of whether the King's fate is a punishment or a reward.

"Peter and Rosa"

"Peter and Rosa" is a story about a boy and a girl who have entered into the dangers of adolescence. The mentality of adolescence appears to have been something that interested Dinesen artistically. There are numerous female adolescents in Dinesen's tales, such as Calypso in "The Deluge at Norderney" and Athena in "The Monkey," to name only two. The female adolescent is at that point in life when culture asks her to move from individual to symbol, and it is not always an easy transition, especially when the transition to the traditional female role is perceived as a move from freedom to confinement. Adolescent males are fewer in number in Dinesen's tales, but Simon in "The Sailor-Boy's Tale" has much in common with Peter. Adolescent boys have reached a stage where they must decide how their interest in the opposite sex can be reconciled with a yearning for a life of adventure.

The nature symbolism in "Peter and Rosa" echoes the confusion and the state of flux that the two adolescents are experiencing. The season is changing from winter to spring and from a deep freeze to a thaw. The solid ground has liquified and the water is deceptively solid. Peter identifies especially with the birds of passage and mentally quotes the Swedish romantic poet Esaias Tegnér's poem "The Birds of Passage" (1812): "Northward! Northward!" (*WT,* 252). Peter imagines himself traveling with the birds and the strong instincts that propel them are similar to the forces at work in Peter's soul: sexual desire and a longing for freedom and adventure. Rosa's conflicting feelings are expressed in her actions towards the butterfly. At first, she wants to capture it and keep it, but then she decides to set it free. Rosa is confused by her attraction to the safety of her home and her own longing for freedom.

Given that Rosa is a girl in a conservative society, freedom is merely a theoretical point, since short of becoming a "fallen woman," Rosa cannot be free. The two maternal role models in the tale point to her apparent options: a sainted wife on a pedestal or a despised sexual being no better than a servant. Some of the anger Rosa feels towards Peter stems from the fact that he has an escape route from the parsonage, and she is not certain whether she should capture him, like the butterfly, or allow him to be free: "If she did tell her father of his project, there would be no ships in Peter's life, no rounding of the Horn, no drowning in the water of all the oceans. She sat on her bed, crouching on the thought, like a hen on her eggs" (*WT,* 270). Robert Langbaum interprets these lines to mean: "In the contrast between the two lines of imagery, we see the contrast between the male principle of boundless desire and the female principle which is precisely to make boundaries and to establish nests."[76] However, Rosa also has a longing for freedom, which is destined to be frustrated if she remains at home: "A prison is a good, safe place for human beings to be in" (*WT,* 276). Just as the butterfly would surely die if held in captivity, so would Rosa's spirit also fade. Rosa perhaps faces a future comparable to the sisters in "The Supper at Elsinore," whose talents are wasted in Denmark while their brother is a pirate on the high seas, a future in which "She had been let down and deserted by someone, and left in a cold world, from which all colour and life were gone" (*WT,* 269).

Although Peter and Rosa share the turmoil of adolescence, they experience it differently and find it difficult to communicate with each other, in part because they barely understand their own feelings. Peter's plans of adventure seem clear to him until he catches sight of Rosa in the window in the act of releasing the butterfly and sees her as the figurehead of a ship. The vision prompts Peter to want to share some intimacy with Rosa, at first in the form of telling her his secrets. The scene in which they lie side by side is charged with sexual tension, and when he leaves, Peter resolves to come again: "It was something more absolute which he meant to yield up to her, it was himself, the essence of his nature, and at the same time it was eternity. . . . He could not go away until it had been consummated" (*WT,* 267). Although he does not put this name to it, Peter is overwhelmed by his own sexuality and would be likely to attempt a seduction the following night. There is a parallel here between Peter's feelings and the story he tells of the skipper who has a figurehead that resembles his wife. The skipper must live his life of action, but likes to be reminded of his wife as a symbol and inspiration while he is at sea. He returns to harbor when he wants a kiss. Peter sees Rosa as the figurehead of a ship, and even as a female deity of the sea, but at the same time, the promise of a kiss from her might persuade him to stay in the harbor.

Rosa has gone through a phase where she has resented Peter for his physical size and for the very fact that he is male. She is dimly threatened by his sexuality and disapproves of the fact Peter's father was a seducer. She has wished him away at sea, so that she could reign supreme at home. When she tells Peter that she has wanted him to go to sea, Peter misinterprets the comment as a sign that she has understood him. Rosa has lived in a dream world, where she can be everything she wants to be. She fears Peter because: "She could no longer, she felt, be sure of her dream-world. Peter might find the 'Sesame' which opened it, and encroach upon it, and she might meet him there any day" (*WT,* 256). In some sense, Peter and Rosa are the two locked caskets, each of which contains the key to the other, that will be mentioned in "A Consolatory Tale." Thomas Whissen sees the story of Peter and Rosa as a tale of the interaction of opposites: "[Peter and Rosa] require each other, they define each other, and they suffer a common fate when the ice floe on which they are symbolically sailing breaks apart beneath them and sends them to the bottom of the sound. . . . Opposites fulfill their destinies through the agency of one another. Separately they have no roles to play."[77] In a fit of resentment, Rosa betrays Peter's secrets to her father and walks away with thirty pieces of silver like Judas. She realizes that "now she had sided with that room, with the prison, with the grave" (*WT,* 277). Like Judas, she contemplates suicide to avoid her shame.

Not realizing Rosa's mood, Peter plays into her hands when he suggests that they go to see the ice breaking up. Rosa's young brother in a moment of clairvoyance predicts that they will not return. The two young people find themselves out in nature which reflects all of their inner tumult, and the sensation goes to their heads. Rosa has lived her life in a dream world, and she takes Peter into her imaginative world as they play their game on the ice. They are heading for the ship Esperance, whose name means "hope." As they come to the large floe of ice, which is the Esperance, Peter asks: "Am I to board her now, Rosa?" Rosa responds "Yes, we will go aboard now" (*WT,* 281). Only in this dream world would Rosa be allowed to board the ship and run away with Peter and he is thrilled by her audacity. One might argue that Rosa is leading Peter to his death, having already decided to commit suicide herself. In part, she is certainly motivated by her fear of Peter learning of her betrayal. On the other hand, consigning Peter to the spiritual death of the parsonage might be a worse fate than the beautiful death at sea he has imagined for himself. Adrift on the ice floe, Peter and Rosa symbolically make love and are swept to their deaths as one. Depending upon one's point of view, the ending can be interpreted as either happy or tragic: happy, because they die united before the world has had a chance to ruin them; tragic, because like Romeo and Juliet, the two cannot find happiness in this world.

Dinesen commented on this tale in the context of her discussion of Nemesis in a letter to Johannes Rosendahl. She counts Rosa as one of her characters who is reluctant to embrace her destiny: "Rosa wants to 'get off cheaply' and is only saved by Peter, to whom such a thing has never occurred" (*KBD,* 1:392). At the end of the tale, Rosa has embraced her destiny and pays the highest price for it. Dinesen's admiration for Peter is also suggested by the fact that he expresses in a halting fashion views that Dinesen expressed as her own in *Out of Africa:* "Pride is faith in the idea that God had, when he made us" (*OA,* 250). Peter has stumbled on the notion that God has meant him to be a sailor, and he will pursue that destiny no matter what the cost. He is fully prepared to die at sea, and even thinks of it as a beautiful death.

Dinesen's critical view of Rosa's actions is further implied in the extended version of the inset tale "The Blue Eyes" which Dinesen performed for Danish radio in 1959. It is clear, in both versions of the tale, that the skipper's wife has not understood her husband and does harm to both herself and him when she steals the jewels from the eyes of the figurehead. Rosa identifies with the captain's wife and sees her own betrayal of Peter echoed in the theft of the jewels. In the radio version of "The Blue Eyes," when the wife is going blind and hopes to reverse the effects of her betrayal, she seeks the help of a Lapp woman named Sunniva, like the witch in "The Sailor-Boy's Tale." Sunniva informs the captain's wife: "The Powers we call upon—they refuse to help us. They say that a wrong has been committed and they take the part of those Powers that we wish to fight."[78] The powers of Nemesis that draw a man to the sea are evidently not to be trifled with and Rosa is in the wrong when she betrays Peter, a fact she realizes herself. In several of Dinesen's stories it has been mentioned that women flare up with hostility at the mention of the sea. For example, the imaginary Madame Knudsen in *Out of Africa* will not go there. The sailor and his wife in the harbor seem to represent an image that expresses a crucial misunderstanding between the sexes. Men enjoy the adventure and freedom of the sea, whereas women prefer the security of the harbor. There are exceptions to this rule, and the women who long for the freedom of the sea, like Eliza, Fanny, or Rosa, are bound to meet with tragic fates.

"A Consolatory Tale"

Charlie Despard, who was featured in the first story in *Winter's Tales,* is once again in crisis. He has finished his second book, which was a success, but now is experiencing another creative slump. Charlie appears to have assimilated the lessons he learned in the first tale. He has abandoned his bourgeois existence by sending his wife back home to her people and by becoming a wayfarer without roots. To all appearances, this sacrifice successfully released Charlie's artistic energies. Even so, Charlie "still had in his heart a constant, slight nostalgia for London, and his old life there" (*WT,* 289). In a Parisian café, the melancholy author runs into an old acquaintance, Æneas Snell, and vents his spleen about the relationship between the author and his public. In the English version of the story, Æneas offers Charlie in return "a consolatory tale." The Danish title is more accurately translated "an edifying tale."

Some critics have noted that Charlie and Æneas appear to be doubles.[79] They physically resemble each other, have traveled extensively, and each is capable of creating narratives. Elisabeth Tykesson notes, however, that whereas Charlie represents the author of fiction, Æneas is the born storyteller.[80] As Æneas prepares to tell his story, it is said "the prim bailiff faded away, and in his seat sat a deep and dangerous little figure, consolidated, alert and ruthless—the storyteller of all the ages" (*WT,* 296). Æneas's storytelling technique is described as follows: "He would not let his own person play any big role in his tales, but he would tell even his strangest story as if it had taken place before his own eyes, which indeed it might often have done" (*WT,* 291). This describes Dinesen's own narrative voice in the majority of her tales and is perhaps part of what gives the tales their oral quality.

Æneas's unusual name calls to mind Virgil's *Aeneid,* which was an attempt by a literary figure to emulate the epics of oral tradition. Aeneas, the hero of the *Aeneid,* narrates part of the epic as he recounts his adventures to Queen Dido. Thus, Aeneas is an oral storyteller embedded in a literary epic. Similarly, his namesake in "A Consolatory Tale" contributes an "oral" narrative to an otherwise literary tale. In "The Young Man with the Carnation," Charlie found creative inspiration in the tales told by sailors. Now in a second slump, Charlie returns to the well of oral tradition and comes away refreshed. The final lines of the tale indicate that Charlie's creative imagination is already appropriating Æneas's tale: "Not a very good tale, really, you know. But it has moments in it that might be worked up, and from which one might construct a fine tale" (*WT,* 313).

What is the nature of the consolation or edification that Charlie receives from Æneas's story? The tale presents another set of doubles: Prince Nasrud-Din and the beggar Fath. Prince Nasrud-Din is inspired by the example of the Caliph Harun al Rachid of *The Arabian Nights,* who was in the habit of moving about in disguise among his subjects. There are certain resemblances between Æneas's story and "The Tale of the False Caliph" from *The Arabian Nights,* in which Harun al Rachid, while in disguise, encounters a man who is impersonating him. In the original tale, the impostor is pretending to be the wealthy and powerful caliph. Dinesen's version adds an additional twist in that the impostor is imitating the Prince in his beggar's disguise, raising the question "Who is imitating whom?"

Prince Nasrud-Din might have felt further encouraged in his escapades by some of the tales of Western literature told to him by Æneas, in particular Eugene Sue's *Mysteries of Paris* (1842–43). One of Sue's characters, Rudolphe, is a mysterious prince who lurks about the Paris underworld in disguise, punishing evil and rewarding virtue. The theme of great power in disguise is a popular one in Dinesen's tales. One need only think of "The Dreamers" or "Converse at Night in Copenhagen." The Prince's advisors are worried about the political repercussions of a royal personage learning too much about his subjects. Their fears might be justified. Karl Marx was a great fan of *Mysteries of Paris,* because of its descriptions of conditions among the poor and wrote a substantial essay on the novel. Learning of the complaints of the poor is the first step toward changing their condition.

The Prince goes to meet Fath with the expectation that the impostor is trying to win some personal gain, either financial or political, from the resemblance between them. Instead he meets a beggar who has turned begging into an art form. Fath has no need of the gold the Prince tries to give him, but values his profession, the art of begging, more highly. Fath and the Prince are both in disguise, but Fath is the more skilled impostor. Fath critiques the Prince's performance as a beggar: "You did not, when you walked the streets as a beggar, endeavour to be any wiser or greater, any nobler or more magnanimous than the other beggars of the town" (*WT,* 307). The Prince did nothing to enhance the prestige of the beggar's profession. Fath, on the other hand, is better at playing his role than the Prince was. He refuses alms and remains by the wall for three days without food in order that the people will think the best of the Prince they believe him to be. The Prince comes to see that his reputation is in better hands with Fath than in his own. Fath encourages the Prince to return to his royal duties and perform them as well as he can, for this will enhance Fath's prestige as well: "but a beggar of Teheran has harnessed me to his wagon, and from now on, awake or asleep, I shall be labouring for Fath" (*WT,* 308). Grethe Rostbøll sums up their compact as follows: "The beggar honors the prince by being a beggar. In exchange, the prince must fulfill his role in a proper manner—not by being a beggar himself, but by avoiding the misuse of power and capriciousness."[81]

The edifying/consoling impact of Æneas's tale perhaps lies in the moral that each must play his or her role to the utmost and in the vision of the interdependence of opposites encapsulated in Fath's cryptic sayings: "Life and Death .... man and woman. ... the rich and the poor of this world, are two locked caskets, of which each contains the key to the other" (*WT,* 303, 309, 312). As mentioned in the first chapter of this book, the dynamic interaction of opposites is a major theme throughout Dinesen's work. Opposites may reach a type of reconciliation, but not at the cost of compromising the integrity of either part. Thus, opposites form a unity but remain distinct. The caskets remain locked. The doubling effect that has run throughout "A Consolatory Tale" mirrors this theme. The Prince impersonates the beggar and the beggar impersonates the prince, but the Prince remains a Prince and the beggar remains a beggar. Each will inspire the other to greater deeds. The writer of fiction imitates oral tradition and the oral storyteller borrows from the classics of literature. The writer of fiction and the oral storyteller inspire each other. Even Charlie's worries about his relationship to his public may be addressed in this way. The author and his public may inspire each other if they play their roles responsibly. The author must remain true to his artistic vision, and the public must remain attentive. Neither can show mercy to the other.

CHAPTER 5

Last Tales

Fifteen years elapsed between the publication of *Winter's Tales* (1942) and *Last Tales* (1957), although Dinesen was not silent. In 1946, *The Angelic Avengers* appeared in English under the pseudonym Pierre Andrézel. The book was written for her own amusement during the Nazi occupation, and she did not like to have it considered as part of her serious work. The fifteen years between the two collections were troubled by spells of poor health, making it difficult for Dinesen to summon the concentrated strength she needed to produce a complete new collection of tales: she told Robert Langbaum that much of *Last Tales* was dictated while lying on her back on the floor.[1] From time to time, Dinesen published tales in magazines. Three of the stories in *Last Tales* were published before their inclusion in the volume: "The Caryatids" (1938 in Danish), "Converse at Night in Copenhagen" (1953 in Danish), "The Cloak" (1955 in English).

There are signs that Dinesen had become less comfortable expressing herself in English over time. Contrary to her previous practice, "Converse at Night in Copenhagen" and "Copenhagen Season" were both written in Danish first, before being recast into English. Frans Lasson notes that just before the publication of *Last Tales,* Dinesen sought the help of Hugh F. Pooley (1883–1971), a British school rector and family friend, who went over her English manuscript for her.

Although Dinesen did not lack creative inspiration as well as the ambition to write long, polished, and intricate collections, she realized that her strength was failing and that what was finished should be published as soon as possible. Both *Last Tales* and *Anecdotes of Destiny* were ready for publication at the same time, and Dinesen wanted them released simultaneously. Her publishers felt that was unwise, so Dinesen, with characteristic irony, insisted that *Last Tales* be published first. She believed that *Last Tales* was a stronger collection than *Anecdotes of Destiny,* and wished to put her best foot forward after such a lengthy hiatus. At one point, Dinesen told Johannes Rosendahl that she wanted her next book to be published in America, England, Sweden, Norway, and Finland—but not Denmark, an indication that Dinesen's awkward relationship with her Danish public continued to bother her (*KBD,* 2:256).

Last Tales was not greeted with the same critical enthusiasm that her previous collections had received. It was not selected by the American Book-of-the-Month Club or the English Book Society, perhaps because the reference to syphilis in "The Cardinal's Third Tale" was too shocking in the conservative 1950s.[2] Reviews in America, England, Sweden, and Denmark were respectful, but tinged with disappointment. Some reviewers found merit in a few of the tales, if not all of them. The Danish critic Klaus Otto Kapel felt that "The Cardinal's First Tale" and "A Country Tale" were the only two worthy tales in the collection.[3] Cornell professor Victor Lange similarly named "A Country Tale" as his favorite, as did William Dickey, who also felt that "Copenhagen Season" and "Echoes" would stand the test of time.[4] Even if the critics responded lukewarmly to the collection, Dinesen still had her fans. Jørgen Gustava Brandt wrote to Dinesen about a woman he knew who called in sick from work for fourteen days, in order to read *Last Tales* ceremoniously and repeatedly when it first came out (*KBD*, 2:377).

Dinesen divided the tales under three headings: "Tales from *Albondocani*," "New Gothic Tales," and "New Winter's Tales." The Gothic tales include "The Caryatids," which Dinesen had finished writing by 1934, but simply not included in *Seven Gothic Tales*, and "Echoes," which takes up the character of Pellegrina Leoni from "The Dreamers." Dinesen's selection of new "Winter's Tales" confirms the observation that the original collection had a strong Danish thrust to it. All three new "Winter's Tales" are set in Denmark.

The first seven of the tales in the collection are designated as belonging to *Albondocani,* an elaborate novel on which Dinesen was working during the final years of her life.[5] When she spoke of the project, she described it as one hundred, two hundred, or as many as a thousand and one separate, but connected, tales.[6] The numbers are suggestive, since they appear to invoke both the hundred tales of Boccacio's *Decameron* and the thousand and one *Arabian Nights*. Dinesen told one interviewer, "*Albondocani* is actually not a novel but chapters loosely connected through recurring characters, and the stories can be read independently of each other."[7] "Albondocani" was the alias used by the Caliph Harun al Rashid, whenever he wanted to move about Baghdad in disguise in *The Arabian Nights*. Aage Henriksen remembered being told by Dinesen that the central figure of the work "would be a man, who lived incognito in society but possessed great power and riches, due to the fact that he could always secretly renew his resources from the castle he came from—until the day his secret contact did not appear and the castle denied all knowledge of him."[8] Such a central figure appears to be absent from the existing tales of *Albondocani,* but the tales are linked by the recurring characters of Cardinal Salviati and Pizzuti, the puppet master, as well as a certain thematic unity.

"The Cardinal's First Tale"

Dinesen wrote to her Danish publisher, Ole Wivel, that "The Cardinal's First Tale" "contains a sort of program for the whole novel [*Albondocani*]" (*KBD*, 2:271). Toward the end of the tale, the Cardinal allows himself a small lecture on the difference between the story and the novel, which may have been prompted by queries as to why Dinesen used such an old-fashioned form, instead of keeping up with the times. In a Swedish interview, Dinesen spoke of how Eyvind Johnson and Harry Martinson (who later shared the Nobel Prize in 1974) "asked me why I did not write a novel when I had so much material."[9] The very question implies that the story is an inferior genre to the novel, so Dinesen perhaps felt the need to come to its defense.

The tale begins with the question "Who are you?" (*LT*, 3). This particular inquiry has played a significant role in Dinesen's previous fiction. In "The Deluge at Norderney," Jonathan Mærsk responds to the query by telling the story of his troubles in Copenhagen. Lincoln Forsner drives Pellegrina off a cliff with the same question, later to be answered by a tale from Marcus Cocoza. In *Out of Africa,* when Dinesen crafts Jogona's experiences into a narrative, she claims, "I had created him and shown him himself" (*OA,* 115). In "The Cardinal's First Tale," similar words are used by the lady in black to describe the service the Cardinal has rendered for her: "You have shown me myself! I might tell you that you had created me" (*LT,* 4). The Cardinal has evidently fashioned a story out of the lady's experiences. Her question to the Cardinal prompts yet another story in answer to this central question.

There are some suggestive and noteworthy details about this narrative frame. The conversation between the Cardinal and the mysterious lady in black takes place in a library, a literary, rather than a religious, space. The confession process itself seems to have been an artistic process in which "fragments have been united into a whole" (*LT,* 4). When the lady in black exclaims, "To the eyes of the world, it is true, I am standing at the edge of an abyss, or walking in a blizzard in wild mountains" (*LT,* 4), one's thoughts might be drawn to the climactic scene in "The Dreamers," in which Pellegrina flees her pursuers up a mountain in a blizzard and then hurls herself into the abyss. Is the lady in black Pellegrina? There is a further, curious connection between Pellegrina and the Cardinal: both have received a scar on their neck in a fire. What might these echoes signify?

145

Some have suggested that the Cardinal is a fictional alter ego of Dinesen, and Dinesen claimed Pellegrina as such a fictional representation of herself. Could this be a case of two of Dinesen's fictional selves interrogating each other? Pellegrina would represent the Dinesen of the early thirties, just after she lost the farm and began her new career as an artist. This younger self asks the older, "Who are you?" In return, the Cardinal tells a story that explains Dinesen's current artistic program.

The Cardinal begins by describing his parents. Prince Pompilio, as his name suggests, is a pompous representative of patriarchal society. He marries a girl of fifteen, who has been brought up as a caryatid-type, prepared to maintain the family name and honor at the cost of her personal fulfillment. When she becomes with child, she sees herself "as a fragile, precious vessel, within which a rare seed had been laid down to germinate, and at the end of the term it had been her husband's old name to which she had given birth" (*LT*, 6). Thus, she has perfectly performed her duties as a caryatid. Susan Hardy Aiken suggests that Ercole, the heir, literalizes the phallic nature of patriarchy: "the child was delicate and had but one eye" (*LT*, 5) and "only distinguished himself by growing up to a most unusual height" (*LT*, 19).[10] Because of the poor health of the first child, a doctor recommends that Prince Pompilio not sleep with his wife again for three years.

During this period, Princess Benedetta discovers her own erotic nature and lays the groundwork for her future career as a blossom-type, who will transgress the rules of patriarchy without seeming to break them altogether. Benedetta's passion for reading as well as her love for music are presented in the tale as symbolic adulteries. During a performance of Metastasio's *Achilles at Scyros,* Benedetta's eyes lock with those of the castrato Marelli, and a sort of spiritual insemination takes place. This conception is different from the first, breaking the bounds of both biology and gender. Marelli is undoubtedly singing the role of Achilles who is hidden at the court at Scyros dressed as a girl.

During her ensuing pregnancy a dispute arises between Benedetta and Pompilio about the name of their next child. Pompilio wants to name the child Atanasio after St. Athanasius, "the Father of Orthodoxy," and have as sponsors Cardinal Rusconi and the Bishop of Beri. Benedetta wants to name the child Dionysio after Dionysus, "the God of inspired ecstasy" (in Danish, "the God of inspiration's ecstasy," *MU* 5:236), and to have as sponsors the poet Gozzo, the composer Cimarosa, and the sculptor Canova (*LT*, 11). The familiar opposition between the Apollonian and the Dionysian is set up: one represents order, the other, a type of creative chaos. The fact that Benedetta gives birth to twins recalls the tale of Alkmene, who gave birth to the god Hercules and a normal mortal after sleeping with Zeus and Amphytrion on the same night. Perhaps one of Benedetta's children is in fact the offspring of the celestial union between herself and the artist Marelli, while the other was begotten in the more conventional embrace of her husband.

An additional three paragraphs have been inserted into the Danish edition of the tale at the point when Pompilio returns to his wife after she has given birth and agrees to have one of the children baptized Dionysio. In the English version, Pompilio resolves to forgive his wife when he learns that she has borne twins, and thus he can have his way and be generous at the same time. Upon seeing her, he tells her immediately of his decision. In the Danish version, more is made of the perilous state of Benedetta's health after the birth. In fact, she is so feverish that she does not even remember giving birth. When Pompilio approaches her bed, she reaches out a hand and says, "Oh, how late you have come, my dear" (*MU,* 5:238). This is the first time that Benedetta has ever spoken to him with such an intimate, loving voice. She urges him to prepare for the baptism of his son Dionysio and, deeply touched, Pompilio agrees. Since Benedetta does not remember she has given birth to twins, this seems to her to be a full concession from her husband: "This was yet another of those—in themselves understandable but questionable—steps, whereby the Prince precipitated unforeseen consequences in his marriage. The memory of having denied or held back his son Atanasio's existence, on such a solemn occasion before the child's own mother, passed through his mind in the coming years from time to time like a cold shudder and a slight sense of uneasiness" (*MU,* 5:238–39). Since the Prince is the first to withhold information, it might vindicate Benedetta in her future duplicity towards her husband.

Six weeks after the two children are baptized, a fire engulfs the villa and only one of the twins survives. Pompilio claims the survivor is Atanasio, but Benedetta secretly believes him to be Dionysio, the proof being the scar the infant presumably received when the blue ribbon he wore around his neck burned off. She calls him Pyrrha, the nickname of Achilles when he was disguised in Scyros. As in "The Dreamers," the fire precipitates a drastic shift in identity for the victim. Atanasio is raised with a double nature. His father treats him like a future patriarch of the church and his mother treats him like an artist. The story tells us: "He kept his small head by adopting and perfecting, in the innocent manner of a child, the doubleness of his elders. He saw the lovely and beloved form of his mother with the eyes of a priest. . . . He saw his father with the eyes of the artist. . . . In this way the hand of a child out of the elements of an anomalous family life produced a reconciling synthesis" (*LT,* 19). The Cardinal is not either Atanasio or Dionysio, he is both, and one never knows to whom one is speaking. The synthesis does not prioritize one identity over the other, and, miraculously, the integrity of both identities does not appear to have been compromised. They both still exist. This duplicity might also be said to be a quality of Dinesen's fiction. The reader of a Dinesen text may not be certain whether he or she is hearing from a supporter of aristocratic tradition or a subverter of patriarchal order. Both seem to exist at the same time.

According to Susan Hardy Aiken's interpretation of "The Cardinal's First Tale," the Cardinal is not a fictional representation of Dinesen and his comments at the end of the tale should not be taken as her own. Aiken sees condescension in the attitude of the Cardinal towards his mother at the end and feels that Benedetta's transgressions are subsumed back into patriarchal order through the ceremony of extreme unction. Another possibility is that the Cardinal speaks with compassion when he notes that the lives of most ladies involve "smiles . . . and tears, dauntlessness and fear, unconquerable hope and the certainty of failure" (*LT,* 20). His mother was as much a reconciliation of opposites as he is.

Although it is always wise to hesitate before ascribing the thoughts and feelings of Dinesen's fictional characters to the author herself, the Cardinal's exposition about the divine art of the story and the nature of God is congruent with similar sentiments expressed elsewhere in Dinesen's fiction. The Cardinal reports a conversation with God, along the lines of Charlie Despard's encounter in "The Young Man with the Carnation." God asks the Cardinal before his ordination if he believes that God has created "a sublime world with all things necessary to the purpose in it, and none left out?" (in Danish, "a sublime world with possibilities for both the most glorious and dreadful of things?" *MU* 5:250). Life is an artwork for which both comedy and tragedy, white and black are aesthetically necessary. *Seven Gothic Tales* was riddled with allusions to God as the artist and puppet master controlling the fates of his human marionettes. Mortals must keep the ideas of the divine author clear. When the Cardinal compares himself to the bow of the Lord, he identifies himself as both a tool and cocomposer of this divine artwork: "The divine art is the story. In the beginning was the story. At the end we shall be privileged to view, and review it—and that is what is named the day of judgement" (*LT,* 24). The story as a literary genre emphasizes plot over character, in contrast to the art of the novel which sacrifices plot for the sake of getting to know its characters. The character of a story is a symbol, but the character of the novel is an individual. The story shows humans in the grip of the powers of fate, whereas the novel leaves them to their own devices in the secular world. In one paragraph, the Cardinal whisks through a catalog of great stories:

> The [hero and the heroine] need not distress themselves about material for
> the burnt offering [Genesis 22], for the story will provide. It will separate

the two, in life, by the currents of the Hellespont [*Hero and Leander*] and unite them, in death, in a Veronese tomb [*Romeo and Juliet*]. It provides for the hero, and his young bride will exchange an old copper lamp for a new one, and the Chaldeans shall make out three bands and fall upon his camels and carry them away [*Aladdin*], and he himself with his own hand shall cook, for an evening meal with his mistress, the falcon which was to have saved the life of her small dying son [*Decameron*]. The story will provide for the heroine, and at the moment when she lifts up her lamp to behold the beauty of her sleeping lover it makes her spill one drop of burning oil on his shoulder [*Amor and Psyche*]. The story does not slacken its speed to occupy itself with the mien or bearing of its characters, but goes on. It makes the one faithful partisan of its old mad hero cry out in awe: "Is this the promised end?"—goes on, and in a while calmly informs us: "This is the promised end" [*King Lear*].

Evidently, the Cardinal and Dinesen include both God and Shakespeare among the great storytellers. This paragraph is not only a dizzying example of Dinesen's use of literary allusions, but it also serves to establish the credentials of the story as both ancient and enduring.

"The Cloak"

"The Cloak" is part of a trilogy of tales that includes "Nightwalk" and "Of Hidden Thoughts and of Heaven." Collectively, Aage Henriksen has referred to them as "The Cardinal's Second Tale," which is otherwise conspicuously absent in the *Albondocani* suite.[11] Cardinal Salviati does play a brief, but crucial, role in "The Cloak" when, at his urging, Angelo is allowed to take his master's place in prison for the night. As a recurring character, the Cardinal provides one of the links that holds the diverse stories of *Albondocani* together.

After examining Dinesen's notes for the story, Ulla Albreck deduces that the stories were probably first written in Danish.[12] There are, however, significant passages included in the Danish version but not in the English, and vice versa. These discrepancies will be pointed out as need arises.

All three tales in the trilogy deal with the fate of Angelo, the young apprentice of the sculptor Leonidas Allori. Dinesen herself had been a student at an art academy, and some of the lessons she learned there undoubtedly surface in these three stories. Dinesen once wrote in a newspaper about the impact that exposure to the laws of perspective had upon her: "I had not before, in my daily schooling, made the acquaintance with strict regularity. I became in some strange way delighted by the unyielding regularity of the laws of perspective drawing. If I behaved correctly, the result could not avoid being correct—but if I allowed myself the least carelessness, it would be revenged at the end of the exercise, invariably, and with a terrible power!"[13] Dinesen once wrote to her Aunt Bess from Africa: "I feel that out here I have come to understand the value of distance or perspective, (it is true to say that something of this dawned on me when I attended the Academy and learned to draw perspective, which I count as one of the experiences of my life, but whose significance I only recently understood how to apply to practical life)" (*LA,* 356). This quote implies that the rules of art may also be applied to life. This is what the apprentice Angelo needs to learn.

The story begins with a love triangle. Angelo is in love with Leonidas's wife, Lucrezia, at the same time he is devoted to his teacher. Leonidas is Angelo's "spiritual father," the master who must teach Angelo the rules of art, if Angelo is to be his true disciple and heir (*LT,* 27). Lucrezia has a more elemental essence, and Leonidas compares her to the four elements: "the earth, the sea, the air, and the fire" (*LT,* 36). In a sense, Angelo is torn between Apollonian and Dionysian forces, but his great passion for Lucrezia has given the Dionysian the upper hand. Angelo is out of balance. This imbalance is signified by his obsession with Lucrezia to the exclusion of any knowledge of the peril Leonidas faces, and the fact that Angelo goes to see "a recently unearthed Greek statue of the god Dionysus" (*LT,* 33; in the Danish version the Greek statue is not identified, *MU* 5:264). Leonidas is himself preoccupied by the idea of his impending death but still seems to live within the rules: "He spoke no word of his danger to the people surrounding him, because these people, in the course of a few weeks, to him had become infinitely distant and thus, in accordance with the law of perspective, infinitely small" (*LT,* 29–30). When Leonidas steps out of his isolation, he soon realizes that Angelo is need of a lesson in faithfulness to the rules of proportion.

It is almost certain that Leonidas has overheard Angelo and Lucrezia planning their tryst: "All this they discussed in Lucrezia's room next to the studio where the master was working, and with the door open" (*LT,* 31). Moreover, Leonidas is able to repeat with striking detail the plans for the meeting, including throwing a pebble against Lucrezia's window and wearing the cloak. Why does Leonidas act as he does? Possibly, he may be getting revenge on his faithless pupil by pricking his conscience—"I thank you for your faithfulness throughout our long happy years"—and depriving him of the assignation that had filled Angelo's thoughts. Another possibility is that Leonidas seeks to teach Angelo an art lesson: "faithfulness is the supreme divine factor by which the universe is governed" (*LT,* 35). Faithfulness applies to the rules of both art and life: "I enjoin and implore you: keep always in your heart the divine law of proportion, the golden section" (*LT,* 36). The "golden section" is a formula developed during the Renaissance to calculate the proportions of a perfect rectangle, which when applied to art was thought to create an aesthetically pleasing effect. The formula sets forth a relation between three points that will determine the fourth.[14] The love triangle that Leonidas and his pupil are involved in is distorted, and the relationship between the three points is not as it should be. A great artwork will never come of it.

Leonidas takes Angelo's cloak and impersonates him at the lovers' rendezvous. Robert Langbaum sees a parallel between the story of when Leonidas saved Angelo's life in the mountains by throwing his cloak over him and his present action: "Leonidas is saving Angelo's life a second time—saving this time his spiritual life by preventing him from committing the sin he plans."[15] An actual betrayal at this point would have thrown all their lives out of proportion.

Angelo spends a painful night in the cell. At first, his guilt causes him to lash out at the thought of the woman who tempted him to betrayal. He fears that his passion for Lucrezia would have sapped his creative strength. Even if he can deny the Dionysian forces while awake, when he falls asleep sexual jealousy returns with a vengeance: "Gone was the disciple's reverence for his master, the great artist; in the darkness the son ground his teeth at his father" (*LT,* 41). A second dream is missing from the English text that is included in the Danish version. Angelo sees Leonidas in his masculine nakedness, adored by Lucrezia. When he wakes from this dream, Angelo thinks of Ham, who was cursed for having seen his father, Noah, naked: "No, he was not Ham" (*MU,* 5:274). This dream suggests filial rebellion to Angelo, but, at the same time, it provides a vision of male/female and Apollonian/Dionysian forces in balance. In his sleep, Angelo tries to reject the Apollonian and dreams of murdering his "father." Langbaum assesses Angelo's spiritual dilemma as follows: "The son must obey and revere his father, yet he must psychologically overthrow him and biologically replace him. It is in God's scheme that we rebel even against Him in the course of our moral development."[16]

For a moment, when Angelo thinks that Leonidas might not return to the cell in time and that he is to be executed in Leonidas's stead, he is relieved and grateful, in much the same way as Rosa, in "Peter and Rosa," embraces death rather than have her betrayal exposed. Leonidas does return, places the cloak on Angelo's shoulders, and kisses him on the cheek. In draping Angelo with his mantle, Leonidas claims Angelo as his successor in the manner of the prophet Elijah who throws his mantle to Elisha (2 Kings 2:13). The kiss strikes Angelo as a parallel to the biblical scene in the Garden of Gethsemane when Judas betrays Christ with a kiss. Angelo feels that he is the betrayer, but Leonidas, like Judas, is the one who does the kissing. It is possible that this is a kiss of reconciliation, although Angelo, riddled with guilt, cannot see it that way. Angelo cannot remember the look that Leonidas gives him before the kiss. It is an appropriate "blank page" that leaves the tale open in its ambiguity.

"Night Walk"

It takes a while for the lessons of "The Cloak" to sink in. Angelo's experiences in prison have cured him of his preoccupation with the Dionysian, but he has not yet forgiven himself for his betrayal of the Apollonian. By choice, Angelo refuses to sleep. While asleep in the cell, Angelo had had dreams of murdering his father figure, and he does not wish to recall those dreams. Angelo is punishing himself for a crime he committed in spirit, though not in deed. He avoids Lucrezia and considers himself an unworthy disciple of Leonidas.

In a tavern, Angelo meets Pizzuti, "the philosopher" and puppet master (*LT*, 46). Pizzuti plays a major role in another tale of *Albondocani,* "Second Meeting," that did not find its way into *Last Tales.* In that story, we learn that Pizzuti as a young man was a double for Lord Byron and saved his life. Moreover he claims to be related by blood to Scheherazade (*CV,* 329). So many links with Dinesen's favorite themes should make us take notice. Pizzuti coaxes a confession from Angelo by making a comment in the Danish version of the tale that is not included in the English: "He understood without difficulty how a conscienceless young person might be plagued by pangs of conscience, and commented sadly: 'Yes, it is difficult for a hedgehog to have lice'" (*MU,* 5:280). Dinesen fortunately explained this cryptic comment in a note among her papers: "It is difficult for a hedgehog to have lice. It cannot scratch itself. (About a proud man, who cannot, or will not, complain of his humiliation.)"[17] Angelo does unburden his soul and Pizzuti tries to comfort Angelo with the thought: "It is a good thing to be a great sinner. Or should human beings allow Christ to have died on the Cross for the sake of our petty lies and our paltry whorings?" (*LT,* 47) Although the idea does not cure Angelo's insomnia, it nonetheless makes an impression upon Angelo who repeats the sentiment seven years later in "Of Hidden Thoughts and of Heaven" (*LT,* 56).

Angelo eventually becomes desperate to sleep, but is unable. He buys a sleeping draught, "but it only conveyed to him a row of novel, quite confused sensations of distance, so that objects and times which were far away were felt by him as quite near, while such objects as he knew to be within reach—his own hands and feet and the stone steps of the stairs—were infinitely far off" (*LT,* 48). The laws of artistic perspective are out of joint for Angelo.

Angelo finally returns to the tavern where he met Pizzuti in order to search for the cloak that he has forgotten. Grethe Rostbøll interprets this as a sign that

Angelo has come to the point where he wants to take up the mantle again that Leonidas has given him, but to do so he must look deep within himself.[18] Mariana the Rat gives Angelo some unusual advice: "Walk from the broadest street of the town into a narrower one, and from this narrow street into one still narrower, and go on like that. If from your narrowest alley you can find your way into a tighter passage, enter it, and follow it, and draw your breath lightly once or twice. And at that you will have fallen asleep" (*LT,* 49). Passing from a broader space into a narrower seems like a Jungian image for the subconscious, or a descent into hell. When Angelo steps into the final, narrow space he finds a stranger. In typical "Dinesenian" fashion, the reader is not told explicitly who the stranger is, but sufficient clues are given for an accurate guess. The stranger is "red-haired," and he plays with silver coins, arranging them in piles of two, five, six, ten, and fifteen (*LT,* 50–51). A bit of elementary math leads to the deduction that the stranger has thirty pieces of silver. The stranger is Judas, who boasts, "But no one, . . . no one in the world could ever seriously believe that I myself did sleep—on that Thursday night in the garden" (*LT,* 51).

Somewhere during Angelo's night walk, the bounds of the plausible were crossed. The meeting with Judas cures Angelo of his insomnia, but why? Robert Langbaum posits that Angelo has learned "only the great sinner has a spiritual intensity equal to that of the saint."[19] Aage Henriksen suggests, "He has met his higher self in the form of the lost apostle Judas."[20] Hans Holmberg reads this meeting in a manner consistent with the lessons in art that have riddled this trilogy: "Only Christ and Judas know what really happened. Judas is proud because he knows that his role was necessary in the divine drama. . . . The rewards of Christ's role as a savior, his role as a hero, depend upon or are conditioned by how Judas plays the role of betrayer. The bigger the villain the greater the hero is the message of this applied aesthetic balancing act."[21] By meeting Judas, Angelo certainly comes to terms with his feeling of betrayal. Perhaps he realizes that his actions were aesthetically necessary and set off a chain of events that would eventually turn him into a great artist. After all, his fate has been manipulated by two other great artists: Cardinal Salviati and Leonidas.

"Of Hidden Thoughts and of Heaven"

Seven years have passed between "Night Walk" and "Of Hidden Thoughts and of Heaven." Angelo has married Lucrezia, become a famous sculptor, and, in every way, seems to have taken up Leonidas's artistic mantle. Pizzuti, the puppeteer, appears suddenly for a chat after all this time. He confesses that he has fallen in love with "a great lady traveling from England," "tall like a statue," and "her hair was like red-golden silk!" (*LT,* 56). This mysterious woman with the "goddess glance," whom Pizzuti cannot name, might very well be Lady Flora Gordon of "The Cardinal's Third Tale." Angelo confesses in return that he does not know what happened between Lucrezia and Leonidas the night he spent in prison, because he has not dared to ask his wife: "For the entire being of a woman is a secret, which should be kept" (*LT,* 58). These three tales have been rather male-dominated. As the male characters philosophize and negotiate about the rules of life and art, Lucrezia has been the silent model and source of inspiration for her two husbands. Rostbøll notes that the Christian Trinity has no room for the feminine: the Father, Son, and Holy Spirit exclude the Virgin Mary, just as Lucrezia has been excluded from the deliberations of Leonidas and Angelo.[22]

Pizzuti describes a fantasy in which he imagines what happened to the thief Demas (traditionally, Dismas) when he tried to get into heaven after the crucifixion. Christ was not there to receive him, as St. Anne explained, "My grandson has been delayed, for He has found it necessary to descend into hell" (*LT,* 61). Before Christ could assume his throne in heaven, he literally had to go through hell. In a similar fashion, Angelo of "Night Walk" descends into hell, so that he can obtain the paradise of domestic bliss and artistic success. Pizzuti asks Angelo if he thinks he is going to heaven, and, in reply, Angelo pronounces a judgment upon his character in the three stories of the trilogy. The Angelo of the first story will not go to heaven: "He was too light of weight to mount so high." In retrospect, Angelo dismisses the passionate imbalances of his youth as frivolous. The Angelo of the third story will not go to heaven either: "Because he is not at all eager to go there." Having discovered harmony on earth, Angelo does not find it necessary to seek it elsewhere. The Angelo of "Night Walk," however, "will go to heaven." The Angelo that went through hell will find his way to paradise (*LT,* 62).

The English version of this tale contains a passage that is absent from the Danish, but worthy of serious contemplation. Angelo has arranged the three equestrian figures he is working on in a specific configuration: "These three tiny toy figures are placed to mark three corners of a rectangle, in which the width is to the length as the length to the sum of the two. These, you know, are the proportions of the golden section" (*LT,* 62). In "The Cloak," Leonidas enjoined Angelo never to forget the proportions of the golden section, and this shows that he has not. It also points to some interesting numerology that has been present through the entire trilogy. There were three participants in the love triangle and three stories in the trilogy. Angelo has three children, but is expecting a fourth. Lucrezia was said to represent the four elements. Pizzuti has seven fingers and seven years have elapsed between "Night Walk" and "Of Hidden Thoughts and of Heaven." Threes, fours, and sevens are important numbers in the symbolism of religion and art.

The artists who decorated and constructed Gothic cathedrals, such as the one at Chartres, practiced a type of mystical numeric symbolism. The Virgin was associated with the number seven, in part because that number is composed of three (the Holy Trinity) and four (the material world of four seasons, four elements, four directions, and four winds).[23] Thus, three represents the spiritual and four represents the physical world. Pizzuti with his seven fingers may have achieved a balance between the spiritual and the physical. Angelo after seven years has achieved a similar harmony, recalling the rules taught to him by his spiritual father while conjoining with the four elements represented by Lucrezia. Their union has been fruitful in many respects. According to the law of the golden section, three points will generate the fourth. There are three children and there will soon be four. There are three stories: Will there be a fourth? That is a "blank page" left to be filled in by our imaginations.

"Tales of Two Old Gentlemen"

In "Tales of Two Old Gentlemen," it is important to bear in mind at all times who is speaking. Our storytellers are two old aristocratic men, who have outlived their wives and look upon the world with a sense of superiority. The topic of their discussion may be seen as an elaboration of Angelo's observation in the previous tale that the nature of a woman is a secret. The two old men watch young ladies dancing, "moving with such perfect freedom in such severely regulated figures" (*LT*, 66). This image conjures in a nutshell the challenge that women met growing up in the patriarchal society of one hundred years ago. The restrictions upon them were many and the challenge was to find freedom within the boundaries laid down for them.

Matteo relates his grandfather's notion that the irrationality of the universe can be explained if one considers that God is a woman. This, of course, reiterates the standard stereotype of the irrationality of women. Men are associated with rational, ordered relationships: "tutor and pupil, or . . . commander and soldier" (*LT*, 65). Providence provides humankind with blood and tears, which Matteo claims to be the natural element for women: "What little girl will not joyously shed her blood in order to become a virgin, what bride not hers in order to become a wife, what young wife not hers to become a mother?" (*LT*, 65). One might reply, "Any number of Diana figures in Dinesen's fiction." Matteo's assumptions about women are a far cry from the tragic maiden's prayer given in "The Monkey": "From being a success at court, a happy congratulated bride, a mother of a promising family, good Lord, deliver me" (*SGT*, 142). Matteo also claims that there are no genuine female atheists. Lady Flora Gordon of "The Cardinal's Third Tale" will test this assumption as well.

The anecdote of King Alexander and the Sibylla is meant by Matteo to illustrate the irrationality of women, but, on another level, it shows a woman playing on a man's greed and getting the better of him. King Alexander wants to possess the secrets of the Sibylla and pays a high price for them. He parts with his most precious ruby in order to gain a final piece of information, but this information is the undoing of all the rest: "At the moment when you gaze in the smoke, you must not think of the left eye of a camel. To think of its right eye is dangerous enough. But to think of the left is perdition" (*LT,* 66). King Alexander was better off not knowing this part of the secret. With the admonition ringing in his ears, how can he avoid thinking of the left eye of a camel and ruining the spell? He might not have run the risk without the last piece of advice from the Sibylla.

Matteo further elaborates on the suitability of the convent education for producing a woman of the world. In the convent, everything is kept from a young woman that she will be expected to excel in once she is married: mirrors, fashion, men. He claims confidently, "But a young girl agrees with her mother, with her mother's mother and with the common, divine Mother of the Universe, that the only method of turning out a dazzling and adorable woman of the world is a convent education" (*LT,* 67). Perhaps the reader may be permitted to question this statement as much as Matteo's earlier pronouncements about women.

Matteo produces an anecdote that he feels supports his point. A nobleman marries a young girl fresh from the convent and ceremoniously gives her possession of all that he owns. At the end of this ritual, he strips his bride and turns her toward a mirror: "There . . . is the one thing of my estate solely reserved for me myself" (*LT,* 69). Matteo maintains that twenty years later, the wife of the story expressed approval of this behavior, "If you had not included in your directions that last clause of yours, I should have felt disdained and betrayed! My God, I should have been lost!" (*LT,* 69–70). On one level, the husband has not given anything away since he retains possession of his wife. The wife, however, seems to have understood the gesture as illustrating her relative importance in the household.

The final anecdote is told by Thaddeo and does not express quite Matteo's confidence in feminine submission to the whims of patriarchy. From notes left in Dinesen's papers, the story seems to have been inspired by a tale told by her Aunt Bess: "The girl . . . who was the last of nine sisters, all born . . . because the family wanted a son and heir, and who felt that a great injustice had been done her from the beginning, and that she had the power to exist in her own right."[24] This comment is illuminating because it shows the situation from the point of view of the woman, rather than filtered through the male perspectives of both Thaddeo and the woman's husband. The nobleman of Thaddeo's story marries the youngest of seven sisters, "blanks drawn by their ancient house in its lottery on life and death" (*LT,* 70). The husband is proud of how his wife blossoms, but he also expects gratitude from her for having taken her away from her spartan circumstances. When her husband finally takes her to task for the coldness she has shown him in the third year of their marriage, she responds: "Surely you will realize that to an ambitious woman it comes hard, in entering a ballroom, to know that she is entering it on the arm of a cuckold" (*LT,* 72). As Matteo's previous anecdote indicated, in this patriarchal culture, the female body is meant to be under control, not free to be disposed of by its owner. This woman has rebelled against the restrictions placed upon her and found a certain sort of freedom within these "severely regulated figures" (*LT,* 66). We assume that her husband is shocked at her ingratitude, and Matteo and Thaddeo are similarly baffled at a woman who would not accept being raised from impoverished circumstances with humility and gratitude. Dinesen's note hints at the woman's perspective: she had the right and the power to exist in her own right and not merely submit to the dictates of society.

"The Cardinal's Third Tale"

As mentioned earlier, "The Cardinal's Second Tale" is conspicuously absent from the *Albondocani* group of tales. Although Henriksen seemed to think that the stories about Angelo the artist might have been meant to hold this status, Dinesen explained to her American publisher, Robert Haas, "If the book is ever finished, there will be several chapters in between those included in 'Last Tales,' and it is for this reason that I have named two of the chapters 'The Cardinal's First—' and 'The Cardinal's Third Story,' without giving a second!" (*KBD,* 2:161). The omission is a promise for the future that could not be kept.

In "The Cardinal's Third Tale," Cardinal Salviati tells the story of Lady Flora Gordon, a wealthy Scottish noblewoman who traveled through Italy and became changed forever. Dinesen sets up her familiar north/south polarity. Lady Flora comes from the cold Protestant north, and has been brought up "in one of those North-European denominations which most of all despise and abhor beauty" (*LT,* 75). Catholic Rome, with its abundance of artwork, forms an antithesis to all that Lady Flora has known before. She adopts as her confidante the diminutive, poor and humble Father Jacopo, her opposite in many respects.

Lady Flora is herself the product of opposites. Her mother, like Lady Flora, was a woman of unusually large dimensions, and her father was a witty, small man and a libertine, who tormented his wife because of her size. Cardinal Salviati, who was also raised by two opposites, managed to produce a reconciling synthesis out of this childhood. Lady Flora also possesses traits from both her parents: her mother's size and her father's wit. The combination, however, does not seem to be a happy one. Lady Flora's traumatic childhood has made her shut herself off from any trace of an erotic life. She is a Diana figure, and is, in fact, called Diana as a nickname by her fellow inmates in the sanatorium at the end of the tale. She is a fanatic about preserving her physical integrity. Her motto is "Noli me tangere" (Do not touch me). She refuses to shake hands, shuns any conversation that takes up an erotic topic and does not blush. In Dinesen's fiction, the blush is a sign of erotic sensibilities and one of the defining traits of the blossom type. Lady Flora states, "My own oneness is my integrity. I have not married, I have taken no lover; the idea of children repels me—all because I want to be one, and alone in my skin" (*LT,* 84). Father Jacopo sees her metaphorically dressed in a heavy impenetrable armor, and wonders if secretly "she had at times vaguely desired to meet an opponent worthy of her" (*LT,* 82).

Father Jacopo patiently tries to break through Lady Flora's isolation and to convince her that she is part of the community of mankind. He brings up the point that Christ died for the sins of us all. Lady Flora rejects the doctrine of atonement: "Never in my life have I asked any human being—much less any god—to die for me, and I must insist that my own personal account be kept altogether outside this statement . . . what I have neither ordered nor paid for I will not receive" (*LT,* 87). Dinesen also treats the doctrine of atonement in "The Heroine" from *Winter's Tales,* and from passages in her letters, it appears that Dinesen was in sympathy with Lady Flora's pronouncement (*LA,* 374).

Father Jacopo eventually takes Lady Flora to San Pietro, where she is impressed by a statue of St. Peter. Evidently, this same statue may have once represented Jove, but "the thunderbolt in his hand has been replaced by the key" (*LT,* 90). Lady Flora herself was described as possessing "goddess-like dimensions" (*LT,* 74). Father Jacopo had earlier held forth upon how likeness is love: "For we love that to which we bear a likeness, and we will become like to that which we love" (*LT,* 85). In the statue of St. Peter, Lady Flora seems to have met her match, and the first chink in her armor appears.

Later in the story, Lady Flora tells the Cardinal what happened to her on her last night in Rome. She returns to gaze at the statue and imagines that it tries to speak to her. A young man goes up to kiss the statue's foot, who leaves in his wake "a smell of sweat and stable, a smell of the people" (*LT,* 98). Father Jacopo had earlier predicted, "It is by the low, rough roads of humanity; it is by the streets, lanes, and highways trudged by the feet of human beings that my high-flying lady must walk to Heaven" (*LT,* 84). Moreover, the young man is slightly built, "with a perfect gracefulness in all his movements" (*LT,* 98). Jørgen Dines

Johansen has noted that this same phrase is used to describe Lady Flora's father (*LT,* 77).[25] The sight of the young man kissing the foot of St. Peter may invoke the reconciliation of the forces that plagued Lady Flora's childhood. Lady Flora goes up to St. Peter and kisses the foot in the same spot as the young man, and, in doing so, contracts the disease that will transform her.

In an odd parody of the immaculate conception, Lady Flora contracts a venereal disease without ever having sex. Without explicitly naming the term "venereal disease," Cardinal Salviati hints at it when he remarks that the affliction is "named after the goddess of love of our own Roman ancestors" (*LT,* 94). The Latin saying that he quotes reads: "An hour with Venus, ten years with Mercury" (*LT,* 94). This alludes to the traditional use of mercury as a treatment for venereal diseases. How has this disease worked such a remarkable transformation? In one respect, it is the answer to a prayer to Cupid uttered by Prince Scipione Odesalchi at the beginning of the tale: "Sweet Cupid, God of Love, deign to let the shadow of one of your pinions fall upon our guest, for it is a disgrace to all of us that she should leave the Eternal City the same as she came!" (*LT,* 86).

Moreover, the disease has brought Lady Flora into a communion with humanity. Dinesen has embedded a naughty joke in this tale. Earlier in the story, the pious Jacopo had held forth on the theological issue of a true humanity. If one rereads the paragraph with venereal disease in mind, the significance of the whole passage changes: "But there exists a true humanity, which will ever remain a gift, and which is to be accepted by one human being as it is given to him by a fellow human. The one who gives has himself been a receiver. In this way, link by link, a chain is made from land to land and from generation to generation. Rank, wealth and nationality in this matter all go for nothing. The poor and the downtrodden can hand over the gift to kings, and kings will pass it on to their favorites at Court or to an itinerant dancer in their city. The Negro slave may give it to the slave-owner or the slave-owner to the slave. Strange and wonderful it is to consider how in such community we are bound to foreigners whom we have never seen and to dead men and women whose names we have never heard and shall never hear, more closely even than if we were all holding hands" (*LT,* 87–88). Lady Flora's disease has brought her in touch with her true humanity in a way that Jacopo had undoubtedly not foreseen.

Lady Flora has indeed changed. Before, her clothing was never embellished with ribbons or bows, but now she wears a "tasteful trimming of ribbons and lace," which indicates "the wish to charm" (*LT,* 96, 75). She now happily engages in conversations of "an amorous nature," whereas, she shunned them before (*LT,* 96). Lady Flora has also learned to blush, an indication of erotic sensibilities. Her nickname at the sanatorium is Principessa Daria, after Dromedaria. According to legend, the dromedary has been entrusted with the hundredth name of Allah: "Therefore she gazes round with pride and keeps aloof, conscious of her superiority as keeper of the secret of Allah. She says to herself: *I know the name*" (*LT,* 95). Lady Flora has the pride of the initiated. She discovered the sore on her lip in Missolonghi, curiously, the place where Lord Byron died. Byron's mother was a Gordon, thus forging an additional link with Dinesen's favorite dark romantic hero.[26] Lady Flora tells the Cardinal: "My English doctor, who accompanied me, at once diagnosed the disease and named it to me. I was not ignorant. I knew the name" (*LT,* 98). This repetition of the phrase points to a curious doubling of both theological (the name of Allah) and erotic (venereal disease) issues in this tale.

In the final lines of the story, Lady Flora looks at the sore in the mirror and thinks of Father Jacopo: "To what, I thought, does this bear a likeness? To a rose? Or to a seal?" (*LT,* 98). The reference brings our attention back to their earlier conversation about the Song of Solomon. The Song of Solomon is a notoriously ambiguous text. On one level it is an erotic love poem, but it has been harnessed for religious purposes by turning it into an allegory of the relationship between Christ and his church. As previously noted, it is not always apparent in this tale when Lady Flora and Father Jacopo are discussing theology and when they are discussing sex. Is the venereal sore like a rose of Sharon, having turned Lady Flora into an erotic blossom type? Or is it a seal?: "Set me as a seal upon thine heart, as a seal upon thine arm, for love is strong as death; jealousy is cruel as the grave" (*LT,* 86). In Lady Flora's century, venereal disease was often fatal, thus the sore becomes a seal signifying both love and death.

Dinesen on a number of occasions expressed sympathy for the character of Lady Flora. It is now well known that Dinesen suffered from syphilis which she contracted in Africa, probably from her husband Bror Blixen. At the time the story appeared, it was only a rumor. On one occasion when Dinesen sent Aage Henriksen a photograph of herself, she remarked: "I look just like Princess Dromedaria from 'The Cardinal's Third Tale'" (*KBD,* 2:203). Bjørn Poulsen once wrote to Dinesen that he found Lady Flora to be "a demonic figure, with all the demonic's aversion against being touched at all" (*KBD,* 2:11). Dinesen commented in a letter to Thorkild Bjørnvig, "Lady Flora was not demonic, she was a decent person" (*KBD,* 2:12).

"The Blank Page"

"The Blank Page" is the final tale of the *Albondocani* suite, and, in a sense, constitutes a sort of bookend to the series with "The Cardinal's First Tale." Both stories examine the art of the story. In the first tale, the highly educated and noble Cardinal Salviati holds forth on the difference between the story and the novel. In "The Blank Page," a poor, illiterate, two-hundred-year-old storyteller gives her listeners a lesson in the art of storytelling. She has told "one more than a thousand" tales, linking her with the fabled Scheherazade. The important lesson of storytelling is that "where the story-teller is loyal, eternally and unswervingly loyal to the story, there, in the end, silence will speak" (*LT,* 100). The storyteller tells a tale of a Carmelite cloister—a monastic order characterized by a vow of silence—in which the stained bridal sheets of the noble houses of Portugal are collected in a sort of art gallery. Among all the framed sheets, there is one that is completely white from corner to corner. This is the sheet that causes the nuns to "sink into deepest thought" (*LT,* 105).

On one level, Dinesen illustrates by this story the art of innuendo, at which she excels in her fiction. The technique is related to the romantic use of literary fragments, and the result is to engage the reader and to compel him or her to participate in writing the story. Dinesen seeks the "excellent and imaginative listener," like Mira Jama who happily recomposes Lincoln's tale in "The Dreamers" (*SGT,* 354). The mysteries, clues, double entendres and games of Dinesen's fiction are meant as a challenge to her readers to participate. Dinesen often falls silent at a crucial moment, trusting her reader to fill in the blanks. Examples from the *Albondocani* suite include Dinesen's refusal to name Judas in "Night Walk" or to name "venereal disease" in "The Cardinal's Third Tale." The reader must make that deduction. In the same way, it takes only three points to extrapolate the perfect artistic rectangle, according to the law of the golden section. If the original three points have been arranged properly, then the fourth point will come of itself. If the elements of the story have been arranged correctly, loyally, then the silences will speak for themselves.

In "The Blank Page," the reader is invited to create the story that led to the one sheet in the gallery remaining unstained. Some critics have happily risen to the task: "the snow-white square could mean that the bride was not a virgin, that someone had claimed *jus primae noctis,* that the marriage was not consummated, even that the bride had been visited by a god" or "Did she, perhaps, run away from the marriage bed and thereby retain her virginity intact? Did she, like Scheherazade, spend her time in bed telling stories so as to escape the fate of her predecessors? Or again, maybe the snow-white sheet above the nameless plate tells the story of a young woman who met up with an impotent husband, or of a woman who learned other erotic arts, or of a woman who consecrated herself to the nun's vow of chastity within the marriage."[27] The possibilities are limited only by the reader's imagination.

"The Blank Page" has received considerable critical attention as a text about sexuality and textuality. The connection between sexuality and narration is invoked in some of the very first lines of the tale by our storyteller: "I have told many tales . . . since that time when I first let young men tell me, myself, tales of a red rose, two smooth lily buds, and four silky, supple, deadly entwining snakes" (*LT,* 99). According to Gail Petersen, the symbols of this tale "evoke a mental image of lips, breasts and legs entwining in coitus."[28] The Danish edition adds the image of "two mountain lakes," which may perhaps be construed as eyes (*MU,* 5:341). Mark Kemp notes that, in this passage, "the man's tale signifies seduction."[29] Thus, narrative can be construed as a type of seduction.

Susan Gubar, coauthor of the feminist classic *The Madwoman in the Attic* (1979), has written a well-known article on "The Blank Page." Mustering considerable erudition, Gubar documents a prevalent theme throughout centuries of literature: "[The] model of the pen-penis writing on the virgin page participates in a long tradition identifying the author as a male who is primary and the female as his passive creation."[30] A similar sexual metaphor was undoubtedly not far from Dinesen's thoughts when she put the following double entendre into the mouth of her storyteller: "When a royal and gallant pen, in the moment of highest inspiration, has written down its tale with the rarest ink of all—where, then, may one read a still deeper, sweeter, merrier and more cruel tale than that? Upon the blank page" (*LT,* 100). The "royal and gallant pens" of the noble grooms have written their tales in the virgin blood of their brides in a moment of orgasmic inspiration. Gubar sees the blank page as a "mysterious but potent act of resistance."[31]

Christine Froula seconds this thought: "The 'blank page' of linen in the convent's gallery tells the story of escape from the patriarchal sexual economy with its fetish of virgin blood on matrimonial sheets, not only in the specific instance it memorializes but in the many which echo it in the story—Achsah, the Virgin Mary, the sisterhood, the storyteller, and the spinster."[32] Achsah (Joshua 15:17–19), from whose fields the linseeds come, shows a spark of resistance when she demands a present from her father in compensation after she has been traded away as a bride. The air-blue flax flowers on the hillside invoke the Virgin Mary at the time of the Annunciation, when she learned that she was to give birth without the help of a man. The nuns and the court spinster have withdrawn from the sexual economy of the patriarchal court, and the storyteller is a woman of sexual experience who does not seem to care who knows it.

Marianne Stecher-Hansen objects to Gubar's suggestion that there is a "feminist rage" in Dinesen's text, whereby the sex act is always seen as a "painful wounding": "Notably absent in her tale ["The Blank Page"] is the view, much cherished by Gubar's brand of feminist criticism, of woman as *victim.* Rather, there is in Dinesen's tales an implied sense of feminine superiority."[33] Indeed, both Gubar and Froula seem to "sink into deepest thought" in front of the blank page and assume that the destinies of all the other women are known and the same. The story suggests otherwise. We are told that some spectators find the marks of the Zodiac in the stains on the sheets, "or they may there find pictures from their own world of ideas: a rose [erotic awakening], a heart [love], a sword [a phallic victory]—or even a heart pierced through with a sword [love (for another?) destroyed by sex]" (*LT,* 103). In the Danish version of the tale, an additional item is added to the list: a tree [family continuance] (*MU,* 5:346). The fates of this long string of caryatids have not been the same. Some may have been martyrs, but others were reconciled to their role and may have even embraced it. Although the caryatid figure in Dinesen's fiction is not viewed with envy, she is viewed with respect, as the next tale in the collection will demonstrate.

"The Caryatids, an Unfinished Tale"

"The Caryatids, an Unfinished Tale" was "finished" in 1934, but not included in *Seven Gothic Tales.* It was published in 1938 in Danish in a Swedish magazine, and it is unlikely that Dinesen ever meant to finish it. She told Georg Svensson, the editor of the magazine, "It is best that the story ends where it does. Best for the characters and best for us. I did not dare to continue."[34] To a Danish interviewer, Dinesen said, "If Schubert could write an unfinished symphony, then I can certainly write an unfinished tale."[35] Else Cederborg suggests that the story needed to remain unfinished because a closed ending in which we find out Childerique's fate would have resulted in a moral judgment on her actions: she will be either rewarded or punished.[36] A lack of closure allows the reader to make up his or her own mind about the events of the tale and to write whatever fate seems appropriate on the blank pages of the future.

The tale begins with a scene that resembles an idyllic landscape painting. The picture includes "delicately rosy clouds . . . which might forebode thunder on the morrow" (*LT,* 107). Indeed, at the end of tale, a storm seems about to break: "Will the lightning strike in the forest of Champmeslé?" (*LT,* 151).[37] No doubt lightning, of a sort, will strike in the general vicinity of the mill. The family has been brought together for a picnic so that the men of the neighboring estates can discuss boundaries. As Susan Hardy Aiken notes: "The figure is a telling one, for the text is in every sense a 'question of . . . boundaries' and the consequences of their displacement and alteration by forces beyond the control of the patriarchal economy."[38]

The relationship between the estates of Haut-Mesnil and Champmeslé is an intricate one. Childerique's mother, Sophie, was evidently a blossom figure, like Ulrikke of "A Country Tale" or Sophie of "Sorrow-Acre." Married into the life of a caryatid, she fell in love with the owner of the neighboring estate and became his lover, thus transgressing the rules of patriarchy in order to fulfill her own erotic needs. To the eyes of the world, however, she appeared to continue as a caryatid, holding up the honor of her house, even though she gave birth to the daughter of her lover and did not produce a male heir for her husband. This is the secret that Philippe discovers as he reads through the old love letters: he and his wife are brother and sister. He burns the letters and assumes that with the destruction of those documents, the secret will remain buried in his heart forever. Philippe has failed to notice that one other person, at least, knew of the affair between his father and Sophie: the gypsy Udday, who happens to be the father of the miller's widow.

Childerique's father remarried, and his second wife gave birth to a son. Thus, Childerique and her "brother," Childeric, are not related at all. Instinctively, it appears that Childerique has an inkling of these circumstances. Her behavior towards Philippe is that of a proper wife and mother, but he does not seem to command her erotic passion: "But with the young Lord of Haut-Mesnil . . . she showed all the attributes of a passionate and jealous mistress" (*LT,* 129). Sensing that this description could lead to some misunderstandings, Dinesen clarified to her friend Birthe Andrup, "There is one thing I want to say to my various readers: Childerique is not in love with her 'brother.' An amount of coquetry and amorousness, that she has inherited from Sophie and that cannot properly be expressed toward Philippe because of their sister-and-brother relationship, is expressed toward Childeric, but it is not a deep erotic feeling. Childeric, on the other hand, loves her and turns to Simkie, because he cannot have her" (*KBD,* 2:392). Childeric is the unfortunate victim of the gypsy curse laid upon his "father and all his descendants" by Simkie's father, old Udday (*LT,* 115).

"The Caryatids" is, in large part, a tale of Childerique's psychological development. In the introductory chapter to this book and later throughout the various analyses, references have been made to four types of female characters: Dianas, witches, caryatids, and blossoms. At different points in her life, Childerique moves through all four states. As a young girl, Childerique was "a Diana of Dordogne, a kind deity, but with bow and arrows." She regretted that she had not been born a boy, and she was "unusually tall for her age." Moreover, "she had no desire to be desired," and the narrator speculates that if Actaeon has walked forthrightly up to her bathing pool, she would have invited him in for a dip. Had he played the role of the peeping-tom, she would have "enjoyed the sight of his dismembering" (*LT,* 122). As a young girl, Childerique thus has many of the traits we have seen in other female characters in Dinesen's fiction: Athena, Lady Flora, the young Malin Nat-og-Dag, and others.

Childerique has been trained to be a caryatid, named for the stone pillars of Greek architecture made in the image of women and representing, in this culture, the women of the noble houses who maintain the family honor. Childerique perhaps makes this transition with relatively little fuss, because she admires her mother and believes Sophie to have been a caryatid as well. When Childerique finally gives birth to a son and heir—the acme of a caryatid's career—"she made all the house and land of Champmeslé clap their hands at this master-stroke of hers. She wanted the child named first after his father and then after hers" (*LT,* 127). A caryatid has been raised to participate in the sacred continuance of patriarchy. Significantly, "Childerique had given up hunting after the birth of her little boy" (*LT,* 112). Having become a full-fledged caryatid, Childerique puts her Diana-ways behind her.

Childerique's stepmother is another classic caryatid, "a highly bigoted, dry woman, with little knowledge of the world or the heart, no imagination and no faculty for loving" (*LT,* 120). The Countess has clearly been warped by her upbringing as a caryatid and is metaphorically "made out of stone," but, even so, the tale does not scorn her (*LT,* 133). She possesses "a rare talent for being a friend" and shows considerable forbearance with Childerique's escapades as a young Diana (*LT,* 121). One possible derivation of the Greek term "caryatid" is "Maiden of Caryae," perhaps connected with the female dancers who performed at Caryae in honor of Diana (Artemis).[39] This might explain a caryatid's sympathy for the adventures of Diana, who, after all, is still a model of chastity.

As a defender of her family's honor, Childerique is outraged to learn that her "brother" plans to marry Simkie and bring disgrace to the family. Her anger brings her into the sphere of witchcraft. The widow at Masse-Bleue, "the mill witch," appears to deserve the name, since she can actually perform magic. Gypsies in Dinesen's fiction are attractive and wild figures outside the boundaries of the civilized world. Alkmene tries to run off with the gypsies, and Benedetta of "The Cardinal's Third Tale" threatens to do the same. Simkie is several times compared to a snake. In a sense, she is the snake that tempts Childerique to eat of the Tree of Knowledge, which may result in a fall from paradise.[40] Her mill is a dark den of magic, and she offers Childerique a three-legged chair, an appropriate tripod for the Pythia of the Delphic Oracle. As the daughter of Udday, Simkie is surely initiated into the secrets of Childerique's family tree. She knows exactly what she is doing when she suggests the wording of the spell, "a charm to turn the heart of your brother, your father's son, entirely away from the woman whom he now loves, and thinks of as his wife" (*LT,* 142). If these words are spoken, the spell will turn Philippe's heart from Childerique, not Childeric's heart from Simkie. According to Dinesen, a witch is a woman who exists "independently of a man and [has] her own center of gravity" (*DG,* 33). Simkie is feared by both Philippe and the groundskeeper, who echo each other's thoughts: "If only . . . we could get rid of the miller's widow at Masse Bleue" (*LT,* 109). She is a serious threat to the ordered lives on the estates.

Simkie gives Childerique a glimpse into the world of witchcraft and "once a woman has turned to witchcraft there is nothing in the world that can turn her off it, not love, children nor virtue" (*LT,* 115). Simkie shows Childerique a scene from the past, which Childerique mistakenly interprets as her mother meeting her father in the forest. Childerique does not yet realize that she has been shown her mother in an illicit rendezvous with Philippe's father. Childerique enjoys the vision and is captivated by the power of witchcraft. She can barely wait for tomorrow when she will participate in more spells: "how the time would be filled with longing" (*LT,* 149). Childerique's feverishness and disquiet after this experience indicate that in the untold events to come, she may very well turn to witchcraft and become a witch.

For a brief moment, during the vision and on the path home, Childerique experiences what it is like to be a blossom figure. She has taken pleasure in witnessing the act that made her mother Sophie a blossom, even though she may not have consciously recognized what she has seen. On her way home, "she thought of her husband, and for the first time in her life she felt an overwhelming longing for his embrace" (*LT,* 149). The vision has brought about an erotic awakening, but because of the secrets that surround her, Childerique's "blossom potential" does not last for long. When she does meet Philippe, "she felt disappointment and insecurity" (*LT,* 150). Perhaps the true import of the scene in the forest has begun to filter into her consciousness. Perhaps the lure of witchcraft is simply too strong.

It appears that Erik Carstens delivered a lecture on "The Caryatids" in 1958 which Dinesen was unable to attend. She asked her friend Birthe Andrup to tell her about it. Evidently, Carstens at some point questioned whether Sophie and Childerique were particularly good examples of caryatids and whether the story ought properly to be called "The Caryatids." Dinesen wrote to her friend:

> The title "The Caryatids" is defensible, even if the story's own characters should prove not to be the perfect examples of the role. It may be a matter of a discussion or a definition of the concept caryatid. If a novella or a drama was called "The Vestals," that title would not be unjustified, even if the vestals fell short in their vestal duty—one might actually expect from the beginning that something like that would happen. The designation "caryatid" is also not, in the sense that the novella makes out, so inflexible, that it might not turn out in the long run that Sophie by her power and

sweetness, despite her moral misstep, has been a caryatid for her house. Childerique takes her duty as a caryatid seriously, when she tries by all means to break her brother's relationship with Simkie. There is no departure from her duty to the idea. (*KBD*, 2:391–92)

Dinesen goes on to make a startling suggestion about one possible outcome of the tale: "But who can say for certain that Simkie could not—perhaps by being turned upside down and put in her place—become a caryatid?" (*KBD*, 2:392). That would indeed be an interesting reversal.

Torben Glahn wrote to Dinesen with some questions about "The Caryatids," including what she meant by the whole thing. Glahn suspected there was some sort of romantic connection between Childerique's family and the gypsies. Dinesen's reply to him was: "As I recall, I believe I thought something like this: there are dangerous powers that it is unsafe to tangle with, even in jest, even in friendliness and sympathy. They lash out, unexpectedly, like a grass fire that is thought to be extinguished, and a weakness, a departure from the safe path, plays us—in an unreasonable, unexpected and crazy way—into their hands. I do not believe that I thought there was any direct connection, through blood, between the noblemen's and the gypsies' world" (*KBD*, 1:578). The reader is left to determine what they think Childerique's fate will be. What price will she pay for her flirtation with the dangerous powers of witchcraft?

"Echoes"

"Yet I can tell you that the Lord likes a jest, and that a *da capo*—which means: taking the same thing over again—is a favorite jest of his," confides Pellegrina to Niccolo (*LT,* 160). Evidently, Dinesen enjoys a *da capo* as well, since she has chosen to resurrect in "Echoes" the main character of "The Dreamers," so that she might perform for us one more time. Dinesen confided to Thorkild Bjørnvig that she was Pellegrina: "The loss of her voice corresponds to my loss of the farm in Africa."[41] She did not mind letting Robert Langbaum know that "Echoes" was a fictional treatment of her relationship with the young Thorkild Bjørnvig, who later became a major Danish poet.[42] Thorkild Bjørnvig's account of their creative and turbulent friendship can be found in his book, *The Pact* (1974).

Unlike "The Dreamers," "Echoes" gives us direct access to Pellegrina's thoughts. The Pellegrina of "The Dreamers" is much more of a mystery, and the story provides only hints and glimpses of her motivation. In "Echoes," Pellegrina's thoughts and feelings are now an open book. In the first part of "Echoes," Pellegrina meets an old sailor named Niccolo, who as a young shipwrecked boy ate the right hand of the ship's chaplain in order to survive. He has not been to sea since, even though he still wakes up at night in order to see "whether it is a south wind or north wind, east or west wind" (*LT,* 162). Pellegrina feels a sort of kinship with Niccolo: "you are a traveler of my own kind" (*LT,* 158). Even so, their fates have been the opposite of each other. In his youth, Niccolo was a traveler, whose trauma at sea then fixed him in one place for sixty-five years. Pellegrina originally was fixed in one identity, but the crises of the opera house fire compelled her to become the eternal wanderer that she now is. Pellegrina is able to bring comfort to Niccolo, and, in the voice of his mother, forgives him his sins. His body shakes as though a tremendous weight had been lifted from it.

In the second part of the story, Pellegrina hears the boy Emanuele sing in church and feels that she has found her lost voice. She undertakes to train Emanuele, so that Pellegrina might sing again. At first, the two seem to possess an uncanny understanding of each other. Emanuele knows her true identity, and they appear to read each other's thoughts. A turning point occurs when Pellegrina pricks his fingers and draws three drops of blood, which she then brings to her lips for a kiss. This frightens Emanuele. Although he has the potential of becoming a great artist, another part of him is a superstitious peasant from a provincial, inbred town. He thinks that Pellegrina is a vampire who wants to drink his blood. It is possible that he fears Pellegrina means to castrate him, turn him into a *castrato,* so that Pellegrina's voice will live on for another lifetime, not only three to four years.

"The Dreamers" hinted at a subtext wherein Pellegrina, like Faust, had made a pact with demonic forces so that she could become many people. "Echoes" takes this theme up explicitly. Pellegrina tells Niccolo, "I was an angel once," indicating that she is now a fallen angel, a Lucifer (*LT,* 161). She also reflects that "she had on her forehead the mark of Cain," which affiliates her with another dark hero from romanticism. The townspeople are puzzled by the sources of her wealth and her mysterious friend who never appears. Emanuele accuses her: "You have sold your soul . . . to the Devil" (*LT,* 185). Pellegrina blithely responds, "Whatever my friend the Devil has got from me, he has got as a present" (*LT,* 185). When Emanuele throws a stone at her, she grows angry: "What is a coward's soul worth? Must you sit on that soul of yours as a young miss on her maidenhood, with all your wooden, squinting friends sitting round you, praying that it may be preserved!" (*LT,* 187).

Pellegrina feels that Emanuele was wrong when he thought she wanted to drink his blood; instead, she wanted to mingle blood, as "two friends or two lovers mix blood," as the Danish text states more specifically (*MU,* 2:312). Then in a moment of self-reflection, Pellegrina admits to herself, "And then, maybe, he was not as mistaken as all that" (*LT,* 188). Part of Pellegrina has wanted her voice back, her soul back, and to stay in only one place. What lengths might she have gone to in order to reverse the conditions of her pact with fate? She begs pardon "from the north wind, and the south wind, from the east and west wind," echoing the words of the sailor Niccolo (*LT,* 189). She has become a traveler once more.

The final lines of the tale constitute another echo. Niccolo had advised her, "One may take many liberties with God which one cannot take with men. One may allow oneself many things, toward Him, which one cannot allow oneself toward man. And, because He is God, in doing so one will even be honoring him" (*LT,* 165). When Pellegrina wanders back into the church, the congregation has been taking communion. She looks at an old woman and sees "that the wrinkled lips and toothless gums were still moving and munching a little with the consummation of the Host" (*LT,* 190). The act of communion entails the ritual consumption of the body and blood of Christ in the form of bread and wine. The first part of "Echoes" brought up the theme of cannibalism, and the second of vampirism. In communion, the eating of human flesh and the drinking of blood is turned into a holy ritual that honors God. One may not, however, take such liberties with men.

In a letter to Dinesen, Aage Henriksen responded to "Echoes" by fabulating his own story about a meeting between Pellegrina and Ahasuerus. In that story, Pellegrina asks to drink the blood of the Wandering Jew. In reply, Dinesen, very politely, felt the need to protest: "Of course, she has admitted to being a vampire, but that was under unusual circumstances and in excitement. She is, in reality, not a vampire and, in general, very much likes to avoid drinking other people's blood" (*KBD,* 2:335).

"A Country Tale"

It has been suggested that in "A Country Tale," Dinesen has returned to the subject matter of "Sorrow-Acre," in order to take up the same issues again in a way that would not elicit the negative responses that she received to her earlier tale.[43] The two stories are set more or less in the same milieu and in the same time frame and treat the historical shift from the old manorial culture to modern ways of thinking. Since "A Country Tale" was hailed by both Danish and English-speaking critics as one of the best in *Last Tales,* it appears that Dinesen succeeded. Robert Langbaum pronounced: "Its plot is the best in all Isak Dinesen."[44]

The story deals with two families, one noble and one peasant, whose roots are "too tightly intertwined" (*LT,* 235). The manor house is built on the spot where the peasant family used to have its farm. Thus, as Yvonne Sandstroem has pointed out, "the lords' house is in a very real sense built upon the ruin of the peasants."[45] In the past, one of the lords on the estate caused the death of a peasant, Linnert, by having him sit on the timber mare in the sun for hours after he had been gored by a bull. The lord's son, Eitel, has grown up feeling the shame of this deed and has wanted to make up to the peasants for the crime of his father. Eitel's wet-nurse, Lone, was the daughter of Linnert and was taken into the house by the lord's wife as an act of kindness. Twenty-five years later, Lone's own son, whom she abandoned to take care of Eitel, has been condemned to death for murder. On the eve of his execution, Lone comes to Eitel to tell him that she switched her own child with the child in the manor, and, therefore, Eitel is her son, a descendent of Linnert's and not the son of the lord. The lord's true son is now condemned to be executed.

The primary ambiguity in the tale is whether or not Lone is telling the truth. Have the children been switched or have they not? Langbaum put this question to Dinesen and as Langbaum describes, "Isak Dinesen said to me of 'Country Tale' that she began it with the idea that the boys were not changed but that the story itself seemed to tell her, as she wrote it, that the boys were changed. 'You can tell they have been changed,' she said, 'by comparing their characters to the characters of the fathers.'"[46] Langbaum seems to take the matter as settled that the children have been switched, but there is something coy about Dinesen's response. She puts herself in the position of a reader of her own tale which magically seems to have written itself. Her favorite interpretation of the tale is that the boys have been switched, but there still remains some ambiguity in the text itself.

The case for the children not being switched rests primarily on the testimony of Mamzell Paaske, who tells Eitel that Lone was not hired as a wet-nurse until after the christening, thus making Lone's tale impossible. Mamzell Paaske claims that Lone has always been a bit touched, especially during a full moon. Eitel is eager to believe her. If the boys have not been switched, do the sons take after their fathers? Young Linnert appears as strong as old Linnert. It takes three men to subdue him, which is the same number of men it took to control the bull that Linnert rode to death. Eitel's speech about his noble name, family honor, and his duties to the past make him sound the thorough aristocrat (*LT,* 199–200). When Eitel meets young Linnert for the first time, he thinks he has seen the expression on his face recently, "Was it the hard glint of triumph in Lone's face?" (*LT,* 246). If the boys have not been switched, then it is natural for Linnert to resemble his mother Lone.

The primary argument for the boys having been switched is, as Dinesen herself pointed out, the characters of Eitel and Linnert. It is possible to brush aside

Mamzell Paaske's testimony, if one assumes that she knows why Lone was there and she means to preserve the status quo. Lone makes her announcement of the switch just as Eitel's valet enters the room. It is possible he overheard and relayed the news to Mamzell Paaske who hastens to smooth things over. The expression that Eitel thinks he has seen recently could well be the smile on the portrait of the old lord that he has lately stared into. The main similarity between Eitel and old Linnert is their insistence on justice: old Linnert goes to his death insisting upon it. Despite young Linnert's impoverished condition there is something aristocratic about him. He enters into conversation with Eitel as though it were "some humble game or pastime" (*LT,* 243). This playfulness was a characteristic of the old lord, who thought he and old Linnert were playing a game with each other. Young Linnert is compared to a wild animal, "which will keep more deadly still than any domestic animal" (*LT,* 241). Dinesen is virtually quoting herself in *Out of Africa* (*OA,* 15). In that book, the wild animals are the aristocrats and the domestic beasts are the bourgeois.

Further proof of young Linnert's aristocratic nature may be found in the similarities between him and, surprisingly, Ulrikke. Like Linnert, Ulrikke "talked as if she played" (*LT,* 193). Ulrikke also knows "not shame nor remorse, nor rancor" (*LT,* 194). Similarly, young Linnert has not shown guilt or remorse for his crime and does not seem to hold it against anyone that he is to die for it. When Eitel worries about how difficult it would have been for the first farmers before the land was tamed, Ulrikke responds, "And they will . . . have had real fine hunting with those bears and those wolves" (*LT,* 193). Even on his last day on earth, young Linnert's thoughts are with the hunting he has done and could yet do in the forest. When Eitel expresses the hope that those farmers might "forget the wrongs done to them," Ulrikke replies, "Oh, yes . . . It is all a long time ago" (*LT,* 193). When Eitel tells young Linnert that Lone claims they were switched after birth, he responds similarly, "That will have been a long time ago" (*LT,* 245).[47] The echo in the Danish version is more striking since a Danish idiom has been used, "there has been both drizzle and pouring rain since that time," which might roughly correspond to "there has been a lot of water under the bridge since then" (*MU,* 5:9, 71). Ulrikke's lineage is indisputably aristocratic, and these common traits indicate that Ulrikke and young Linnert might have made a pair. They met in their youth and Linnert has clearly not forgotten her, since he has named his dog after her and, as a last request, wants to be shaved and not have his hair cut off until he is on the scaffold. Ironically, it is Eitel that Ulrikke loves, not the man that she seems closer to by nature.

The technique of using strategically repeated phrases has been with Dinesen since *Seven Gothic Tales* ("The Monkey"), but she seems particularly to relish the tactic in her later tales. The concluding scene of "A Country Tale" is especially resonant, as the two central characters recreate a crucial scene between the older generation. Young Linnert raises his hand and "the smell of it was nauseating to Eitel" (*LT,* 246). This recalls old Linnert's earlier comment "I smell no mercy on your hand" (*LT,* 206). Is it the smell of mercy that offends Eitel, or is it the humbling act to follow? Young Linnert, playing that he is the lord and Eitel the vassal who has enjoyed his estates at his pleasure, uncannily quotes the old lord's words to Linnert: "Wilt thou then . . . go down on thy knees to kiss my hand, and thank me for my mercy?" (*LT,* 246, 206). Eitel, unlike old Linnert, kisses the condemned man's hand. Why does Eitel kiss his hand? Perhaps he does it because it is the only thing he can do to give a doomed man pleasure on his last day. Perhaps it is because he has learned humility; whereas old Linnert did not at the cost of his life. The final line of the tale, which ostensibly refers to the removal of Linnert's chains so that he can scratch his lice bites—"It was well that thou didst set me loose"—fulfills a wish that Eitel had expressed earlier in the tale: "All my life I have felt my father to be a prisoner in the chains of guilt and hate, and I have believed that the moment would come when I would hear him say to me: 'It was well that you set me loose.' But when, now, will these words be spoken?" (*LT,* 210). At young Linnert's words, Eitel has, in a sense, been freed from his own chains of guilt. Justice, it seems, is a divine matter, as indicated by the inset tale "The King of Portugal." In this case, justice has been delayed a generation. The old lord could not be punished for manslaughter, but young Linnert will pay the price. Old Linnert could not compromise, but Eitel has learned to bend.

Just to complicate the relationships in this story a bit further, it might be worth considering Yvonne Sandstroem's suggestion: "The crowning joke of the whole affair is that Eitel is not only the grandson of Linnert, but the son of the Old Lord."[48] Sandstroem's argument is based on Eitel's comment, "For the maidens of that old peasant stock were cow-eyed and red-lipped . . . and my father was a lusty youth, and might have cast his eye upon a pretty girl on his own estate" (*LT,* 202). Not much mention is made of Lone's husband; she is a recent widow at the time of Eitel's birth. If Sandstroem's theory is true, then it would take a great deal of arrogance on the part of the old lord to seduce the daughter of a man whose death he had caused, and this might have created an even greater thirst for revenge in Lone. Other hints in the text that might support the idea that the men are half-brothers is the fact that both Eitel and Linnert are exactly the same height. Also, when Eitel tells Linnert that he is his milk-brother, "the word echoed through his mind, 'Brother'" (*LT,* 243). Note that it is the word "brother" and not "milk-brother" that sticks in his thoughts.

Ulrikke's role in this drama is worth some more attention. In many ways, she is the consummate blossom type. She blushes easily, is compared to both a rose and a dahlia, and is having an illicit love affair while keeping up the appearance of being a caryatid. Her costume is even appropriate, as it is "Greek in drapery like that of a dryad" (*LT,* 192). At the same time that she is a kindred spirit to young Linnert, she also forms a contrast to the guilt-ridden Eitel. She, like young Linnert, does not seem to hold a grudge for the wrongs done in the past. Ulrikke appears to have forgiven her vampire-like mother for having married her off to an older man. She has the grace to comfort her tormented mother, and her act of loosening her mother's corset—"let me undo them for you and set you loose!"—is an ironic parallel to loosening the chains from which both the old lord, young Linnert, and even Eitel have been freed. Ulrikke is easily able to absolve her mother of her past sins.

If "A Country Tale" is meant to form a parallel to "Sorrow-Acre," then Ulrikke's role in this tale will correspond to Sophie Magdalena's. Ulrikke, like Sophie, might be interpreted as symbolic of Denmark itself. Her past has been bound up with aristocratic values, but her present is linked to the young man with modern ideas of reform. It is therefore appropriate for Ulrikke to choose Eitel, just as Denmark chose to break with its feudal past and move towards its democratic future.

"Copenhagen Season"

"Copenhagen Season" (Danish title, "Ib and Adelaide") was one of the last tales to be finished for the collection and was written first in Danish. Despite Cardinal Salviati's lecture on the superiority of the story over the novel, Dinesen felt that in "Copenhagen Season" she had attempted a "short novel."[49] This story has more descriptive passages than the average Dinesen tale, and it allows the reader thorough access to the thoughts of Ib and Adelaide. Nonetheless, it still bears the hallmarks of the typical Dinesen tale: disguise, coincidence, aristocrats, and tragedy.

Dinesen described "Copenhagen Season" as "a sort of fantasy of my father as a youth."[50] Wilhelm Dinesen's clan somewhat resembled the Angels. Dinesen's father was said to have been in love with his cousin Agnes Frijs, but could not win her. The social gap between them may have played a role, as it does between Ib and Adelaide. Like Ib, Dinesen's father also went off to fight in the Franco-Prussian War. Dinesen wrote to her publisher, Robert Haas, "['Copenhagen Season'] is different from my other tales, and I do not know if you will like it. It has amused me to write down what I myself have been told as a child about conditions, individuals and happenings of my father's generation,—before knowledge of these things has been altogether lost" (*KBD*, 2:347). Even though Dinesen clearly has a close personal relationship to the material, as usual, one should be cautious about assuming too much approval of the customs described. Dinesen herself cautioned Johannes Rosendahl: "In 'Ib and Adelaide,' I think that the author's ironic attitude towards the mentality depicted by him is noticeable to a high degree" (*KBD*, 2:387).

In "Copenhagen Season," the tale "turns upon two families, which, although closely bound by blood, were still socially widely parted" (*LT*, 254). The von Galen family is noble and one of the finest families in the land. The Angels are related to the von Galen family though a young sister of the Count, but they are not, strictly speaking, noble. They are a "middle thing" between the ancient noble families that are experiencing a last historic flowering and the growing bourgeoisie. Dinesen takes the time to characterize the differences between the aristocratic and bourgeois classes, making special note of the different attitudes towards women. The aristocratic world rests upon inherited wealth and a noble name, individual talents and characteristics are immaterial. The bourgeois have earned their fortune through their own initiative, but are not allowed to display that coveted piece of metal, a family crest, upon their carriages. The women of the aristocracy are described as "supporter[s] of civilization" (*LT*, 250). The men tend to agriculture and hunting, while the women learn languages and read French novels. Although legitimacy is "the primary law and principle" of the aristocratic world, once the heir is produced, "a casual slip from virtue was condoned"; in fact, it is held that "the third or fourth child of a big house did in reality derive from the neighboring estate" (*LT*, 250–51). In contrast, among the bourgeois, the "upholding of intellectual values fell to Adam's sons" (*LT*, 249). On the other hand, "Eve was to be found at her lace pillow or her household accounts or watering the flowerpots in her windows. She was the pure and demure guardian angel of the hearth; her mental color was white and her principal virtues more passive than active" (*LT*, 249). The lot of aristocratic women seems here to be glorified somewhat more than it has been in Dinesen's other tales.

The central constellation of "Copenhagen Season" is a romantic quadrangle consisting of two sibling pairs: Leopold and Adelaide von Galen and Ib and Drude Angel. The social complexities of these relationships resemble those found in Mayne Reid's *Osceola* (1859). (Osceola was one of the first pseudonyms Dinesen took as a young writer.) In that novel, there are two brother and sister pairs: the half-caste Seminoles, Osceola and Maiimee, and the plantation owners, George and Virginia. George's love for Osceola's sister Maiimee is condoned in the novel. Even though Osceola is the hero of the story, his love for the white Virginia is thoroughly condemned, so it is fortunate he dies a hero's death. Oddly enough, the same anthropological codes apply to Copenhagen of the 1870s that applied to Florida of the 1830s. Women's hearts may move up the social ladder, but men who aspire to women above their class are social villains. It is, in some way, acceptable for Drude to run away with Leopold von Galen, even if it may mean her social ruin. Adelaide's mother has impressed upon Ib "the sad outcome of mésalliances in general" (*LT,* 265). His code of honor demands that he not compromise Adelaide; she is out of his reach. As Ib himself says, "I would rather die" (*LT,* 305). Ib quotes Victor Hugo's *Ruy Blas* (1838), which deals with another tragic outcome of a mésalliance: "My name is Ruy Blas, and I am a lackey" (*LT,* 305). The servant, Ruy Blas, is disguised as a nobleman by his evil master, in order to gain revenge upon the Queen of Spain. Ruy Blas and the queen fall in love, and, when they are tricked into meeting in an empty house, Ruy Blas kills his master and then himself, rather than compromise the queen.

Professor Sivertsen, the artist, provides the aesthetic commentary to the tale. He has predicted a future of tragedy for the Angel children. At a gathering, he holds forth on the nature of tragedy. Some of the thoughts are familiar from other Dinesen tales. God cannot experience tragedy, so tragedy is the realm of human beings, and a delight to God: "I have done well in making him, for he can make things for me which without him I cannot make" (*LT,* 275). Tragedy is a rebellion against "necessity and routine" (*LT,* 275). There is a chance, however, that mankind as it progresses may lose the ability to write a tragedy, primarily because it will have lost its sense of honor. Tragedy is as necessary to the aesthetics of human existence as the color black is in painting: "tell me whether I should possibly have got any black into the crimson and scarlet of my lobster shells, or into the greenish-gray of my oysters, if I had not seen tragedy going on all around me?" (*LT,* 277).

Part of the doom of the Angel family is that they always remain loyal to "the law of tragedy" (*LT,* 263). In his first flush of anger with Leopold at having seduced his sister, Ib wants to kill him, and he reflects that he was "in danger of committing a sin against a higher law than that broken by Leopold. He found that he could not name this supreme law, but he knew that it was there, and must be obeyed" (*LT,* 300). That law is, of course, the law of tragedy. In the end, Ib does not prevent his sister Drude from participating in her own tragedy. Later, the story explicitly states one of the tragic laws: "tragedy will allow its young maiden to sacrifice her honor to her love and with quiet eyes will consent to the ruin of Gretchen, Ophelia and Héloise" (*LT,* 304). The rule, however, does not apply to both genders: "tragedy forbids its young man to do the same thing" (*LT*, 304). Hence, Ib cannot sacrifice his honor to obtain his desire, so he rejects Adelaide and will seek a death on the battlefield. Adelaide's name may have been inspired by a poem by Friedrich von Mathisson (1761–1831), "Adelaide," set to music by Beethoven, in which the poet suffers from unrequited love and envisions his own grave in the final stanza.

Up to this point, Dinesen has followed some fairly conventional tragic plot lines, but she diverges from these traditions when she follows Adelaide from the rendezvous with Ib. Her honor has been saved at a great sacrifice, but Adelaide does not appear particularly grateful. At first, she is a woman scorned and would like vengeance. Then, Adelaide is overcome by a powerful urge to weep, which she dimly connects to the loss of a sense of smell. This harkens back to Professor Sivertsen's lecture on the loss of tragedy, which he connected to the loss of the aristocratic nose and a superior sense of smell. Professor Sivertsen might explain to her "you are in reality grieving because tragedy has gone out of your life. You have left tragedy with your friend, in the room of Rosenvænget, and you yourself, upon a flat, smooth path of life, have been handed over to comedy, to the drawing-room play or possibly to the operetta" (*LT*, 311).

There are two substantial passages in the Danish version of the story that are not included in the English. After the paragraph in which Adelaide recalls a magical summer evening with Ib and regrets that she did not kiss him (*LT*, 309), the Danish version includes an additional paragraph in which Adelaide wonders whether if she had given Ib permission to die, he might not have sent her away. She thinks it unfair that she wants Ib to live, but he can only be made happy by being sent to his death: "Life and death were mixed,—for her, death had always been the great shadow, was it possible that it could shine now? She no longer knew what it was, nor what life was, either" (*MU*, 5:155). After the paragraph in which she notes that her own path in life will be smooth, but that Ib's will be rough (*LT*, 309–10), the Danish version inserts a long section that includes a Danish poem of seven stanzas. The poem is said to be one that Adelaide composes spontaneously on her walk, though it may include the echoes of other songs she had heard before. The poem was composed by Dinesen herself. It describes the despair of a young girl who has been deserted and betrayed by her lover. Dinesen once presented this poem to Thorkild Bjørnvig for his opinion, claiming that it had been written by her nephew. Bjørnvig writes, "I found it utterly hopeless: pastiche, inversions, conventional rhymes and rhythm devoid of any tension, even though it was moving, particularly the last stanza. She took it all very nicely, considering that she had written it herself, as I found out later."[51] In "Ib and Adelaide," the poem becomes the work of an unliterary young girl, a suitably ironic context. Dinesen evidently did not feel the need to subject her English readers to it.

Adelaide is eventually able to pour out her grief in a churchyard at the grave of a sea captain named Jonas Andersen Tode. Tode's last name is ominous, invoking the German word for death. Agnes Frijs, the model for Adelaide, died of typhoid at a very young age, and Tode's name may be a delicate allusion to that fact. The inscriptions on the tombstone are slightly different in the English and Danish versions. The English inscription reads: "Loyal to his King and Country he sailed his ship steadily from coast to coast. Faithful in friendship, a helper of the afflicted, steadfast in adversity" (*LT*, 314). The captain's bourgeois stability together with the comment that Adelaide has been condemned to the realm of comedy—the preferred genre of the bourgeois—may point to a happy, but dull, bourgeois existence in the future. The Danish inscription is "I delight to do Thy will, oh my God; yea, Thy law is within my heart, Ps. 40" (*MU*, 5:163). The reference to God's law invokes the "law of tragedy." Together with Tode's ominous surname, this might lead to a darker view of Adelaide's future.

"Converse at Night in Copenhagen"

"Converse at Night in Copenhagen" was published in Danish in the journal *Heretica* in 1953 before being included in *Last Tales*. As in "The Fish" in *Winter's Tales*, "Converse at Night in Copenhagen" contains many references to people and poetry that should be part of the cultural knowledge of any well-educated Dane. Recognizing that an English audience is not as likely to be familiar with the sources, the English edition begins with a brief biography of King Christian VII (1749–1808) and the poet, Johannes Ewald (1743–81). The Danish audience is expected to know about these figures. Some allusions to Danish poetry have been cut out of the English edition to the story's detriment. Dinesen worked very hard to refine these allusions in Danish and enlisted the help of Thorkild Bjørnvig at one point.[52] If the poetic resonances were difficult to craft in Danish, they were next to impossible to recreate in English. This is one clear case in which the reading experience of the tale in Danish is superior to that of the English version, although this is not always so with her other tales.

In the initial paragraphs, Copenhagen is described as an underwater world where windows in the dark alleys "revealed themselves, like phosphoric jellyfish on the bottom of the sea" (*LT*, 315). The laughter of the nightlife is compared to "a whirlpool" and coaches are like ships on voyages (*LT*, 316). The story pays attention to two travelers in particular: "Two Copenhagen burghers . . . seemed to draw a tiny sweet wake of cinnamon and vanilla through the fluctuating swell of the alley's reek" (*LT,* 316). These characters represent bourgeois morality as they discuss profits and business, but they pause long enough to disapprove of the life of the young monarch of the country. The young king himself becomes separated from his party and waits "silent as a fish" (*LT,* 319). When he realizes that he is finally alone, he becomes "giddy or seasick with it, then it lifted him up like a wave" (*LT,* 319). After contemplating "the promised apotheosis," the king glimpses a light coming from above (*LT,* 319). It is the light coming from beneath the door of Lise and Ewald's room.

Symbolically, the room that the king comes to is a small piece of heaven. Even the furniture hints at it. "A large four-poster" in Danish is a "Himmelseng" (literally, a "heaven-bed"). The imagery and symbolic tension of the story may have been suggested to Dinesen by the first stanza of a hymn by Hans Adolph Brorson (1694–1764), the second stanza of which is quoted later in the tale. The stanza reads: "Oh, it is good to land / in the sweet harbor of Heaven / From the world's wild beaches, / from foreign lands and cities; / From robber's nests to a party of Angels / From the pig sty to the Father's arms! / Oh, it is good to land / in the sweet harbor of Heaven." Despite the several references to heaven, this is certainly an earthly heaven. Ewald refers to the place as "our little temple" where Venus and Bacchus preside (*LT,* 321). The king, the poet, and the prostitute form a sort of earthly holy trinity, representing power, art, and the erotic as holy spirit.[53] Lise, the prostitute, never says a word through the entire story, but calmly chews on her baked apple, as though she were Eve perfectly content with the Fall.

The room becomes a small stage for role-playing, dancing, and creativity. When Ewald greets the king, he calls him "Soudane Orosmane," thus identifying him with a role the king played in Voltaire's *Zaire* (1732) the previous year. Langbaum explains the designation: "Since Voltaire's Orosmane is a king and lover who is driven mad and destroyed by the moralizing force of Christianity, Ewald is saying in effect that a king and especially a Mohammedan king . . . symbolizes the kind of spirituality that has its source in the erotic instinct."[54] Many of the French quotations in the story come from this play. Further, Ewald hints that the king is like the Caliph Harun al Rashid, who visits his lowly subjects in disguise. Ewald takes the name Yorick, which is a triple allusion to the jester from Hamlet's court, the narrator of Laurence Sterne's *Sentimental Journey* (1768), and the echoes of Sterne in Ewald's own autobiography, *Life and Opinions* (1804–8), written at Rungstedlund, Dinesen's home. From time to time, Dinesen joked about being the reincarnation of Johannes Ewald.[55]

Orosmane and Yorick share a drink and the intoxication brings on some inspired conversation. Orosmane tells a salacious story from the Garden of Eden which suggests that woman pleases man best when she is down on all fours.

Yorick responds by talking about Lise and compares her to a lamb "down by the babbling brook, down in the live, green shades," which is a reference to Ewald's own verse drama *Adam and Eve* (1765), in which the Fall is seen as a fortunate occurrence. A later reference to this work has been cut: "if God wants to be held worthy . . . in law, in judgment and punishment, he would be just!" (*MU*, 5:186). Yorick goes on to wish that he were almighty, and Orosmane quotes a verse that assures him that as an absolute monarch he is almighty. He then suggests that perhaps the poet is almighty as well. We are in familiar territory when the conversation turns to the relationship between God and the artist. Yorick, the artist, yearns for a type of eternal life, but it is primarily to be remembered on earth that he seeks.

Yorick elaborates upon the concepts of *logos* and *mythos*. *Logos* (the word) is the power of creation, so, in a sense, a human being is created by *logos*. It is the task of human beings to create their own *mythos,* equated with "speech" in Yorick's lecture, but another Dinesenian term might have been used: "story" or "tale." As Yorick explains, "From His divine Logos—the creative force, the beginning—I shall work out my human mythos—the abiding substance, remembrance" (*LT*, 333). Christian VII will be remembered as one of Denmark's kings, but he will not have a *mythos,* because the historians will seek to suppress it. "Converse at Night in Copenhagen," in some way, supplies Christian VII with a *mythos,* a story. Orosmane seems to accept his destiny not to have a mythos, and he becomes "light as a bird"; whereas before he was "silent as a fish" (*LT*, 336). This lightness or defiance of the laws of gravity is a positive quality, as we have seen before in "The Poet" and "The Pearls."

The imagery shifts to that of the dance, where there is "music to the scene" and the king performs "his own solo," in which he rises, "spiritually, on tiptoe" (*LT*, 336). Later, "Yorick rose and fell into step with his partner" (*LT*, 338). Yorick tells Orosmane his thoughts when he identifies the three sources of perfect happiness: "to feel in oneself an excess of strength . . . to know for certain that you are fulfilling the will of God . . . the cessation of pain" (*LT*, 338–39). As Yorick tells Orosmane his thoughts, Orosmane speaks Ewald's poetry: "a drinking song, which rang in the halls of our palace and resounded in our streets of Copenhagen!" contains an echo of Ewald's "The Joys of Rungsted" (*LT*, 339). Orosmane goes further to quote from Ewald's "Cantata for the Coronation of Christian VII and Caroline Mathilda 1767," but this passage has been deleted from the English version (*MU*, 5:190). The two, poet and king, are becoming one, although they include Lise in their trinity. The trinity becomes a unity. When Yorick names the third perfect joy, "in a last, flying, completely weightless leap—as in the language of the ballet is called *grand jeté*—he finished off his solo" (*LT*, 339).

Earlier Orosmane had quoted the second verse of Brorson's hymn (*LT,* 332), and he does so again during this *pas de deux* (*LT,* 338). In the English version of the tale, the quotations are both identical. In the Danish version, the second quotation has been significantly altered:

> How sweet it is to taste the flavor
> Of what the house may call its own,
> And of one's due inhale the savor
> Mid those who stand before the throne.
> Oh, there [here] to see
> The Persons Three
> Is risen human's greatest favor.
>   (*LT,* 338, MU 5:189)

The verse refers to the harbor of heaven and the holy trinity to be found there. Changing the word "there" to "here" indicates the difference between a spiritual heaven and a "heaven on earth." Thus, it is a further enhancement of the religious/secular tension that has run throughout the tale.

The moment of intoxication passes and it is time for Yorick to take his leave. He suggests that they celebrate their unity by Orosmane staying with the prostitute, Lise: "King and Poet can mingle their innermost being—just as in times of old the Nordic Vikings in confirmation of sworn brotherhood—a pact of life and death—let their blood mingle, to soak into the earth's mute, bounteous womb" (*LT,* 340). On his way out, Yorick meets a party searching for the king and misdirects them, leaving the king in his heaven for a short while longer. Ewald himself heads "downwards," the direction that the king himself will take, spiritually and literally, before long (*LT,* 341).

CHAPTER 6

Anecdotes of Destiny and *Ehrengard*

The current American edition of *Anecdotes of Destiny* (originally published in 1958) has included *Ehrengard* (1963) in the volume, which can be misleading, since the two works were not originally associated. *Ehrengard* was first published as a book the year after Dinesen's death, although it had been printed as "The Secret of Rosenbad" in the *Ladies' Home Journal* in 1962. Even though not originally part of *Anecdotes of Destiny,* in tone and style *Ehrengard* is much in keeping with the collection. Three out of the four stories in *Anecdotes of Destiny* appeared in the same magazine venue as *Ehrengard,* the *Ladies' Home Journal:* "The Ring" (1950), "Babette's Feast" (1952), and "The Immortal Story" (1953). "The Diver" was published in the Danish journal *Vindrosen* in 1954. "Tempests" is the only story that appeared for the first time in the collection of 1958.

During the long hiatus between *Winter's Tales* (1942) and *Last Tales* (1957), Dinesen was in need of funds, and so she began to write for American magazines, which paid very well. To a certain extent, Dinesen adapted her style to the needs of the market. Dinesen characterized *Anecdotes of Destiny* as follows: "This is played on a lighter instrument. . . . You might say it was played on a flute, where the others were played on a violin or cello."[1] She also used a musical metaphor to describe the collection to her editor, Robert Haas: "I myself look upon them as pieces of music played on different instruments from my other stories,—say, clarinets and bassoons,—and in the manner of such compositions, they are not to be taken too seriously. But this definition does not, to my mind, necessarily affect the question of their *quality* as works of art. Even a very serious composer may be free to give himself up, from time to time, to lighter games!" (*KBD,* 2:160).

Reviewers noticed the "lightness" of the collection, but did not seem to hold it against Dinesen. Overall, the reviews in both Denmark and America have a more positive tone than the reviews for *Last Tales.* A number of critics signaled relief that *Last Tales* was not Dinesen's last collection after all. Jean Martin of *The Nation* wrote, "The *Anecdotes* is more asymmetrical, wilder and thinner than her previous *Seven Gothic Tales, Winter's Tales* and *Last Tales,* but the style is still similar to that in which the Madwoman of Chaillot might have written had she been sane and a writer."[2] Robert Glauber was particularly impressed by "Babette's Feast," claiming that it ranked "with the best Dinesen has ever written."[3]

The somewhat more streamlined plots of *Anecdotes of Destiny* seem to have made them particularly suited to adaptations into other media. Orson Welles made a film out of "The Immortal Story" in 1969, and Gabriel Axel's filmatization of "Babette's Feast" (1987) won an Oscar for best foreign film. "The Ring" was turned into an opera by Bo Holten in 1979, and Danish Television produced a film version of the same story in 1988.

"The Diver"

In the case of "The Diver," Dinesen's own reading of her story seems to be at odds with the majority of interpreters. The story falls into two parts. In the first part, the young Softa Saufe dreams of meeting the angels on wings he will construct. In the second part, the same man, now called Elnazred, has become a pearl diver and a prosperous man. Even though the two parts of the story mirror each other in a strange way, they are in opposition. One part speaks of rising and falling, while the other praises floating and being supported on all sides. Evidently, after its publication in Danish in 1954, some critics interpreted the tale as a "revolt against the pretentious idealism that Saufe, according to their opinion, personified."[4] Similarly, two of Dinesen's most attentive American readers have felt that Elnazred's way of life is valorized above Saufe's. Robert Langbaum sees the move from constructor of wings to pearl diver as a Kierkegaardian move to the realm of the finite: "the Saufe who dives has, in fact, made an advance over the Saufe who aspired to fly."[5] Susan Hardy Aiken sees Elnazred's world as a "feminine undersea world, operating outside the linear, hierarchical world of man."[6] In the context of Aiken's reading, this, too, indicates that Elnazred's realm has a more positive value. The Danish critic, Grethe Rostbøll is somewhat more neutral: "The world of the fish is depicted by the narrator just as positively as the world of the angels."[7] Only the Swedish critic, Hans Holmberg, by taking cues from Dinesen's secretary, Clara Svendsen, and from Dinesen's papers, has suggested that Saufe's winged world might have captured the author's sympathy.[8]

Dinesen expressed her own view of the tale in a letter to her friend, Birthe Andrup: "The philosophy of the cowfish is not the author's creed. It is a slightly melancholy, slightly jovial, slightly bitter complaint over the fact that *The Angelic Avengers,* far above any of my earlier books, was praised as a beautiful achievement, even as an effort on behalf of the nation. I have tried to provide you wings, but then I could not please you. Now, when I have resolutely sought the depths, you reward me with applause and prosperity. The happy diver's name among the fish, Elnazred, is an anagram of Andrézel. But in the midst of the resignation, the author nevertheless allows a glimpse of the pleasantries that *The Angelic Avengers* accorded her" (*KBD*, 2:403). With this heavy hint from the author, it may be worthwhile to see if the text itself supports Dinesen's reading. "The Diver" presents us with an instance in which the English and Danish versions are substantially different from each other. Almost a page of text is included in the Danish version that is not included in the English. The English version has over a paragraph of text that the Danish version does not have. It may be small wonder that the critics have been misdirected. It is useful to read both the Danish and English versions in tandem.

"The Diver" reintroduces two characters that link *Anecdotes of Destiny* to two of Dinesen's other collections. The story is told by Mira Jama, the storyteller who listened to Lincoln Forsner's narrative about Pellegrina in "The Dreamers" from *Seven Gothic Tales.* Saufe's plans to build wings so that he can speak to the angels is foiled by a scheme concocted by Mirza Aghai, who is apparently the same minister who sought to prevent Prince Nasrudin from finding out how his subjects truly fared in "A Consolatory Tale" of *Winter's Tales.* In "The Diver," Mirza Aghai conceives of the notion to introduce a lovely dancer, Thusmu, to the naive young theologian, who promptly mistakes her for an angel. In both cases, Mirza Aghai is concerned with preserving the status quo and fears what changes might arise if the truth were to be known.

The first part of the tale is described as "a sad tale" loved by "princes, great ladies, dancers," and "the beggars by the city walls" (*AD*, 13–14). The second part is a "tale that ends well" demanded by "the men of business and their wives" (*AD*, 14). This echoes a sentiment expressed in *Out of Africa:* "The true aristocracy and the true proletariat of the world are both in understanding with tragedy. . . . They differ in this way from the bourgeoisie of all classes, who deny tragedy, who will not tolerate it, and to whom the word of tragedy means in itself unpleasantness" (*OA,* 196–97). Throughout Dinesen's work, bourgeois values take a back seat to the aristocratic view of life. Thus, one might already begin to suspect where Dinesen's sympathies lie.

Young Saufe spends his youth trying to escape the law of gravity: he wants to fly. He studies the movements of birds, who strive to reach the heights. The risk of life in the bird world is falling, but one is blessed by the ability to see creation from above. Saufe's world is driven by hope: "For God does not create a longing or a hope without having a fulfilling reality ready for them" (*AD*, 4). Saufe is poor, but he has a "lovely face, and his unexpended vigor made him a great lover" (*AD*, 8). The "celestial understanding" that Saufe reaches with Thusmu brings him in contact with the element of fire, which, according to the hierarchy of the elements in Ovid's *Metamorphoses,* is the highest of the elements above air, water, and earth in descending order. Saufe, through his erotic relationship with Thusmu, has come into contact with the divine. He learns to appreciate his hands: "I realize that God, when He gave men hands, showed them as great a loving-kindness as if He had given them wings" (*AD,* 8). When Saufe discovers that he has been deceived, he quotes the Koran: "Taste ye pain of burning, this shall ye suffer for what your hands have done" (*AD,* 9).

The life of Elnazred is in every way opposed to the life of Saufe. He has become a pearl diver, who swims to great depths and brings up treasures from the sea. He is prosperous and is now "a pretty, fat man" (*AD,* 12). His element is water, and he associates with fish, not birds. Instead of the lovely dancer Thusmu, his cicerone is an old cowfish. The cowfish is proud of being a fish: "We fish are supported on all sides" (*AD,* 15). The fish cannot fall, and it views the world from below. There is no risk and no hope in the sea: "one may quite well float without hope, ay, that one will even float better without it. Therefore, also, our creed states that with us all hope is left out" (*AD,* 17). There is a wry echo in this fishes' creed. In Dante's *Inferno,* the gates of hell bear the inscription: "Abandon every hope, who enter here" (canto 3:9). One might infer that the fishes' existence is hell in Dinesen's view. Unlike humans, "fish have no hands, so cannot construct anything at all, and are never tempted by vain ambition to alter anything whatever in the universe of the Lord." The bird's world is characterized by change, whereas the fish live in a world of stasis. Love appears not to be a risk among the fishes, and the old cowfish offers the diver "one of my own nieces, quite unusually salty young creatures, who will never make a lover taste any pain of burning" (*AD,* 17).

The major differences between the English and Danish texts exist in the transition from one part of the story to the other. These passages contain extensive commentary on the nature of the story. In the English version of the tale, Elnazred insists that what happened to him after he left Shiraz "makes no story at all" (*AD,* 14). He repeats this assertion three more times in two short paragraphs that are not included in the Danish version. In the first part of the tale, a certain refrain was struck by Thusmu and Saufe: "For without hope one cannot dance. . . . I have no hope, and without hope you cannot fly" (*AD,* 9, 10). The Danish version adds a third item to this list when Elnazred agrees to tell Mira his story: "I would like . . . to give you something in return for a beautiful story—because it was beautiful, Mira—just as I would not want to take the hope from a young poet, because without hope, one cannot tell stories" (*MU,* 6:21). Where there is no development, risk, hope of rising or fear of falling, there can be no stories. Events are not narratable unless something happens.

Elnazred goes on to explain: "You must know . . . that after the young Softa Saufe wandered out of the town of Shiraz's gate, the last thing he wanted was to be in a story. On the contrary, this seemed to him to be the most annoying and futile thing of all, and he would have, I believe, angrily ordered any person away from him who had told our lovely story to him. It might have been difficult to stick to this principle if a lucky coincidence, or perhaps a final sensible inspiration, had not led him to the water and to the fishes' world" (*MU,* 6:21). In the Danish, Elnazred shows a small sign of regret when he asks whether or not Thusmu still dances at the rose festival. Mira informs him that within a year of his departure, Thusmu married a rich merchant. This cynical fact appears to banish whatever regret Elnazred might have had. Elnazred feels safe in the world of the fishes because he runs no risk of falling or burning or failing, and there will be no story made of him.

According to Elnazred, "fish have, because of their being and form, very little sense of or interest in stories—and you know yourself, Mira, that a story that is shaped *à la queue-de-poisson* (like the tail of a fish) is only a mediocre work" (*MU,* 6:22). A fish tail generally consists of two fins joined in the center and pointing in opposite directions. "The Diver" has two parts joined by a transition that also point in opposite directions, thus, one might infer from this metafictive comment that Dinesen has deliberately written a mediocre work. The second part of the tale (tail) "makes no story." Considering the strong esteem that the story as a genre has in Dinesen's fiction, imagine Dinesen's dismay when the majority of her critics took the second part of the story to be her new creed and valued it above the first part of the tale! As in the case of *The Angelic Avengers,* her public's view of mediocrity did not coincide with Dinesen's own.

Having been tipped as to Dinesen's thoughts about "The Diver," it is not difficult to find consistent imagery in her other tales. Dinesen's love for birds and wings has been evident throughout her authorship. The episode in *Out of Africa* when Denys takes her flying has the nature of an epiphany. Wings represent freedom in a youthful poem by that title: "In my prison my heart sings / only of wings, only of wings."[9] Dinesen's home, Rungstedlund, is now a bird sanctuary. On the other hand, the bourgeois Jensine in "The Pearls" wonders if she is "a deep-water fish that felt at home only under the pressure of existence" (*WT,* 116). In "Converse at Night in Copenhagen," Orosmane is able to move from water-world of Copenhagen and momentarily fly in the company of Yorick, the poet.

There is only one story in the fishes' realm, the story of the biblical flood. It is a curious reversal of the human view of things. For humans, the deluge was a punishment for their fallen state. For fish, it was a reward. "The Diver" ends abruptly with the maxim: *"Après nous le déluge"* (After us, the flood, *AD* 18). The Danish version has translated this phrase from the French into Danish, thus

185

it loses its allusive resonance. The line is attributed to Madame de Pompadour (1721–64), who was the mistress of Louis the XV. Through Louis, she controlled the politics of France for almost twenty years to the country's detriment. Thus, the original context of the phrase is one of self-indulgence and a lack of concern for the future. The fish are similarly content with the present and a future deluge holds no threat to them, only the humans. It is a selfish philosophy. Curiously, Madame de Pompadour's maiden name was Poisson (fish).

"Babette's Feast"

Judith Thurman tells an amusing story about the genesis of "Babette's Feast." A friend bet Dinesen that she could not write a story that would be acceptable to the *Saturday Evening Post.* Dinesen took the bet and inquired about the requirements for the market: "Write about food . . . Americans are obsessed with food."[10] "Babette's Feast" was duly written, but later rejected by the *Saturday Evening Post,* which took instead another tale which Dinesen did not esteem as highly, "Uncle Seneca," retitled "The Uncertain Heiress." The tale was further rejected by *Good Housekeeping,* who expressed the concern that the tale would only interest "those in the upper income brackets."[11] "Babette's Feast" finally found a home in the *Ladies' Home Journal.*

Heeding Mira Jama's advice—that businessmen and their wives like a tale that ends well—Dinesen wrote a comedy (*AD,* 14). Part of the comic effect comes from a familiar contrast: the cold Protestant north versus the warm Catholic south. Babette, "known all over Paris as the greatest culinary genius of the age," lands on the doorstep of two pious sisters in a small town in Norway as a refugee from the Paris Commune and becomes their maid (*AD,* 50). Her introductory letter states laconically: "Babette can cook" (*AD,* 30). Babette finds herself in foreign territory. The sisters teach her to make split cod and an ale-and-bread soup, and, during the lesson, "the Frenchwoman's face became absolutely expressionless" (*AD,* 32). One can only imagine the emotions that are being concealed. Luxurious food is a sin; only the food for the poor is important. Babette takes instruction well, and "the soup-pails and baskets acquired a new, mysterious power to stimulate and strengthen their poor and sick" (*AD,* 32). Since the sisters, Martine and Philippa, care nothing for their food, one can only imagine that the poor have benefitted from being Babette's creative outlet in this aesthetic desert.

Martine and Philippa are maiden caryatid figures, consecrated to the task of perpetuating their father's, the old Dean's, memory, but they may not be entirely made of stone. As a young woman, Martine had touched the heart of a young officer named Lorens Loewenhielm, who sat mutely at the Dean's table and, seeing that Martine was beyond his reach, left town to make a brilliant career in the military. Martine has not been unmoved by her young suitor. Later, when her young sister Philippa brings up the young man in conversation, Martine would "find other things to discuss" (*AD,* 25). Similarly, Philippa, who has a marvelous voice, is given singing lessons by the great French opera star, Achille Papin. Papin plans a splendid future for his protegé, but when they are practicing the seduction duet from *Don Giovanni,* Papin—caught up in his role—kisses Philippa. Philippa cancels all future lessons, because she was "surprised and frightened by something in her own nature" (*AD,* 28).

Babette, on the other hand, is an artist and a witch. Her kitchen has a three-legged chair, where she sits as "a Pythia on her tripod" (*AD,* 33). The same piece of furniture was owned by Simkie, the witch at Masse-Bleue in "The Caryatids," and Lise, the prostitute of "Converse at Night in Copenhagen." It is a sign of occult power. Babette suddenly wins ten thousand francs in a lottery, which is felt by the inhabitants of Berlevaag to be an "ungodly" affair, and Babette seems in possession of a "magic carpet" (*AD,* 36, 33). Babette requests that she be able to cook for them "a real French dinner" in honor of the Dean's birthday (*AD,* 37). As the time for the meal approaches, Babette is like "the bottled demon of the fairy tale," and the meal compared to a "witches' sabbath" (*AD,* 39, 40). Babette and her red-haired helper are "like some witch with her familiar spirit" (*AD,* 42).

The members of the religious sect, fearing the French dinner as something "of incalculable nature and range," agree not to speak of the food or drink at all (*AD,* 39). Lorens Loewenhielm, who is now a general and has spent several years in Paris, plans to attend and finally dominate the conversation and prove to himself that he has made the right choices in life. When Babette learns of this last guest, she "seemed pleased with the news" (*AD,* 42). Lorens Loewenhielm is necessary to the magic of the evening. Without him, Babette's feast would be the tree falling in the proverbial forest. The general is the only person at the table capable of appreciating Babette's art, and his astonishment and commentary inform the reader of what a remarkable meal it is. The general's amazement is comic, as are the responses of his fellow guests. As Tone Selboe has written, "Berlevaag's naive inhabitants behave in a worldly fashion, while the man of the world cannot conceal his surprise. Naiveté seems urbane, while urbanity becomes naive."[12] The dinner seems to reconcile many of the opposites of the story, as Ann Gossman points out: "The feast itself, then, is a kind of sacramental union of Christian righteousness with the happiness of artistic fulfillment."[13] The experience makes Lorens Loewenhielm recant the lament of his youth: "Fate is hard, and . . . in this world there are things which are impossible" (*AD,* 24).

Instead, "Grace is infinite" and "in this world anything is possible" (*AD*, 52, 54). The pious guests stumble home, drunk for the first time in their lives, and they undergo a "celestial second childhood," which is "a blessed joke" (*AD*, 55). The fact that no one wakes up until the afternoon of the next day is attributed to the snowstorm, not a hangover.

As the true artwork requires both black and white, so this little comedy needs a stroke of tragedy to create its aesthetic effect. There is something tragic and paradoxical in Babette's destiny. She has fought on the barricades against the only people who were trained to appreciate her art. The same Colonel Galliffet, who claimed to Lorens Loewenhielm, "For no woman in all Paris, my young friend, would I more willingly shed my blood," is the same man who ordered Babette's husband and son to be shot, and who executed six thousand Parisians every second day after the Commune (*AD*, 51). Her audience no longer exists. Babette has spent her ten thousand francs on the evening's dinner, so that she could perform her art one last time. Babette quotes Achille Papin: "It is terrible and unbearable to an artist . . . to be encouraged to do, to be applauded for doing, his second best. . . . Through all the world there goes one long cry from the heart of the artist: Give me leave to do my utmost!" (*AD*, 59). She is now doomed to do her second best.

Throughout the story, characters have lacked words and, occasionally, have needed to borrow them from other sources. The young Lorens Loewenhielm was not able to speak at the Dean's table, but later he borrowed the Dean's words both at court and again at Babette's feast. When Achille Papin returns to Paris, the sisters do not speak of him, since "they lacked the words with which to discuss him" (*AD*, 28). Confronted with Babette's tragedy, Philippa, who perhaps has an inkling of what it might be like to be an artist, is able to draw upon what Achille Papin wrote to her about her singing: "In Paradise you will be the great artist that God meant you to be! . . . Ah, how you will enchant the angels!" (*AD*, 59).

"Tempests"

"Tempests" was first written in Danish, and Hugh Pooley helped Dinesen translate it into English. It appears to be a story of a young girl who is torn between a life of love and domesticity and the life of a wandering artist, but not all the critics have been united about this point. When one pursues the threads of some of Dinesen's literary allusions and familiar themes, some other suggestions present themselves.

The young Malli has many of the hallmarks of a Diana figure. Like Athena from "The Monkey," she is somewhat androgynous and "her skeleton is exceptionally noble" (*AD*, 67). Malli is cast in a male role (Ariel) and mistaken for a sailor when she comes off the ship. Moreover, Herr Soerensen notices a certain lightness about her, so that with the help of William Shakespeare's words, she should be able "to do away with such a hackneyed regulation as the law of gravity" (*AD*, 68). When Malli turns into a lovely young lady, she has no sympathy for the young men who pursue her: "It is they that shall be my victims" (*AD*, 73).

Malli is in search of a father figure through much of the tale. Her own father, Alexander Ross, was a Scottish ship's captain, who married her mother and left never to return again. In his honor, Malli has been named after a poem by Robert Burns, the famous Scottish poet. Herr Soerensen, the theater director, becomes like a second father to her. In a passage left out of the English version, he refers to Malli as "my daughter" (*MU*, 6:91). Jochum Hosewinckel becomes a possible third father to her: "She felt most at ease in the company of the old shipowner. It was, she thought, because for such a long time she had been long-ing for a father" (*AD*, 86).

These three father figures represent familiar categories in Dinesen's fiction. The ship's captain, Alexander Ross, leads a life of masculine adventure like Morten De Coninck in "The Supper at Elsinore."[14] His element is the dangerous sea that is an anathema to Madam Knudsen in *Out of Africa* and other bourgeois women from Dinesen's tales. Herr Soerensen is the artist, who introduces Malli to the element of the air. The world of art to him is magical, and he wishes that life would resemble art, even to the extent that people should speak in verse. William Shakespeare is his god. Dinesen deleted Soerensen's nightly prayer from the story: "My William, who art in Elysium, hallowed be thy name. Thy kingdom come. Thy will be done, in your works as on my stage. Give me my daily bread. Lead me not into temptation, but protect me from the bourgeois spirit. For thine is the kingdom and the power and the glory, forever. Amen" (*KBD*, 2:243). Jochum Hosewinckel is the kindly bourgeois, who offers Malli comfort and financial security. His element is the earth, though he has made the sea his servant. His ancestor, Jens Aabel, was able to command the wind and the fire not to take his house and business, because he was such an honest businessman.

After Malli heroically rescues the ship and its crew, she is received warmly into the hearts and society of Christiansand. The people of the town predict a marriage between their town's most favored young man, Arndt Hosewinckel, and Malli Ross: "It was once again the happy ending, both surprising and fore-seen, to the old tale in which Cinderella marries the Prince" (*AD*, 97). As we learned in "The Diver," men of business and their wives prefer "a tale that ends well" (*AD*, 14). It is perhaps ominous that the lines that pass through Malli's mind when she realizes she is to marry Arndt are lines from *Romeo and Juliet*, a romantic tragedy (*AD*, 100). Malli is not made of the same stuff as the citizens of the town, but she is an actress and plays the role of Cinderella, even attending a ball.

What occurs that brings about the end of this otherwise perfect situation? The first disruption comes when Arndt must leave on a business trip. Malli watches him depart while she wears the same East Indian shawl her mother had worn when she watched Alexander Ross leave. Malli is being cast into the role of her mother, which she realizes with shock: "My God! . . . If it goes with him as with Father! If he never comes back!" (*AD,* 103). In the next chapter, Malli learns that Ferdinand is dead, and this is not according to the script of *The Tempest,* in which the character Ferdinand survives his shipwreck and marries the lovely Miranda. Malli's encounter with the dead Ferdinand teaches her about fear: "And I understand now, and see well, that in a human being it is beautiful to fear, and also I see clearly that the one who does not fear is all alone, and is rejected, an outcast from among people. But I, I was not in the least afraid" (*AD,* 130). Fear of loss is part of the bourgeois world, as we learned in "The Pearls," in which the bourgeois Jensine tried to teach her aristocratic husband to fear. The realm of art does not fear loss or death, since these are required by tragedy. The adventurous sailor lives every day with the possibility that his ship may go down and he may be lost.

The final blow is the passage Malli reads in Jens Aabel's Bible: "A righteous man, who has never made wrong use of his scales or his measure, showed me the door yesterday evening" (*AD,* 120). The Bible evidently opened to Isaiah 29, although Malli has chosen to quote selectively from the chapter, so that it seems to curse Ariel: "Woe to Ariel, to Ariel! . . . And thou shalt be brought down, and thou shalt speak out of the ground, . . . and thy voice shall be as of one that hath a familiar spirit, out of the ground, and thy speech shall whisper out of the dust!" (*AD,* 129). The original chapter predicts a fall for Ariel (Jerusalem), followed by restitution in that all Jerusalem's enemies will be vanquished.[15] Malli feels herself akin to the air spirit, Ariel, from Shakespeare's *The Tempest,* and she reads the passage as a rejection of her by the bourgeois household she sought to join or perhaps as a threat that she will be confined to the element of earth.

Dinesen's own words about Ariel are interesting in this context: "There is a good deal of heartlessness in this temperament,—where the heart predominates, the character feels most a home on earth where things grow and blossom; a garden and a cornfield can be so full of heart,—and Ariel was in fact rather heartless, as you can see if you read 'The Tempest' again, but so pure, compared with the earthly beings on the island, clear, honest, without reservation, transparent,— in short, like air" (*LA,* 413). Ariel is a heartless spirit of the air, and, thus, cannot thrive on land, in Christiansand, where things grow and are full of heart (and fear).

Hans Holmberg has pointed out another allusive echo in this choice of Bible passage. Dinesen held great admiration for Johanne Luise Heiberg (1812–90), who was a famous Danish actress and author. In an essay about whether or not acting is a morally defensible art, Heiberg claims that an actress must have a strong grounding in reality and even be willing to perform domestic duties: "A person cannot derive all his sustenance from art alone; it would be for him as the prophet says: 'It shall even be as when a hungry man dreameth, and behold, he eateth; but he awaketh, and his soul is empty; or as when a thirsty man dreameth, and behold, he drinketh; but he awaketh, and behold, he is faint, and his soul hath appetite.'"[16] Heiberg uses the same quotation from Isaiah 29, thus, Malli might interpret it as an admonishment against her predilection for art over life, for fantasy over reality.

Since Malli has rejected a bourgeois life symbolized by the father figure Jochum Hosewinckel, two options seem to remain to her: the sea or art. An overwhelming majority of critics believe she chooses to follow Herr Soerensen back to the theatre.[17] In a panic, Malli goes to see Soerensen and explain that she cannot stay in Christiansand. He refers to her as "my girl," and Malli clings to him and caresses him feverishly. Soerensen suggests that he cancel their performance of *The Tempest* and that the two should leave town together. He begins reciting the lines of Prospero and calls Malli back to her role of Ariel. Thus, the general consensus is that the two will continue to perform together as vagabond actors in the future. Malli thereby remains a creature of the air, who can defy gravity and dwell in a world of imagination and art. She has rejected the bourgeois existence that Soerensen sought to fend off with his nightly prayer to William Shakespeare.

Tone Selboe has made another intriguing suggestion. When Malli leaves Soerensen dressed in a cloak from her hometown, "She is in the process of returning to where she came from, not to the present mother but to the absent father—the representative of the sea, of disappearance and death."[18] At the same time that Malli has played the role of Ariel, she has not given up her identification with the sea and Alexander Ross, who, she thinks, might have been the Flying Dutchman. Malli shows herself to be the daughter of a ship's captain, when she saves the ship and all its crew: "Alexander Ross had gone down with his ship an honorable seaman. Indeed his daughter's steadfastness on the *Sofie Hosewinckel* in some mystic way became proof of this fact" (*AD*, 99). The townspeople wonder whether or not "the sea, that ever-present and ever-inscrutable supreme force, had really let go its grip of her" (*AD*, 85). She is even compared to a ghost from the sea (*AD*, 86). In her relationship with Arndt, Malli saw herself in her father's, not her mother's, role. She uses the same line her father said to her mother after she is engaged to Arndt: "Nay, let me lie here . . . This is the most fitting place of all" (*AD,* 75, 102). When she is cast into the role of her patient, long-suffering mother by Arndt's departure, she is perhaps disturbed because she is the one meant to do the leaving: "I betray them all, as Father betrayed Mother!" (*AD,* 121). She emulates her father when she leaves Arndt with a gold coin.

With these thoughts in mind, it is enlightening to review Malli's scene with Soerensen. She clings to him "like a drowning person to a piece of timber," suggesting the threat of the sea (*AD,* 119). Soerensen confesses that he, too, has left a wife who loved him and thought well of him, and Malli sees them as two of a kind: "Oh yes. . . . That is how they talk to us, that is what they believe about us" (*AD,* 122). Her feverish caressing of her mentor may be prompted by the fact that she loves him, and whomever she loves, she must leave. Selboe astutely noticed that Malli never agrees to go with Soerensen: "When will *you* be going?" (*AD,* 124, emphasis added). When the two step back into their roles of Prospero and Ariel, again, some selective quoting takes place. When Malli quotes Ariel's song, "Full fathom five my body lies," she is misquoting (*AD,* 126). The original reads: "Full fathom five thy father lies" (act 1, scene 2). Malli is envisioning herself where her father lies—at the bottom of the ocean. Soerensen then speaks the lines of Prospero which release Ariel from his service.

Tone Selboe believes that Malli is not returning to the theatre, but, instead, going to her death. When Malli goes to see Ferdinand's corpse, "Death's icy chill penetrated through her fingers; she felt it go right into her heart" (*AD,* 105). Malli identifies with Ferdinand: "Her own face the while took on the expression of the dead sailor boy's face; the two grew to resemble each other like brother and sister" (*AD,* 105). Malli is vague about her future plans in the letter to Arndt: "I belong elsewhere and must now go there" (*AD,* 131). She will be sailing away and seems to hope for a storm: "This time I shall clearly understand that it is not a play in the theatre, but it is death" (*AD,* 132). She then paraphrases her father: "I am thinking that it will be fine and great to let wave-beat cover heart-beat" (*AD,* 70, 132). She reverses Guro's final words to Arndt: "I am a lost creature [I have been saved] because I have met you and have looked at you, Arndt!" (*AD,* 89, 132). Guro, of course, met her death by drowning. Malli's final words seem bleak: "Yours upon earth faithless and rejected, but in death, in the resurrection, in eternity faithful, Malli" (*AD,* 132).

As often has been the case, the reader must decide whether Malli has chosen a life of art or a life of action ending in death. Both options have been treated favorably in Dinesen's other tales. If one believes the latter option to be true then Dinesen has once again reinvented the role of a dark romantic hero, in this case the Flying Dutchman, so that it might be played by a woman.

"The Immortal Story"

"The Immortal Story" is said to have been Dinesen's favorite tale in the volume.[19] Henrik Ljungberg has dedicated an entire book to the piece, with the enthusiastic subtitle: "About Karen Blixen's Best Tale."[20] Orson Welles himself played the role of Mr. Clay in his 1969 film adaptation of the story. One may easily see certain resonances between the role of Mr. Clay and Orson Welles's most famous role: Citizen Kane.

The germ of the tale is a sailor's anecdote that Dinesen has borrowed from Karl Larsen's "En Rigtig Sømand" (A true sailor, 1909): "It has been told from generation to generation, and the one who tells it, always claims that it has happened to him himself."[21] A sailor is invited by a rich man in a carriage to spend the night making love to his beautiful young wife, so that he may beget an heir to a fortune. According to Larsen's version, the fee for this service is "always five pounds, and that glorious sum radiates a golden shimmer throughout the entire tale."[22] According to Dinesen's version, "In the story, Mr. Clay, it is always five guineas. That is contrary to the law of demand and supply" (*AD*, 150). Dinesen has perhaps chosen five guineas, so that the single gold coin becomes an image comparable to Judas's thirty pieces of silver. An interviewer once asked Dinesen if she meant to imply by the title of her tale that it was immortal: "Not the story I have written, but the story within the story."[23] The version from oral tradition, which is an expression of a sailor's desire, is the tale that will remain immortal as long as there are sailors.

Dinesen's story revolves around four characters: Mr. Clay, Elishama Levinsky, Virginie Dupont, and Povl. Henrik Ljungberg has suggested that in the story, these four characters are related to the four elements: earth, air, fire, and water, respectively.[24] Mr. Clay's name certainly points to a connection with earth. He is a wealthy merchant of Canton, who, through the blood and sweat of his laborers, has gathered together a million pounds. Mr. Clay appears to have no imagination or sense of beauty. When his former business partner, Mr. Dupont, smashes the objects of art in his house, so that Mr. Clay will not benefit from them when he takes it over, the point is lost on Mr. Clay, who does not seem to appreciate art. When he cannot sleep at night because of his gout, his clerk reads to him out of old account books. Mr. Clay describes himself as hard and dry: "I have a distaste for the juices of the body. I do not like the sight of blood, I cannot drink milk, sweat is offensive to me, tears disgust me" (*AD*, 176). Thus, Mr. Clay possesses several qualities that are generally seen as negative in Dinesen's fiction. He is a man of business with no aesthetic sense and no sympathy for humanity.

Mr. Clay's secretary, Elishama Levinsky, is a Jew whose family was killed in the Polish Pogrom of 1848, and who, afterward, led a highly rootless and imperiled life. His name recalls the leaders of two of the tribes of Israel that wandered with Moses in the desert (Numbers 2–3). Virginie calls him "le Juif Errant" (the wandering Jew), which connects him with the other rootless loners of Dinesen's fiction, such as Pellegrina. Like Niccolo of "Echoes," Elishama likes nothing more than locking himself inside his room while locking out the world and its contingencies. He seeks comfort in numbers, which are reliable, unlike life itself. Elishama, as opposed to most of the businessmen with which he works, has no ambition: "Desire, in any form, had been washed, bleached and burnt out of him before he had learned to read" (*AD*, 140). Robert Langbaum identifies Elishama with the air spirit Ariel from Shakespeare's *The Tempest,* who "without feeling desire himself, fulfills other people's desires."[25] Elishama's connection with the air is supported by his sympathy for birds, whom he visits in their cages in a shop. Although some have been tempted to see Elishama as a soulless tool of Mr. Clay's megalomania, Dinesen's own comment about her character is worthy of note: "Among the characters, I myself like Elishama the best. Yes, he stands overall quite highly in the author's regard" (*KBD,* 2:409).

After many nights of Elishama reading account books aloud to his master, Mr. Clay asks uneasily whether there might be any other kind of books. Neither Elishama's or Mr. Clay's lives have admitted the indulgences of fiction, and the naiveté of these two worldly men is startling. The next evening Elishama brings Mr. Clay a text of a prophecy from Isaiah 35 that he has carried around for many years. Mr. Clay is disturbed to learn that the prophecy has not been fulfilled in over a thousand years and calls it foolish. Trying to bring the text into Mr. Clay's frame of reference, Elishama compares it to profit projections to attract shareholders. Mr. Clay dredges from his memory the story about which the rest of the tale will turn, but is shocked to learn from Elishama that the tale is not true. Mr. Clay has no appreciation for fiction, stories, or prophesies labeling them "pretense" or lies: "It is insane and immoral to occupy oneself with unreal things. I like facts. I shall turn this piece of make-believe into solid fact" (*AD*, 151).

Langbaum sees several connections between this story and "Tempests." In "Tempests," Malli confused reality with fiction. In this tale, Mr. Clay wants to turn fiction into reality. Mr. Clay becomes a degraded Prospero, who sends Ariel/Elishama on his errands, and tampers with the lives of Miranda/Virginie and Ferdinand/Povl. Mr. Clay assumes the role of "cosmic meddler" which has been played before by Prince Pozentiani in "Roads Round Pisa" and the Councillor in "The Poet."[26] Stories and prophecies are generated by desire, by a longing for what one does not have. Elishama wisely notes that Isaiah prophesies rain because he lives in a desert. The sailors dream of being paid for having sex with a beautiful woman, because most often they must pay for the attentions of weathered prostitutes at the docks. Mr. Clay has now become possessed of a desire: to turn fiction into fact.

To enact the immortal story, Elishama must find two more actors, the beautiful girl and the sailor, both, in their way, incarnations of desire. The young woman he locates is Virginie, whose very name suggests the sense of irony attributed to her by her father. Virginie (the virgin) is anything but that. Virginie "had been ruined by her amorous temperament and now lived only for passion" (*AD,* 154). Thus, she becomes the appropriate representative of fire in the tale. Virginie has been raised by a father with aristocratic sensibilities. This aristocratic father was the former business partner of Mr. Clay, the consummate bourgeois, who eventually ruined him financially. In attempting to recruit Virginie to play the role of the beautiful young wife, Elishama speaks to her of patterns: "Sometimes the lines of a pattern will run the other way of what you expect. As in a looking-glass. . . . But for all that it is still a pattern" (*AD,* 164). Dinesen's tales are often filled with such patterns that may only become visible at the end of the story, as in the case of "The Roads of Life" from *Out of Africa.* Virginie creates a pattern of her own when she demands a fee of three hundred guineas for her services, the same sum that caused the ruin of her father. She will also find that her playacting in the evening will return to her the youth and virginity that she had left behind her.

The young sailor, Povl, completes the pattern of the four elements in the story by representing water. As a sailor, Povl is not only connected with the watery element of the sea, but Mr. Clay also notes that Povl is "full of the juices of life," the same essences that the dry Mr. Clay despises. The young Danish sailor can keep pace running with a team of horses, whereas Mr. Clay is virtually lame. Povl is young and innocent; Mr. Clay is neither. In many ways, these two figures are completely the opposite of each other. Several other of Dinesen's tales reveal the fondness she had for sailors as representatives of a life of masculine action: Peter of "Peter and Rosa," the sailor-boy in "The Sailor-Boy's Tale," Morten in "The Supper at Elsinore," Captain Ross in "Tempests," and Captain Mærsk in "The Deluge at Norderney." Povl and Virginie are also, in many ways, opposites, but complementary opposites: masculine/feminine, north/south, proletariat/aristocrat.

The enactment of the immortal story means different things to the different characters involved. Mr. Clay is playing God and enforcing his will on reality. He thinks of Povl and Virginie as "his dolls" and "two young, strong and lusty jumping-jacks within this old hand of mine" (*AD,* 185). Closure is often followed by death in Dinesen's tales, and Elishama predicts: "This story is the end of Mr. Clay" (*AD,* 167). Both Pozentiani and the Councillor meet with death when they attempt to rearrange reality. Mr. Clay also dies when the story is complete and is described as "a jumping-jack when the hand which has pulled the strings has suddenly let them go" (*AD,* 195). Rather than the puppeteer, it appears that Mr. Clay has been a puppet of fate.

As mentioned previously, Virginie gains a sense of poetic justice in exacting three hundred guineas from Mr. Clay. Moreover, at the moment when her encounter with Povl is consummated, she feels an earthquake, which is an echo of the earthquake that struck when she first lost her virginity. In Povl's arms, she is able to feel young and innocent. Povl is being initiated into adulthood, both through the sexual encounter and his acquaintance with loss. He will sublimate his thwarted desire into a ship named "Virginie," as Morten De Coninck sailed the seas on *La Belle Eliza* in "The Supper at Elsinore." The original sailor's tale is a comedy, but the parting of Povl and Virginie echoes two romantic tragedies. When Virginie hears a bird singing and remarks, "The candles are burnt out, the night is over," she echoes lines from act 3, scene 5 of *Romeo and Juliet:* "Night's candles are burnt out." (*AD,* 191). The names of the two lovers recall another tragic tale, Bernardin de Saint Pierre's *Paul et Virginie* (1788), in which two young lovers raised in nature on a deserted island are separated forever by the destructive interventions of civilization.

It is more difficult to see what Elishama gains from his participation in events. He loses his highly prized security with the death of Mr. Clay. Still, he is able to experience the fulfillment of Isaiah's prophecy. When he finds Mr. Clay dead, Elishama quotes the words of "his Prophet": "And sorrow and sighing shall flee away" (Isaiah 36:10, *AD* 195). Another line from the prophecy might also have occurred to him: "Behold, your God will come with a vengeance" (Isaiah 35:4). When he hears the sound of Virginie's tears—the sound of a sexually experienced woman weeping like a young innocent—Elishama quotes: "In the wilderness shall waters break out, and streams in the desert. And the parched ground shall become a pool" (Isaiah 35: 6–7, *AD* 196). When Elishama leaves the house he notes: "The trees and flowers of Mr. Clay's garden were wet with dew, in the morning light they looked new and fresh, as if they had just this hour been created" (*AD,* 198). One might find here an echo of "The desert shall rejoice, and blossom as the rose" (Isaiah 35:1).[27] Perhaps the fulfillment of the prophecy, even though it has taken more than a thousand years, will help to soften some of Elishama's world-weary cynicism. The shell that Povl gives to Elishama for Virginie is another symbol of desire. It is shaped like a knee—like Virginie's knee which was their first point of physical contact—and contains the sound of the sea, the sound of desire. When Elishama puts the shell to his ear, his face gains a look of "strange, gentle, profound shock" (*AD,* 199). Although

Elishama has been described as a man who has had desire burned out of him by harsh fate, he nonetheless recognizes the sound as something he heard "long, long ago" (*AD,* 199). If the night has made a virgin out of Virginie, then, possibly, the immortal story will be able to restore to Elishama some of the humanity that the harshness of life had taken from him and reacquaint him with the creative force of desire.

"The Ring"

"The Ring" may be a short tale, but it is densely packed with symbolism. Interpreters are generally agreed that the tale describes a young woman's moment of epiphany, initiation, or coming of age, but the exact nature of the epiphany is under dispute. "The Ring" was first published in *The Ladies' Home Journal* in 1950, which suggests that the English version of the tale may be primary. There are two slight differences between the English and Danish versions, both regarding the characters' names, that may have an impact on how one chooses to interpret the story. In the Danish version, Lovisa has been dubbed Lise by her friends; whereas in the English version her husband is responsible for shortening her name to Lise (*MU,* 6:293; *AD,* 203). Tone Selboe suggests that the English version thus invites the reader to extrapolate a general diminishing of Lise in her relationship with her husband.[28] The husband's name is different in the two versions: in Danish he is Konrad, but in English he is Sigismund. Konrad is an upperclass name with an old-fashioned ring, but Sigismund leads one's thoughts to Richard Wagner's *Ring of the Niebelungs* (1848–53).[29] Wagner's ring is cursed, thus Sigismund's name hints at an ominous future for the marriage.

The story begins with an idyll. Sigismund and Lise have had to struggle for ten years in order to be together and, now, "they were wonderfully happy" (*AD,* 203). The story begins at the point when most fairy tales end with "and they lived happily ever after": "Their distant paradise had descended to earth and had proved, surprisingly, to be filled with the things of everyday life: with jesting and railleries, with breakfasts and suppers, with dogs, haymaking and sheep" (*AD,* 203).[30] Despite having been married for a week, nineteen-year-old Lise still views the world as a child. As she fulfills her limited housewifely duties, "all the time one knew one was playing" (*AD,* 203). When she hears about the trouble with the sheep thief, "she remembered Red Ridinghood's wolf, and felt a pleasant little thrill running down her spine" (*AD,* 205). If the thief is a wolf, as he is explicitly called in the tale, then Lise is a lamb dressed completely in white under a sky where "little wooly clouds" drift (*AD,* 204). The color white, of course, underscores Lise's innocence, despite the blushes at her own thoughts which indicate that Lise has been sexually initiated by her husband. Lise's innocence is spiritual, not physical.

Sigismund's dedication to his sheep places him in some rather unflattering company. In "Alkmene," the tending of sheep became a symbol for the Christian/bourgeois way of life that supplanted the pagan pastoral of erotic shepherds and shepherdesses. "The Ring" begins as a pastoral, but Sigismund becomes taken up with the health and welfare of his livestock and sends his wife on ahead, where she will experience a transforming erotic encounter with Pan (the thief) in the woods. Despite her impatience with the conversation about sheep, Lise is originally as conventional as Sigismund, if not more so. She was happy "because she could never have any secret from her husband" (*AD*, 203). When Sigismund expresses sympathy for the thief, she accuses her husband of being "a revolutionary and a danger to society!" (*AD*, 205).

Lise's decision to leave her hat behind and let her hair blow in the wind has been interpreted as a symbolic gesture through which she leaves her civilized, socialized existence behind.[31] Lise moves from the cultivated pastures into the woods. As the young Osceola, Dinesen referred to the forest as "the home of the unknown, temple of secrets, . . . symbol of the unfathomable" (*OC*, 38). Other female characters, like Emilie in "The Dreaming Child" and Alkmene, have found their true selves in the forest. Lise heads to a place which feels like "the very heart of her new home" (*AD*, 207). Lise is motivated by the childish wish to play hide-and-seek with her husband. The forest appears to be reaching for her as it grabs at her dress and hair. When she reaches the center of the grove, she comes face to face with the thief. Considering the impact the subsequent experience will have on Lise, it appears that this location in the center of the woods is symbolic of a primal, central place in Lise's psyche.

The encounter with the thief takes place in the space of four minutes and is enacted in pantomime. Scholars have interpreted a wealth of meaning into the silence of the gestures. The first move is made by the thief: "He moved his right arm till it hung down straight before him between his legs. Without lifting the hand he bent the wrist and slowly raised the point of the knife till it pointed at her throat" (*AD*, 208). Although Rolf Gaaslund sees this gesture as a symbolic murder that clears the way for Lise's spiritual rebirth, Ted Billy sees it as a symbolic erection.[32] Lise offers the thief her wedding ring, which he spurns, taking instead her handkerchief. On one level, this might be interpreted as nobility in a hunted animal, in the manner of young Linnert in "A Country Tale." The thief chooses the chivalrous token of a lady's esteem rather than robbing her. On another level, the thief spurns the symbol of a conventional, social union, and symbolically takes Lise's innocence in the form of the white handkerchief. The movement with which the thief reaches toward the hand holding the ring reenacts the scene of God giving Adam life in Michelangelo's painting in the Sistine Chapel.[33] This supports the notion that Lise is somehow being recreated. Placing the knife in the handkerchief and thrusting it into the scabbard has been seen by many as symbolic intercourse.[34] During this action, the thief's face "grew whiter till it was almost phosphorescent" (*AD,* 209). Although apparently caused the by the pain of using his broken arm, the thief's whiteness has been associated with erotic excitement and a union of the two characters who both are now white.[35]

There is little unity among scholars about how to interpret the aftermath of this encounter. The story itself says that Lise has wedded herself to "poverty, persecution, total loneliness. To the sorrows and the sinfulness of this earth" (*AD,* 210). The clear sign of Lise's transformation is that the story ends with a lie. Lise, who earlier could not imagine having any secrets from her husband, now has a secret she withholds from him. There is some disagreement about what the thief symbolizes. Some scholars feel that Lise has encountered "a hidden side of her own personality," while others suggest that the thief might actually be a sort of double for Sigismund, who, after all, expresses sympathy for the thief.[36] The character Sigmund in *The Saga of the Volsungs,* the Old Norse inspiration for Wagner's *Ring of the Niebelungs,* was a man by day and a wolf by night, suggesting perhaps a similar dual nature for Sigismund.

According to Robert Langbaum, "Only now, we are to understand, when she has this secret from her husband, is her marriage to him fully consummated."[37] On the contrary, Leif Søndergaard feels the outcome is tragic and that the experience has isolated the couple from each other forever.[38] Tone Selboe argues that the story reflects the idea that marriage as an institution is predicated on loss, "a consciousness that sexuality must be institutionalized and sublimated so that it will not appear as wild, destructive."[39] Rostbøll feels the message is that women "would rather be loved by a real man than carefully tended by a polite husband."[40] Gaaslund believes we have seen the birth of the modern woman, "a hybrid monster: feminine woman on the outside and bloody wild man on the inside."[41] Anders Westenholz feels that the experience has been liberating for Lise, who is now free of the bonds of convention in the form of the ring.[42] The ambiguities of this tale obviously leave a great deal of room for the reader's own speculations.

Ehrengard

Although *Ehrengard* was published on its own, small details connect it with other parts of Dinesen's production. Ehrengard von Schreckenstein shares a surname with Boris of "The Monkey" in *Seven Gothic Tales.* If Boris and Ehrengard come from two branches of the same family, then Boris's peccadillos as a young officer are quite out of character for the clan which is famous for its moral rectitude. Moreover, Herr Cazotte is, at one point, said to be in Rome painting the portrait of Cardinal Salviati (*AD,* 224). This reference connects the story with *Albondocani,* the great work of interconnected tales that occupied Dinesen in her final years, since Cardinal Salviati is a character who appears three times in the existing *Albondocani* stories. Ehrengard was written in English, and Dinesen never had the time to cast it into Danish herself. The Danish version has been translated by her secretary, Clara Svendsen.

Although *Ehrengard* did not appear until 1962, Dinesen had evidently written it in the early 1950s under the influence of her friendship with Kierkegaard scholar Aage Henriksen. When she submitted it to the *Ladies' Home Journal* in 1962, she suggested, "You might call it . . . 'The Seducer's Diary'—which is, of course, a quotation from Kierkegaard, but which is here to be taken ironically and might from the beginning give the reader an idea of the nature of the story."[43] *Ehrengard* consists of a playful answer to Søren Kierkegaard's "Diary of a Seducer" (1843), in which the character Johannes plots the seduction of Cordelia as an intellectual/aesthetic exercise with no thought to the consequences for her. When Dinesen sent Henriksen a copy of *Ehrengard* as early as 1952, she wrote deferentially, "It is one of the stories that I, in great need of money, have written for an American magazine. So you know that, in a way, it is a joke—will you think it a good joke?" (*KBD,* 2:118).

Dinesen formulated another imaginative response to "Diary of a Seducer" in a letter to Aage Henriksen in 1954:

> Very much occupied by your book I have read Søren Kierkegaard again, that is to say, the "Diary of the Seducer." I have not come further in this round of reading Kierkegaard. And in order to make a story of it (and because I, as you know, think that Cordelia must be permitted to exist and be a human being, and that Johannes may stand and fall with her in such a way that if she is not a human being then he is not a human being either and if she is not a heroine in a story then he is not a hero), I have imagined or the imagination has appeared with me: I am now Cordelia, or this time Cordelia is speaking. Johannes is dead. Cordelia is old, she has inherited from her aunt and does now possess her own house. Then comes a young devoted nephew, "student and poet," and brings her without an inkling of connection the diary of the seducer which has just been published (historically incorrect). She reads it and recognizes the letters, the conversations, the situation. And with the weight of the many years she is older now than he was when the diary was written, she now thinks (many different things, but among other things): "If I had known this." And at the

very last as she's comparing her sorrow to his: "Oh most unhappy! Could I have saved you? Could I have made more of you than I did?" An echo reaches Johannes's spirit and he thinks . . . ? (*KBD*, 2:243)[44]

The arrogance and pleasure of Kierkegaard's seducer is predicated on the perception of Cordelia as a passive victim of his maneuvers. Their ultimate physical union is meant to bring about the ruin of Cordelia. Dinesen looks at events from Cordelia's point of view and joins her story at a point when it is certain that her life has not been ruined after all by her experiences. Cordelia's pity for the young man she knew undercuts the arrogant triumph Johannes felt at her fall.

In *Ehrengard*, Herr Cazotte takes the role of Johannes, the seducer. He is known as "the irresistible Don Juan of his age" (*AD*, 218). He is an artist, accustomed to viewing women as passive aesthetic objects, as his "fresh and pure nudes were bought at fancy prices by the galleries" (*AD*, 218). Herr Cazotte's ideas of seduction are even more rarified that Johannes's, who views physical consummation as the mark of successful seduction: "For what does seduction mean but the ability to make, with infinite trouble, patience and perseverance, the object upon which you concentrate your mind give forth, voluntarily and enraptured, its very core and essence?" (*AD*, 219). Herr Cazotte believes this moment can be captured in a glance or a nod. Like Johannes, however, once the desired result has been achieved, Cazotte would rather not see his victim again.

The object of Cazotte's attention is Ehrengard, who is called to attend the Princess Ludmilla while a small group is attempting to conceal the embarrassingly early birth of the royal prince of the house of Fugger-Babenhausen at the estate of Rosenbad. Ehrengard is the familiar Diana type, a "young Walkyrie. Brought up in the sternest military virtues, in the vast and grim castle of Schreckenstein" (*AD*, 228). Ehrengard has been raised a strict Lutheran, thus making her seem even more out of place in the voluptuousness of the rococo idyll at Rosenbad. Dinesen, once again, presents a familiar north/south, Lutheran/Catholic opposition. Herr Cazotte artistically expounds: "If the Roman Catholic mind has a greater picturesqueness, the Lutheran mind has a steelier armature" (*AD*, 228). Cazotte determines that his seduction of Ehrengard will be achieved by making her blush. Throughout Dinesen's fiction the blush has been a sign of erotic sensibilities. To make Ehrengard, an Amazon made of marble, blush would be a sign of having awakened new erotic feelings in her.

Although Cazotte expresses himself with the same confident arrogance as Johannes, there are signs that Cazotte has misjudged his passive victim. The painter learns that Ehrengard bathes in the nude every morning at six o'clock, and he resolves to make her blush by painting in secret "The Bath of Diana" with her as model. Cazotte places himself in the position of Actaeon who spied upon

Diana taking her bath and was later torn to shreds by his own hounds. His titillation is enhanced by the feeling that he is partaking of her naked beauty without her permission. Ehrengard discovers him, but she does not set her hounds upon him. Instead, she invites him to paint her, thus laying waste to Cazotte's plans to make her blush by surprising her with a painting of her own nude body. Ehrengard has already blushed slightly when Cazotte asked her what she was thinking as they passed by a fountain of Leda and the Swan. Leda was raped by Zeus in the form of a swan, so the image in art is traditionally highly erotic. Ehrengard claims she is thinking of nothing at all, but perhaps Cazotte is wrong to believe her. They are standing by the fountain once again, when Ehrengard gives him permission to paint her. Cazotte is possibly mistaken in his presumption of Ehrengard's complete innocence.

The plot of the story thickens when the lateral branch of the house of Babenhausen contrives to convince a young peasant, Matthias, to kidnap the prince's wet nurse, who is his wife, and the child on the day before the birth is to be announced. They stop at an inn, so that Lispeth can have a chance to nurse the baby, though she is terrified and cannot tell her husband who the baby really is, lest the early birth of the royal heir be discovered. Once the child and his nurse are discovered missing, both Cazotte and Ehrengard take off in hot pursuit. Ehrengard, racing on her steed Wotan, arrives first and starts banging Mathias's head into the wall. As the coincidences of comedy would have it, Ehrengard's fiancé, to whom she has been betrothed since she was a child, is with his fellow soldiers in the inn and goes upstairs to find out what all the fuss is about. Kurt von Blittersdorf is, needless to say, surprised to find his fiancée manhandling Mathias and asks what is happening. Mathias demands that the women tell them who the child is. At this fortuitous moment, Herr Cazotte arrives and seats himself on the bed as though he were a spectator watching a piece of theater. Unable to break her vow of secrecy, Ehrengard heroically claims that the child is her own, even though she believes this means the end of her relationship with Kurt. Kurt asks her who the father of the child is, and Ehrengard declares: "Herr Cazotte is the father of my child" (*AD*, 276). The result of this declaration is charming: "At these words Herr Cazotte's blood was drawn upwards, as from the profoundest wells of his being, till it colored him all over like a transparent crimson veil" (*AD*, 276). The seducer has become the seduced. The blush he hoped to see on Ehrengard, now glows from his own face.

Since this is a comedy, Kurt and Ehrengard are eventually reconciled, but significantly Herr Cazotte has made himself scarce. He has learned that to be seduced is not just "the privilege of women," but he keeps to his edict that the seducer and the seduced should not meet again (*CV,* 220). *Ehrengard* is a seductive story. As Tone Selboe points out: "The seduction is consequently not bound to one person, but is spread out among several: the narrator seduces his reader to believe that Cazotte's seduction will take place. Cazotte himself becomes seduced by his own seduction plans. Ehrengard is seduced by her infatuation for a newborn baby into doing her utmost for the baby's sake. The nurse, Lisbeth, lets herself be seduced by her husband to say things she should not. The husband, on his side, is seduced by jealousy and a wish for honor and status, etc."[45] Dinesen claimed that *Ehrengard* was written as a joke, and part of the joke is on us, the readers. We are seduced to believe in the passivity of Ehrengard and her ultimate conquest by Cazotte. It is pleasantly surprising to learn that our expectations are wrong.

Notes

Chapter 1: Understanding Isak Dinesen

1. Susan Hardy Aiken, *Isak Dinesen and the Engendering of Narrative* (Chicago: University of Chicago Press, 1990), xxiv.

2. Thanks to Rachid Oenniche, who helped me with my limping French, and Niels and Faith Ingwersen, who answered many questions on the nuances of Danish. Any errors in translation are my fault, not theirs.

3. Danielle Gilles, "Karen Blixen ou la Pharaonne de Rungstedlund," *Revue général belge* 99 (1963): 56.

4. Robert Langbaum, *Isak Dinesen's Art: The Gayety of Vision* (Chicago: University of Chicago Press, 1975), 25.

5. Hans Brix, *Karen Blixens Eventyr* (Copenhagen: Gyldendal, 1949), 170; Eric O. Johannesson, *The World of Isak Dinesen* (Seattle: University of Washington Press, 1961), 47; and Donald Hannah, *Isak Dinesen and Karen Blixen: The Mask and the Reality* (New York: Random House, 1971), 159—to name a few of those critics.

6. Jørgen Gustava Brandt, "Et Essay om Karen Blixen II," *Heretica* 6, no. 3 (1953): 302.

7. Christian Elling, *Karen Blixen* (Viby: Strubes, 1976), 25.

8. Gilles, "Karen Blixen," 57.

9. See, for example, Else Gress, "Karen Blixen," in *Danske digtere i det 20. århundrede,* vol. 3, ed. Torben Brostrøm and Mette Winge (Copenhagen: Gads, 1980), 21.

10. Eugene Walter, "Isak Dinesen Conquers Rome," *Harper's Magazine,* February 1965, 48.

11. Niels Birger Wamberg, *Samtaler med danske Digtere* (Copenhagen: Gyldendal, 1968), 42.

12. Erik Egeland, *Ansikt til Ansikt* (Oslo: Gyldendal Norsk Forlag, 1969), 93. Harry Martinson, the friend quoted in this passage, is a Nobel laureate and one of Sweden's premier modernists.

13. Note the title of Langbaum's book, *Isak Dinesen's Art: The Gayety of Vision.* See also: *Karen Blixen i Danmark: Breve, 1931–62,* vol. 1, 383–84.

14. Eugene Walter, "Isak Dinesen," *Paris Review* 14 (autumn 1956): 56.

15. Harald Nielsen, *Karen Blixen: Studie i litterær Mystik* (Copenhagen: Borgens Forlag, 1956), 46.

16. Hans Brix, "Mod er Menneskets Svar paa Livet," *Berlingske Aftenavis,* 21 Sept. 1942.

17. Marcia Landy, "Anecdote as Destiny: Isak Dinesen and the Storyteller," *Massachusetts Review* (spring 1978): 390.

18. Gilles, "Karen Blixen," 57.

19. Annamarie Cleemann, "Karen Blixen fortæller," *Samleren* 19 (1942): 35.

20. Grethe Rostbøll, *Længslens vingeslag* (Copenhagen: Gyldendal, 1996), 11–12.

21. Else Cederborg, introduction to *On Modern Marriage and Other Observations,* by Karen Blixen, trans. Anne Born (London: Fourth Estate, 1987), 14.

22. Langbaum, *Isak Dinesen's Art,* 76.

23. See, among others, Marianne Juhl and Bo Hakon Jørgensen, *Dianas Hævn* (Odense: Odense Universitetsforlag, 1981), translated as *Diana's Revenge* by Anne Born (Odense: Odense University Press, 1985); Sara Stambaugh, *The Witch and the Goddess in the Stories of Isak Dinesen* (Ann Arbor: UMI Research Press, 1988); Robin Lydenberg, "Against the Law of Gravity: Female Adolescence in Isak Dinesen's *Seven Gothic Tales,*" *Modern Fiction Studies* 24, no. 4 (winter 1978–79): 521–52; Annelies van Hees, "Karen Blixen og heksene," *Tijdschrift voor Skandinavistiek* 1, no. 1 (1980): 76–107; and Susan Brantly, "Karen Blixen: Häxor, Kariatyder och Blommor," *Tijdschrift voor Skandinavistiek* 3, no. 1 (1982): 79–94.

24. Aiken, *Dinesen and Engendering of Narrative,* 80.

25. Vidi, "Giv dette Folk endnu to Hundred Aars Fred!," *Politiken,* 3 October 1937.

Chapter 2: *Seven Gothic Tales*

1. Ole Wivel, *Karen Blixen: Et uafsluttet selvopgør* (Copenhagen: Aldus, 1987), 94.

2. Valdemar Rørdam, interview, *Berlingske Tidende,* 16 May 1934.

3. Ibid.

4. Elias Bredsdorff, "Isak Dinesen v. Karen Blixen: *Seven Gothic Tales* (1934) and *Syv fantastiske Fortællinger* (1935)," in *Facets of European Modernism,* ed. Janet Garton (Norwich: University of East Anglia, 1985), 275–93.

5. Lewis Gannett, "Books and Things," *New York Herald Tribune,* 9 April 1934: 13.

6. Jenny Ballou, "These Magic Tales Have an Air of Genius," *New York Herald Tribune Books,* 8 April 1934, VII: 3.

7. Howard Spring, *Evening Standard,* 6 Sept. 1934.

8. Gerald Gould, *Observer,* 9 Sept. 1934.

9. Scap, "Hyldest til Isak Dinesen," *Politiken,* 3 Dec. 1935; and Mario Grut, "Trana i sparvedansen," *Aftonbladet,* 13 Oct. 1958.

10. Frederik Schyberg, "Isak Dinesens, alias, Baronesse Blixen-Fineckes *Syv fantastiske Fortællinger,*" *Berlingske Tidende,* 25 Nov. 1935.

11. Svend Borberg, "Isak Dinesen–Karen Blixen," *Politiken,* 9 March 1936.

12. Vidi, interview, *Politiken,* 1 May 1934.

13. Ibid.

14. Susan Hardy Aiken, *Isak Dinesen and the Engendering of Narrative* (Chicago: University of Chicago Press, 1990), 70.

15. William Maxwell, "Suffused with a Melancholy Light," *New York Times Book Review,* 9 May 1943: 2.

16. Curtis Cate, "Isak Dinesen," *Atlantic Monthly,* December 1959, 153.

17. Eric O. Johannesson, *The World of Isak Dinesen* (Seattle: University of Washington Press, 1961), 28.

18. Sibyl James, "Gothic Transformations: Isak Dinesen and the Gothic," in *The Female Gothic,* ed. Juliann E. Fleenor (Montreal: Eden Press, 1983), 138–52.

19. Vidi, interview, *Politiken,* 1 May 1934.

20. Eric O. Johannesson, "Isak Dinesen, Søren Kierkegaard, and the Present Age," *Books Abroad,* winter 1962, 20–24.

21. Aiken, *Dinesen and Engendering of Narrative,* 88.

22. Pointed out to me by George C. Schoolfield.

23. Aiken, *Dinesen and Engendering of Narrative,* 94.

24. Robert Langbaum, *Isak Dinesen's Art: The Gayety of Vision* (Chicago: University of Chicago Press, 1975), 62.

25. Aiken, *Dinesen and Engendering of Narrative,* 107.

26. Marilyn Johns Blackwell, "The Transforming Gaze: Identity and Sexuality in the Works of Isak Dinesen," *Scandinavian Studies* 63, no. 1 (1991): 58.

27. Aiken, *Dinesen and Engendering of Narrative,* 106.

28. Aage Henriksen, "A Portrait of Karen Blixen," *Orbis Litterarum,* 22, nos. 1–4 (1967): 338.

29. The original quote may be found in Adam Oehlenschläger, *Poetiske Skrifter,* vol. 4, ed. F. L. Liebenberg (Copenhagen, 1858), 206.

30. Hans Holmberg, *Ingen skygge uden lys* (Copenhagen: C. A. Reitzels Forlag, 1995), 15–23.

31. Langbaum, *Isak Dinesen's Art,* 66.

32. Hannah, *Mask and Reality,* 166.

33. Elisabeth Bronfen, "'Scheherazade sah den Morgen dämmern und schwieg diskret': Zu der Beziehung zwischen Erzählen und Tod in den Geschichten von Isak Dinesen (Karen Blixen)," *Skandinavistik* 16, no. 1 (1986): 48–62.

34. Hans Brix, *Karen Blixens Eventyr* (Copenhagen: Gyldendal, 1949), 50.

35. In her later years, Dinesen sometimes asked people which poet they would like to sleep with. Dinesen's own answer to the question was, "For my own part, I think I would choose Aarestrup. . . . I wouldn't have any trouble with him afterward" (Ole Wivel, "Letsind og tungsind," *Dansk udsyn,* 55 [1973]: 166). Perhaps Aarestrup would not have caused any trouble because, despite the steamy eroticism of his poetry, he was a happily married man and father of twelve. Dinesen evidently tried this question out in the United States. To Jean Stafford, she responded, "A Danish poet you wouldn't know" (Jean Stafford, "Isak Dinesen: Master Teller of Tales," *Horizon* 2, no. 1 [Sept. 1959]: 112).

36. Susanne Fabricius, "Vandrende riddere og knuste kvinder," *Kritik* 22 (1972): 72.

37. Gurli Woods, "Lilith and Gender Equality," in *Isak Dinesen and Narrativity*, ed. Gurli Woods (Ottawa: Carleton University Press, 1994), 57.

38. Grethe F. Rostbøll, *Længslens vingeslag* (Copenhagen: Gyldendal, 1996), 37.

39. Thomas Whissen, "The Magic Circle: The Role of the Prostitute in Isak Dinesen's Gothic Tales," in *The Image of the Prostitute in Modern Literature*, ed. Pierre L. Horn and Mary Beth Pringle (New York: Frederick Ungar Publishing, 1984), 50.

40. Søren Kierkegaard, *Either/Or*, vol. 1, trans. David F. Swenson and Lillian Marvin Swenson (Princeton: Princeton University Press, 1971), 68.

41. Johannesson, *The World of Isak Dinesen*, 97.

42. Sara Stambaugh, *The Witch and the Goddess in the Stories of Isak Dinesen* (Ann Arbor: UMI Research Press, 1988), 6.

43. Emil Aarestrup, *Samlede Skrifter*, ed. Hans Brix and Palle Raunkjær (Copenhagen: Henrik Koppels Forlag, 1922), vol. 2, 197.

44. Woods, "Lilith," 58.

45. Ibid., 57.

46. Rostbøll, *Længslens vingeslag*, 39.

47. Aarestrup, *Samlede Skrifter*, vol. 2, 189.

48. Fabricius, "Vandrende riddere," 71.

49. Aiken, *Dinesen and Engendering of Narrative*, 119.

50. Marianne Juhl and Bo Hakon Jørgensen, *Dianas Hævn* (Odense: Odense Universitetsforlag, 1981), 57, 64.

51. Fabricius, "Vandrende riddere," 72.

52. Aiken, *Dinesen and Engendering of Narrative*, 119.

53. Tom Kristensen, "Hekse, herremænd og husjomfruer," *Politiken*, 3 March 1951.

54. Brix, *Eventyr*, 46.

55. Harald Nielsen, *Karen Blixen: Studie i litterær Mystik* (Copenhagen: Borgens Forlag, 1956), 53.

56. Johannesson, *The World of Isak Dinesen*, 29.

57. George C. Schoolfield pointed out to me that another text along similar lines is Aino Kallas's (1878–1956) *Sudenmorsian* (1928), which was translated into English as *The Wolf's Bride* (1930), and was widely reviewed. In that tale, a forester's wife turns into a wolf.

58. Brix, *Eventyr*, 65.

59. Pointed out to me by George C. Schoolfield.

60. Bernhard Severin Ingemann, *Samlede Skrifter*, vol. 12 (Copenhagen: C. A. Reitzels Forlag, 1872), 208.

61. Ibid.

62. Langbaum, *Isak Dinesen's Art*, 88.

63. Juhl and Jørgensen, *Dianas Hævn*, 49.

64. William Mishler, "Parents and Children, Brothers and Sisters in Isak Dinesen's 'The Monkey,'" *Scandinavian Studies* 57, no. 4 (autumn 1985): 425.

65. Dag Heede, "Gender Trouble in Isak Dinesen's 'The Monkey,'" in *Karen*

Blixen—Out of Denmark: Papers from a Colloquium at the Karen Blixen Museum, April 1997 (Copenhagen, 1998), 116.

66. Ibid., 110.

67. Ibid., 112.

68. Mishler, "Parents and Children," 426.

69. Annelies van Hees, "Hemmeligheder i Karen Blixens 'Aben,'" *Edda,* 1984, no. 1: 9–24.

70. Mishler, "Parents and Children," 433; Robert S. Phillips, "Dinesen's 'Monkey' and McCuller's 'Ballad': A Study in Literary Affinity," *Studies in Short Fiction* 1 (1963–64): 73.

71. Robin Lyndenberg, "Against the Law of Gravity: Female Adolescence in Isak Dinesen's *Seven Gothic Tales,*" *Modern Fiction Studies* 24, no. 4 (winter 1978–79): 523.

72. Van Hees, "Hemmeligheder," 16.

73. Rostbøll, *Længslens vingeslag,* 55; Anders Westenholz, *Den glemte abe* (Copenhagen: Gyldendal, 1985), 109.

74. Brix, *Eventyr,* 69.

75. Langbaum, *Gayety of Vision,* 88.

76. Juhl and Jørgensen, *Dianas Hævn,* 51; Vibeke Schröder, *Selvrealisation og selvfortolkning i Karen Blixens forfatterskab* (Copenhagen: Gyldendal, 1979), 82.

77. Mishler, "Parents and Children," 449.

78. Van Hees, "Hemmeligheder," 22.

79. Heede, "Parents and Children," 121.

80. Morten Kyndrup, "The Vertigo of Staging: Authority and Narration in Isak Dinesen's 'The Roads Round Pisa,'" in *Isak Dinesen: Critical Views,* ed. Olga Pelensky (Athens: Ohio University Press, 1993), 334.

81. Casey Bjerregaard Black, "The Phenomenon of Intertextuality and the Role of Androgyny in Isak Dinesen's 'The Roads Round Pisa,'" in *Isak Dinesen and Narrativity,* ed. Gurli Woods (Ottowa: Carleton University Press, 1994), 180–92.

82. Aiken, *Dinesen and Engendering of Narrative,* 161.

83. Else Brundbjerg, *Kvinden, kætteren, kunstneren: Karen Blixen* (Charlottenlund: KnowWare, 1995), 123.

84. *Blixeniana 1980,* ed. Hans Andersen and Frans Lasson (Copenhagen: Karen Blixen Selskabet, 1980), 41. Schimmelman is also a well-known name in Danish history. Heinrich Schimmelman (1724–82) was considered a financial genius and was ennobled by the Danish crown in gratitude for his economic advice. His son, Ernst Schimmelman (1747–1831), followed in his father's footsteps and became the Danish finance minister. Dinesen's point in choosing this name may be that Augustus's family has not been aristocratic for sufficient generations to endow him with the true aristocratic spirit. Moreover, the family's association with economics and business makes them further suspect in the context of Dinesen's fiction.

85. Helene Høyrup, "The Arabesque of Existence: Existential Focus and Aesthetic Form in Isak Dinesen's 'The Roads Round Pisa,'" *Scandinavica* 24, no. 2 (1985): 200.

86. Hannah, *Mask and Reality,* 140.

87. Aage Henriksen, "Karen Blixen og marionetterne," in *Det guddommelige barn og andre essays om Karen Blixen* (Copenhagen: Gyldendal, 1965), 10–11.

88. Hannah, *Mask and Reality,* 119.

89. Although the inspiration for this metafictional moment has been traced to Pirandello, Dinesen probably got the idea first from Johan Ludvig Heiberg's *Julespøg og nytårsløjer* (1818, Christmas jests and New Year's games), in which Harlequin briefly takes control of the play away from the Poet in a similar manner. Dinesen seems to have recognized in Pirandello a kindred spirit.

90. Hannah, *Mask and Reality,* 124.

91. Aiken, *Dinesen and Engendering of Narrative,* 168.

92. Black, "Intertextuality and the Role of Androgyny," 191.

93. Holmberg, *Ingen skygge uden lys,* 110.

94. Bent Mohn, "Orson Welles i Paris," *Politiken,* 9 Oct. 1969.

95. Annelies van Hees, "Karen Blixen: 'Et Familieselskab i Helsingør'—en motivhistorisk og dybdepsykologisk studie," *Meddelelser fra Dansklærerforeningen,* September 1979, 152.

96. Aiken, *Dinesen and Engendering of Narrative,* 179.

97. Van Hees, "Karen Blixen: 'Et Familieselskab i Helsingør,'" 164.

98. Langbaum, *Isak Dinesen's Art,* 92.

99. Brix, *Eventyr,* 98.

100. Aarestrup, *Samlede Skrifter,* vol. 3, 47.

101. Thorkild Bjørnvig, "Who Am I? The Story of Isak Dinesen's Identity," in *Isak Dinesen: Critical Views,* ed. Olga Pelensky (Athens: Ohio University Press, 1993), 210.

102. Gargi Roysircar Sodowsky and Roland Sodowsky, "Myriad Possibilities in Isak Dinesen's 'The Dreamers': An Existential Interpretation," in *Creative and Critical Approaches to the Short Story,* ed. Noel Harold Kaylor, Jr. (Lewiston: Edwin Mellen Press, 1997), 330.

103. Anthony Stephens, "Narrative Structures in Karen Blixen's 'The Dreamers,'" in *Festschrift for Ralph Farrell,* ed. Anthony Stephens et al. (Las Vegas and Frankfurt: Peter Lang, 1977), 133.

104. Judith Thurman, *Isak Dinesen: The Life of a Storyteller* (New York: St. Martin's Press, 1982), 188.

105. Aiken, *Dinesen and Engendering of Narrative,* 55.

106. Peter L. Thorslev, Jr., *The Byronic Hero: Types and Prototypes* (Minneapolis: University of Minnesota Press, 1962), 66.

107. Juhl and Jørgensen, *Dianas Hævn,* 156.

108. Thorslev, *Byronic Hero,* 23.

109. Johann Wolfgang von Goethe, *Faust* (Munich: Deutscher Taschenbuch Verlag, 1983), Part II, act 5, lines 11936–7.

110. In "The Dreamers" this scene is referred to as the letter aria. In the original opera, there is no letter, but Else Brundbjerg (*Kvinden, kætteren, kunstneren,* 270) has found Lilli Lehmann's description of a performance of *Don Giovanni* in which a letter

was included so that other scenes from the opera could be cut. The performance is described in Lehmann's *Mein Weg* (My way, 1913).

111. Kuno Poulsen, "Karen Blixens gamle og nye testament," *Vindrosen* 10, no. 5 (1963): 377.

112. Aage Henriksen, "A Portrait of Karen Blixen," *Orbis Litterarum* 22, nos. 1–4 (1967): 330.

113. Ted Billy, "Werther Avenged: Isak Dinesen's 'The Poet,'" in *West Virginia University Bulletin Philological Papers,* Series 78, vol. 24, no. 5–1 (November 1977): 62.

114. Aiken, *Dinesen and Engendering of Narrative,* 186.

115. Ibid., 190.

Chapter 3: *Out of Africa*

1. Quoted in Judith Thurman, *Isak Dinesen: The Life of a Storyteller* (New York: St. Martin's Press, 1982), 281.

2. Marianne Juhl, "Om 'Den afrikanske Farm': Tilblivelsen, udgivelsen og modtagelsen af Karen Blixens anden bog," *Blixeniana 1984* (Copenhagen: Karen Blixen Selskabet, 1984), 40.

3. Ibid., 115–16.

4. Torgny Segerstedt, "Et trolsk syn," *Göteborgs Handels-och Sjöfartstidning,* 26 October 1937.

5. Juhl, "Om 'Den afrikanske Farm,'" 196.

6. Lewis Gannett, "Books and Things," *New York Herald Tribune,* 2 March 1939, 17.

7. Joseph Henry Jackson, "Isak Dinesen Distills the Strong Essence of Africa," *San Francisco Chronicle,* 27 February 1939, 24.

8. David Garnett, "Current Literature," *New Statesman and Nation,* 15 January 1938, 85.

9. Sir John Squire, "Africa, The Hero of a Book," *Illustrated London News,* 27 November 1937.

10. S. F. D., "Review of *Out of Africa,*" *Journal of the Royal African Society* 37, no. 148 (1938): 410.

11. Helen Macleod, "Karen Blixen," *Book and Magazine Collector,* no. 27 (June 1989): 19.

12. Tone Cederblad-Bengtsson, "Karen Blixen död," *Uppsala Nya Tidning,* 8 September 1962.

13. Carson McCullers, "Isak Dinesen: In Praise of Radiance," *Saturday Review,* 16 March 1963, 29.

14. Janet Sternberg, "Farewell to the Farm," in *Between Women,* ed. Carol Ascher et al. (Boston: Beacon Press, 1984), 216.

15. Eudora Welty, "Cook, Care for the Mad, or Write," *New York Times Book Review,* 7 February 1965, 45.

16. Juhl, "Om 'Den afrikanske Farm,'" 13.

17. Robert Langbaum, "*Isak Dinesen's African Letters:* The Story behind *Out of Africa,*" *Georgia Review* 36, no. 1 (1982): 213.

18. Brenda Cooper and David Descutner, "'It Had No Voice to It': Sydney Pollack's Film Translation of Isak Dinesen's *Out of Africa,*" *Quarterly Journal of Speech* 82, no. 3 (1996): 240.

19. Ngugi wa Thiong'o, "A Tremendous Service in Rectifying the Harm Done to Africa," *Bogens verden* 62, no. 10 (December 1981): 665.

20. Hariclea Zengos, "'A World without Walls': Race, Politics, and Gender in the African Works of Elspeth Huxley, Isak Dinesen, and Beryl Markham," (Ph.D diss., Tufts University, 1989). Much of my information about the early settlement of Kenya derives from this source.

21. Thurman, *Life of a Storyteller,* 177–78.

22. Peter Beard, *Longing for Darkness: Kamante's Tales* (New York: Harcourt Brace Jovanovich, 1975), ch. 3.

23. Rob Nixon, *"Out of Africa," Grand Street* 5, no. 4 (summer 1986): 225.

24. Beard, *Longing for Darkness,* ch. 3.

25. Ibid.

26. Karen Blixen, "Sorte og Hvide i Afrika," *Blixeniana 1979* (Copenhagen: Karen Blixen Selskabet, 1984), 41.

27. Carolyn Martin Shaw, *Colonial Inscriptions: Race, Sex, and Class in Kenya* (Minneapolis: University of Minnesota Press, 1995), 8.

28. Tove Hussein, *Africa's Song of Karen Blixen* (Nairobi: Majestic Printing Works, 1998), 87.

29. Ibid., 55.

30. Erik Egeland, *Ansikt til Ansikt* (Oslo: Gyldendal Norsk Forlag, 1969), 98.

31. Donald Hannah, *Isak Dinesen and Karen Blixen: The Mask and the Reality* (New York: Random House, 1971), 34.

32. Clara Svendsen, *The Life and Destiny of Isak Dinesen,* ed. Frans Lasson (New York: Random House, 1970), 137.

33. Shaw, *Colonial Inscriptions,* 153.

34. Helge Christensen, "Inspiration den højeste lykke, der er til, siger baronesse Karen Blixen," *Berlingske Tidende,* 1 January 1957.

35. Niels Birger Wamberg, *Samtaler med danske Digtere* (Copenhagen: Gyldendal, 1968), 45.

36. Egeland, *Ansikt til Ansikt,* 97.

37. See the articles by Ngugi wa Thiong'o, Rob Nixon; and Auma Ochanda and Kikuvi Mbinda, "Mit Afrika er en fornærmelse mod det kenyanske folks værdighed," in *Out of Africa: Omkring en film af Sydney Pollack,* ed. Aage Jørgensen (Århus: Center for undervisning og Kulturformidling, 1988).

38. Abdul JanMohamed, *Manichean Aesthetics: The Politics of Literature in Colonial Africa* (Amherst: University of Massachusetts Press, 1983), 57.

39. Ibid., 53.

40. Dane Kennedy, "Isak Dinesen's African Recovery of a European Past," *Clio* 17, no. 1 (fall 1987): 45.

41. See the works by Ngugi wa Thiong'o, Hariclea Zengos, and Auma Ochanda and Kikuvi Mbinda; Rashna B. Singh, "Isak Dinesen's *Out of Africa:* A Variation on a Theme," in *Karen Blixen/Isak Dinesen: Tradition, Modernity, and Other Ambiguities* (University of Minnesota Conference Proceedings, 17–20 April 1985); Sidonie Smith, "The Other Woman and the Racial Politics of Gender: Isak Dinesen and Beryl Markham in Kenya," in *De/Colonizing the Subject: The Politics of Gender in Women's Autobiography,* ed. Sidonie Smith and Julia Watson (Minneapolis: University of Minnesota Press, 1992); and Thomas R. Knipp, "Kenya's Literary Ladies and the Mythologizing of the White Highlands," *South Atlantic Review* 55, no. 1 (1990).

42. Else Brundbjerg, "Karen Blixen—afrikanerne og de vilde dyr," *Bogens verden* 63, no. 7 (August 1981): 517.

43. Singh, "Variation on a Theme," 61.

44. Chinua Achebe, "Heart of Darkness: An Image of Africa," *Massachusetts Review* 18, no. 4 (winter 1977): 784.

45. Shaw, *Colonial Inscriptions,* 149.

46. Raoul Granqvist, *Stereotypes in Western Fiction on Africa,* Umeå Papers in English, no. 7 (Umeå University, 1984), 17.

47. Smith, "Other Woman," 429.

48. Shaw, *Colonial Inscriptions,* 192.

49. Tone Selboe, *Kunst og Erfaring: En Studie i Karen Blixens Forfatterskap* (Odense: Odense Universitetsforlag, 1996), 57.

50. Ngugi wa Thiong'o, "A Tremendous Service," 665.

51. Nixon, *"Out of Africa,"* 219.

52. See, for example, Smith, "Other Woman," 428.

53. JanMohamed, *Manichean Aesthetics,* 60.

54. Ibid., 61.

55. Kennedy, "African Recovery," 42.

56. Brundbjerg, "Karen Blixen," 518.

57. Brenda Cooper and David Descutner, "Strategic Silences and Transgressive Metaphors in *Out of Africa," Southern Communication Journal* 62, no. 4 (1997): 340.

58. Mathew C. Wordsworth, *"Out of Africa," Observer,* 14 November 1937.

59. JanMohamed, *Manichean Aesthetics,* 52.

60. Ngugi wa Thiong'o, *Detained, a Prison Diary* (Exeter: Heineman Educational Books, 1981), 36.

61. Ibid., 37.

62. Harald Nielsen, *Karen Blixen: Studie i litterær Mystik* (Copenhagen: Borgens Forlag, 1956), 89–90.

63. Tove Rasmussen, "Karen Blixen og Afrika—endnu engang," *Bogens verden* 65 (1983): 411.

64. Helge Ernst, "Det drejer sig også om menneskets værdighed" (interview),

Social-Demokraten, 19 December 1954; and Karen Blixen, "Omkring den nye lov om dyreforsøg," *Politiken,* 29 November 1952.

65. Robert Langbaum, "Autobiography and Myth in *Out of Africa,*" *Virginia Quarterly Review* 40, no. 1 (1964): 65.

66. Judith Lee, "The Mask of Form in *Out of Africa,*" *Prose Studies* 8, no. 2 (1985): 45.

67. Ibid., 51.

68. Cooper and Descutner, "Strategic Silences and Transgressive Metaphors," 336.

69. Susan Hardy Aiken, *Isak Dinesen and the Engendering of Narrative* (Chicago: University of Chicago Press, 1990), 236.

70. Sirkka Heiskanen-Mäkelä, "Isak Dinesen's *Out of Africa:* Regressus ad Origenem," *Neuphilologishe Mitteilungen* 75, no. 3 (1974): 455.

71. Sandra Hutchinson, "Frontiers of Imagination: The African Writings of Dorothy Livesay and Karen Blixen," in *Canada and the Nordic Countries,* ed. Jørn Carlsen and Bengt Streijffert, Lund Studies in English 78 (Lund University Press, 1988), 147.

72. Susan R. Horton, *Difficult Women, Artful Lives* (Baltimore: Johns Hopkins University Press, 1995), 28.

73. Sarah Gilead, "Emigrant Selves: Narrative Strategies in Three Women's Autobiographies," *Criticism* 30, no. 1 (1988): 44.

74. Zengos, "'World without Walls,'" 11.

75. Horton, *Difficult Women,* 22.

76. Smith, "Other Woman," 412.

77. JanMohamed, *Manichean Aesthetics,* 55.

78. Quoted in Donald Hannah, *Mask and Reality,* 50.

79. Tone Selboe, *Kunst og Erfaring,* 13.

80. Else Brundbjerg, *Kvinden, kætteren, kunstneren,* 86–87.

Chapter 4: *Winter's Tales*

1. Hans Brix, "Mod er Menneskets Svar paa Livet," *Berlingske Aftenavis,* 21 September 1942.

2. Robert Langbaum, *Isak Dinesen's Art: The Gayety of Vision* (Chicago: University of Chicago Press, 1975), 156.

3. Annamarie Cleemann, "Karen Blixen fortæller," *Samleren* 19 (1942): 35.

4. Vibeke Schröder, *Selvrealisation og selvfortolkning i Karen Blixens forfatterskab* (Copenhagen: Gyldendal, 1979), 13.

5. Judith Thurman, *Isak Dinesen: The Life of a Storyteller* (New York: St. Martin's Press, 1982), 294.

6. Else Brundbjerg, *Kvinden, kætteren, kunstneren: Karen Blixen* (Charlottenlund: KnowWare, 1995), 31.

7. Shirley Clouse De Simone, "Alpenglow: Isak Dinesen and the Sense of History," (Ph.D diss., University of Kentucky, 1977).

8. J. S., "Vi elsker det primitive—og ødelægger det selv," *Politiken,* 8 October 1942.

9. Henning Kehler, "Karen Blixens nye Bog," *Berlingske Tidende,* 10 October 1942.

10. Hans Brix, "Karen Blixen: Vintereventyr," *Berlingske Aftenavis,* 18 November 1942.

11. B. B—a, "Karen Blixens nya berättelser," *Dagens Nyheter,* 18 October 1942.

12. William Maxwell, "Suffused with a Melancholy Light," *New York Times Book Review,* 9 May 1943: 2.

13. Hans Brix, *Karen Blixens Eventyr* (Copenhagen: Gyldendal, 1949), 159.

14. Langbaum, *Isak Dinesen's Art* (1975), 157.

15. Several critics have noted this fact, but the historical shift is described most eloquently in Jens Aage Doctor's "Omkring humanism," *Meddelelser fra Dansklærerforeningen* 6 (1979): 3–27; and Poul Behrendt's "Tekst, historie og samfund i Karen Blixens fortælling 'Sorg-Agre,'" *Kritik* 41 (1977): 94–126.

16. Finn Stein Larsen in *Proasaens mønstre* (Copenhagen: Berlingske Forlag, 1971) performs a more detailed reading of Dinesen's verbal painting than is possible here.

17. American readers can find this passage reproduced in Olga Anastasia Pelensky, *Isak Dinesen: The Life and Imagination of a Seducer* (Athens: Ohio University Press, 1991), 178–79.

18. Jørgen Sandved, "Blandt sorte Brødre," *Politiken,* 4 May 1948.

19. Ole Wivel, *Karen Blixen: Et uafslutet selvopgør* (Copenhagen: Aldus, 1987), 127.

20. See, for example, Susan Hardy Aiken, "Dinesen's 'Sorrow-Acre': Tracing the Woman's Line," *Contemporary Literature* 25, no. 2 (1984): 160–64; and Behrendt, "Tekst, historie og samfund," 96.

21. Behrendt, "Tekst, historie og samfund," 121; and Ida Zeruneith, "Begivenhedernes midpunkt—en analyse af Karen Blixens novelle 'Sorg-Agre,'" *Meddelelser fra Dansklærerforeningen* 4 (1977): 342.

22. David H. Richter, "Covert Plot in Isak Dinesen's 'Sorrow Acre,'" *Journal of Narrative Technique,* 15, no. 2 (1985): 85.

23. Behrendt, "Tekst, historie og samfund," 120. Ida Zeruneith feels similarly in "Begivenhedernes midpunkt," 348.

24. Langbaum, *Isak Dinesen's Art* (1975), 36.

25. Thurman, *Life of a Storyteller,* 297.

26. This point is made by both Langbaum, *Isak Dinesen's Art* (1975), 37; and Merry Weed, "Märchen and Legend Techniques of Narration in Two 'Tales' of Isak Dinesen," *Journal of the Folklore Institute* 15 (1978): 36.

27. Donald Hannah, *Isak Dinesen and Karen Blixen: The Mask and the Reality* (New York: Random House, 1971), 81–82.

28. Hans Holmberg, *Ingen skygge uden lys* (Copenhagen: C. A. Reitzels Forlag, 1995), 44–57.

29. Ibid., 48.

30. Hans Brix, *Karen Blixens Eventyr* (Copenhagen: Gyldendal, 1949), 180.

31. Marianne Juhl and Bo Hakon Jørgensen, *Dianas Hævn* (Odense: Odense Universitetsforlag, 1981), 95.

32. Grethe Rostbøll, *Længslens vingeslag* (Copenhagen: Gyldendal, 1996), 143.

33. Aage Henriksen, "A Portrait of Karen Blixen," *Orbis Litterarum* 22, nos. 1–4 (1967): 332.

34. Ulla Albreck, "Karen Blixen og Nordland," *Edda,* 1977, no. 1: 7.

35. Lionel Trilling, "The Sailor-Boy's Tale," in *Isak Dinesen: Critical Views,* ed. Olga Pelensky (Athens: Ohio University Press, 1993), 53.

36. Sara Stambaugh, *The Witch and the Goddess in the Stories of Isak Dinesen* (Ann Arbor: UMI Research Press, 1988), 56–57.

37. Ibid., 57.

38. Antonine M. L. Marquart Scholtz, "Africa and Creative Fantasy: Archetypes in Three of Isak Dinesen's Tales," *Edda,* 1985, no. 5: 32.

39. Shirley Clouse De Simone, "Alpenglow: Isak Dinesen and the Sense of History," (Ph.D diss., University of Kentucky, 1977), 162.

40. Holmberg, *Ingen skygge uden lys,* 126–28; Aage Henriksen, *Guder og galgefugle* (Oslo: Det Norske Studersamfunds Kulturutvalg, 1956), 21.

41. Henriksen, *Guder og galgefugle,* 21.

42. Toby Foshay, "Resentment and the Economy of Narrative," in *Isak Dinesen and Narrativity,* ed. Gurli Woods (Ottowa: Carleton University Press, 1994), 193–203.

43. Ibid., 200.

44. Juhl and Jørgensen, *Dianas Hævn,* 103.

45. George Schoolfield identified this quotation and suggested its significance to me.

46. Charles Baudelaire, *The Flowers of Evil and Other Poems,* trans. Francis Duke (Charlottesville: University of Virginia Press, 1961), 95.

47. Brundbjerg, *Kvinden, kætteren, kunstneren,* 124.

48. Marianne Juhl, "Kvindens rolle—mandens maske: Om 'De standhaftige Slaveejere,'" *Blixeniana 1982* (Copenhagen: Karen Blixen Selskabet, 1982), 309–26.

49. Rostbøll, *Længslens vingeslag,* 134–35.

50. Stambaugh, *The Witch and the Goddess,* 6.

51. Langbaum, *Isak Dinesen's Art* (1975), 166.

52. Holmberg, *Ingen skygge uden lys,* 118–19.

53. Gunnar Unger, "På thé hos baronessan," *Svenska Dagbladet,* 3 March 1957.

54. Henriksen, *Guder og galgefugle,* 33.

55. Henriksen, *Guder og galgefugle,* 31–32; and Langbaum, *Isak Dinesen's Art* (1975), 173.

56. Langbaum, *Isak Dinesen's Art* (1975), 173.

57. Brix, *Karen Blixens Eventyr,* 184; and Hannah, *Mask and Reality,* 106.

58. Stambaugh, *The Witch and the Goddess,* 86.

59. Johan Christian Jørgensen, *Realisme* (Copenhagen: Borgen, 1972), 143.

60. See, for example, David V. Harrington, "Isak Dinesen's 'Alkmene,'" *Discourse:* 9,

no. 4 (1966): 475; Hans Holmberg, "Meningar om 'Alkmene,'" *Danske Studier* 92, no. 8 (1977): 158; and Juhl and Jørgensen, *Dianas Hævn,* 72–76.

61. Pil Dahlerup, "Amphitryon 99. Karen Blixen: 'Alkmene,'" in *Indfaldsvinkler. 16 fortolkninger af nordisk Digtning tilegnet Oluf Friis* (Copenhagen: Gyldendal, 1964), 103.

62. Aage Henriksen gives an analysis of "Alkmene" in his essay on "Det drømmende barn" in *Guder og galgefugle.*

63. Langbaum, *Isak Dinesen's Art* (1975), 179–80.

64. Juhl and Jørgensen, *Dianas Hævn,* 74.

65. Holmberg, "Meningar om 'Alkmene,'" 179.

66. Brix, *Karen Blixens Eventyr,* 203; Langbaum, *Isak Dinesen's Art* (1975), 183.

67. Juhl and Jørgensen, *Dianas Hævn,* 77; Holmberg, "Meningar om 'Alkmene,'" 176.

68. Brundbjerg, *Kvinden, kætteren, kunstneren,* 68.

69. Johan de Mylius, *Litteraturbilleder* (Odense: Odense Universitetsforlag, 1988), 132.

70. Schröder, *Selvrealisation,* 44.

71. Holmberg, *Ingen skygge uden lys,* 30.

72. Ibid., 35.

73. De Mylius, *Litteraturbilleder,* 136; Rostbøll, *Længslens vingeslag,* 156.

74. Svend Bjerg, *Karen Blixens teologi* (Århus: ANIS, 1989), 27.

75. Schröder, *Selvrealisation,* 45.

76. Langbaum, *Gayety of Vision* (1965), 189.

77. Thomas Whissen, "Without Fear: Isak Dinesen's *Winter's Tales* and Occupied Denmark," *International Fiction Review* 3, no. 1 (January 1976): 60.

78. Ragna Lorentzen, *Fortællersprog, talt og skrevet* (Copenhagen: Gyldendal, 1973), 31.

79. Langbaum, *Gayety of Vision* (1965), 193; Rostbøll, *Længslens vingeslag,* 185.

80. Elisabeth Tykesson, "Livets tyngd och dess bouquet," *Tolv Essayer* (Stockholm: Bonniers, 1945), 70.

81. Rostbøll, *Længslens vingeslag,* 185.

Chapter 5: *Last Tales*

1. Robert Langbaum, *Isak Dinesen's Art: The Gayety of Vision,* (Chicago: University of Chicago Press, 1975), 45.

2. Judith Thurman, *Isak Dinesen: The Life of a Storyteller* (New York: St. Martin's Press, 1982), 404.

3. Klaus Otto Kapel, "Nidkært og ubestikkeligt," *Vindrosen* 5 (1958): 190.

4. Victor Lange, "Deceptive Cadenza," *New Republic* 18 (Nov. 1957): 18; and William Dickey, "Isak Dinesen, Last Tales," *Epoch* 8, no. 4 (winter 1958): 258.

5. For more information on *Albondocani,* see Ulla Albreck, "Karen Blixen and *The Thousand and One Nights: Albondocani*—an Analysis," in *Karen Blixen/Isak Dinesen: Tradition, Modernity, and Other Ambiguities* (University of Minnesota Conference

Proceedings, 17–20 April 1985), 162–70; and Susan Brantly, "Karen Blixen and the Mystery of *Albondocani,*" *Nordica* 9 (1992): 179–87.

6. See Langbaum, *Isak Dinesen's Art,* 44; Thurman, *Life of a Storyteller,* 363; and Bernhard Glienke, *Fatale Präzendenz: Karen Blixens Mythologie* (Neumünster: Karl Wachholtz Verlag, 1986), 250.

7. Brita Tigerschiöld, "Konversation på Rungstedlund," *Göteborgs Handels- och Sjöfartstidning,* 30 July 1958.

8. Aage Henriksen, *De ubændige* (Copenhagen: Gyldendal, 1984), 76.

9. Tigerschiöld, "Konversation."

10. Susan Hardy Aiken, *Isak Dinesen and the Engendering of Narrative* (Chicago: University of Chicago Press, 1990), 14. Aiken's reading of "The Cardinal's First Tale" is brilliant, and even if I do not agree with some of her conclusions, much in my own reading is inspired by hers.

11. Henriksen, *De ubændige,* 92.

12. Ulla Albreck, *Kappen* (Copenhagen: Akademisk Forlag, 1981), 53.

13. Karen Blixen, "Til fire Kultegninger," *Berlingske Søndags Magasin,* 24 June 1950.

14. Langbaum, *Isak Dinesen's Art,* 212.

15. Ibid., 208.

16. Ibid.

17. Albreck, *Kappen,* 38.

18. Grethe Rostbøll, *Længslens vingeslag,* (Copenhagen: Gyldendal, 1996), 208.

19. Langbaum, *Gayety of Vision,* 211.

20. Henriksen, *De ubændige,* 78.

21. Hans Holmberg, "Karen Blixens estetiska balansakt," *Studiekamraten* 67, no. 2 (1985): 9.

22. Rostbøll, *Længslens vingeslag,* 211.

23. Marilyn Stokstad, *Art History* (New York: Harry N. Abrams Inc., 1995), 557.

24. Thurman, *Life of a Storyteller,* 363.

25. Jørgen Dines Johansen, "Navnet," in *Analyser af Dansk kortprosa II,* ed. Jørgen Dines Johansen (Copenhagen: Borgens Billigbogs Bibliotek, 1975), 105.

26. George Schoolfield suggested to me that Lady Flora's first name might have been inspired by Flora Macdonald, who helped Bonnie Prince Charlie to escape after Culloden. She is depicted as a heroic figure in Scottish ballads, braver than Charlie.

27. Thomas Whissen, *Isak Dinesen's Aesthetics* (Port Washington, N.Y.: Kennikat Press, 1973), 104; Susan Gubar, "'The Blank Page' and Female Creativity," *Critical Inquiry* 8, no. 2 (winter 1981): 250.

28. Gail J. Petersen, "Sine Materia: The Imprint of the Human Voice on Narrative," (Ph.D diss., University of Wisconsin, 1995), 163.

29. Mark A. Kemp, "The Silent Tale: Pragmatic Strategy in 'The Blank Page,'" *in*

Isak Dinesen and Narrativity, ed. Gurli Woods (Ottowa: Carleton University Press, 1994), 174.

30. Gubar, "'The Blank Page,'" 248.

31. Ibid., 259.

32. Christine Froula, "When Eve Reads Milton: Undoing the Canonical Economy," *Critical Inquiry* 10, no. 2 (December 1982): 342.

33. Marianne Stecher-Hansen, "Both Sacred and Secretly Gay: Isak Dinesen's 'The Blank Page,'" *Pacific Coast Philology* 29, no. 1 (September 1994): 8.

34. Georg Svensson, "Kommentarer," *Bonniers Litterära Magasin* 7, no. 3 (March 1938): 163–34.

35. Illa, "Jeg er Verdens største Snegl, siger Karen Blixen," *Frederiksborg Amts Avis,* 1 November 1957. Other echoes of Franz Schubert (1797–1828) may be found in the tale in the form of the miller's widow. Schubert composed music to a song cycle called "Die schöne Müllerin" (1824, The miller's lovely daughter), the titular heroine of which proves to be something of a *femme fatale,* driving a young man to drown himself for love of her.

36. Else Cederborg, "Mytologien som forløsningsmodel i Karen Blixens 'Karyatiderne. En ufuldendt Historie,'" *Edda,* no. 1 (1984): 2.

37. There is a curious, and apparently minor, discrepancy between the name of the estate in the English version of the tale (Champmeslé) and the Danish version (Champsmelé). The Danish name in French invokes a vague sense of "fields of discord," which could be appropriate. Champmeslé (1642–98) was a famous French actress who also was the mistress of the young Racine, thus, she might have been a fascinating figure in Dinesen's eyes. It is anyone's guess whether this is mistake or calculation.

38. Aiken, *Dinesen and Engendering of Narrative,* 193.

39. *The Oxford Companion to Classical Literature,* ed. M. C. Howatson (Oxford: Oxford University Press, 1989), 117.

40. Cederborg, "Mytologien," 8.

41. Thorkild Bjørnvig, *The Pact,* trans. Ingvar Schousboe and William Jay Smith (New York: St. Martin's Press, 1983), 46–47.

42. Langbaum, *Isak Dinesen's Art,* 225.

43. Poul Berendt, "De forbyttede børn," *Blixeniana 1978,* ed. Hans Andersen and Frans Lasson (Copenhagen: Karen Blixen Selskabet, 1978), 62.

44. Langbaum, *Isak Dinesen's Art,* 119.

45. Yvonne Sandstroem, "The Subverted Plot: Kleist's *Michael Kolhaas,* Andersen's *The Two Baronesses,* and Dinesen's *A Country Tale,*" in *Karen Blixen/Isak Dinesen: Tradition, Modernity, and Other Ambiguities—Conference Proceedings* (University of Minnesota Conference Proceedings, 17–20 April 1985), 30.

46. Langbaum, *Isak Dinesen's Art,* 234.

47. Johan de Mylius, *Litteraturbilleder* (Odense: Odense Universitetsforlag, 1988), 144. De Mylius has had an especially sensitive ear for the verbal echoes in this tale, and I have taken a number of his hints.

48. Sandstroem, "Subverted Plot," 32.

49. Langbaum, *Isak Dinesen's Art,* 236.

50. Bent Mohn, "Talk with Isak Dinesen," *New York Times Book Review,* 3 Nov 1957, 49.

51. Bjørnvig, *The Pact,* 38.

52. Ibid., 71.

53. Bent Østergaard, "Samtale om Natten i København," *Dansk Udsyn* 62, no. 2 (1982): 78.

54. Langbaum, *Isak Dinesen's Art,* 243.

55. Gunnar Unger, "På thé hos baronessen," *Svenska Dagbladet,* 3 March 1957.

Chapter 6: *Anecdotes of Destiny* and *Ehrengard*

1. Curtis Cate, "Isak Dinesen: The Scheherazade of Our Times," *Cornhill* 171 (winter 1959/60): 127.

2. Jean Martin, "Have You Got a Story?" *Nation,* 8 November 1958, 345.

3. Robert H. Glauber, "Tales from Isak Dinesen's Magic World," *Herald Tribune Book Review,* 12 October 1958, 4.

4. Hans Holmberg, *Ingen skygge uden lys* (Copenhagen: C. A. Reitzels Forlag, 1995), 168.

5. Robert Langbaum, *Isak Dinesen's Art: The Gayety of Vision* (Chicago: University of Chicago Press, 1975), 247.

6. Susan Hardy Aiken, *Isak Dinesen and the Engendering of Narrative* (Chicago: University of Chicago Press, 1990), 62.

7. Grethe Rostbøll, *Længslens vingeslag* (Copenhagen: Gyldendal, 1996), 273.

8. Holmberg, *Ingen skygge uden lys,* 157–78.

9. Karen Blixen, *Osceola,* ed. Clara Svendsen (Copenhagen: Gyldendal, 1962), 141.

10. Judith Thurman, *Isak Dinesen: The Life of a Storyteller* (New York: St. Martin's Press, 1982), 329.

11. Ibid., 330.

12. Tone Selboe, *Kunst og Erfaring: En Studie i Karen Blixens Forfatterskap* (Odense: Odense Universitetsforlag, 1996), 117.

13. Ann Gossman, "Sacramental Imagery in Two Stories by Isak Dinesen," *Wisconsin Studies in Contemporary Literature* 4, no. 3 (autumn 1963): 325.

14. There was an Alexander Ross (1783–1856), who was a Canadian pioneer from Scotland. He participated in John Jacob Astor's expedition to Oregon (1810–12) and described the first settlement on the Columbia River.

15. Toril Moi, "'Hele verden en scene': En analyse av Karen Blixens 'Storme,'" *Edda,* 1986, no. 2: 158.

16. Holmberg, *Ingen skygge uden lys,* 194.

17. Holmberg, *Ingen skygge uden lys,* 191; Langbaum, *Isak Dinesen's Art* (1975), 262; Moi, "'Hele verden en scene,'" 160; Bo Hakon Jørgensen, "Anekdoter om historien:

En værklesning av Skæbneanekdoter," in *Fortællerens veje: Karen Blixen* (Lysebu rapport, 1994), 69; Annelies van Hees, *The Ambivalent Venus: Women in Isak Dinesen's Tales* (Minneapolis: The Nordic Roundtable Papers, 1991), 39; Merete Stistrup, "Uendelighedens figurer: Om Karen Blixens 'Storme,'" *Kultur og Klasse. Kritik og Kulturanalyse* 76 (1994): 109; Sara Stambaugh, *The Witch and the Goddess in the Stories of Isak Dinesen* (Ann Arbor: UMI Research Press, 1988), 11.

18. Selboe, *Kunst og Erfaring,* 130.

19. Langbaum, *Isak Dinesen's Art* (1975), 262.

20. Henrik Ljungberg, *En elementær historie: Om Karen Blixens bedste fortælling* (Copenhagen: Gyldendal, 1998).

21. Karl Larsen, *Udvalgte Skrifter,* vol. 2 (Copenhagen: Aschehoug, 1930), 122.

22. Ibid., 123.

23. Quoted in Donald Hannah, *Isak Dinesen and Karen Blixen: The Mask and the Reality* (New York: Random House, 1971), 133.

24. Ljungberg, *Elementær historie.*

25. Langbaum, *Isak Dinesen's Art* (1975), 263.

26. Thurman, *Life of a Storyteller,* 356.

27. Stambaugh, *The Witch and the Goddess,* 43.

28. Selboe, *Kunst og Erfaring,* 139

29. Ted Billy, "Isak Dinesen's 'Ring': Matrimonial *Götterdämerung,*" in *Karen Blixen/Isak Dinesen: Tradition, Modernity, and Other Ambiguities* (University of Minnesota Conference Proceedings, 17–20 April 1985), 126. Anders Westenholz in *Den glemte abe,* 69, makes the same connection without the benefit of Dinesen's hint in the English text.

30. Leif Søndergaard, "Syv fantastiske Analyser af Karen Blixens 'Ringen,'" *Kultur og Klasse: Kritik og Kulturanalyse* 73 (1993): 87.

31. Rolf Gaasland, "Syndafald og Initiasjon: En Analyse av Karen Blixen's 'Ringen,'" *Nordlitt* 3 (1998): 12.

32. Gaaslund, "Syndafald og Initiasjon," 14; and Billy, "Isak Dinesen's 'Ring,'" 128.

33. Søndergaard, "Syv fantastiske Analyser," 97.

34. For example, Billy, "Isak Dinesen's 'Ring,'" 128; Gaaslund, "Syndafald og Initiasjon," 15; and Langbaum, *Isak Dinesen's Art* (1975), 273.

35. Søndergaard, "Syv fantastiske Analyser," 86; Gaaslund, "Syndafald og Initiasjon," 12; Selboe, *Kunst og Erfaring,* 141; Billy, "Isak Dinesen's 'Ring,'" 128.

36. Stambaugh, *The Witch and the Goddess,* 28; Selboe, *Kunst og Erfaring,* 142; Gaaslund, "Syndafald og Initiasjon," 22.

37. Langbaum, *Isak Dinesen's Art* (1975), 273.

38. Søndergaard, "Syv fantastiske Analyser," 82.

39. Selboe, *Kunst og Erfaring,* 143.

40. Rostbøll, *Længslens vingeslag,* 300.

41. Gaaslund, "Syndafald og Initiasjon," 23.

42. Anders Westenholz, *Den glemte abe* (Cophenhagen: Gyldendal, 1985), 70.

43. Langbaum, *Isak Dinesen's Art* (1975), 274.

44. Translation taken from Olga Anastasia Pelensky, "Isak Dinesen and Kierkegaard: The Aesthetics of Paradox in *Ehrengard,*" in *Isak Dinesen: Critical Views* (Athens: Ohio University Press, 1993), 323–24.

45. Selboe, *Kunst og Erfaring,* 150.

Selected Bibliography

Additional bibliographical references can be found in the notes.

Works by Isak Dinesen in English

These works are listed here in the order in which they appeared in the United States. See list of abbreviations, at the beginning of this book, for more recent editions.

Seven Gothic Tales. New York: Harrison Smith and Robert Haas, 1934.
Out of Africa. New York: Random House, 1938.
Winter's Tales. New York: Random House, 1942.
The Angelic Avengers. [Pierre Andrézel, pseud.] New York: Random House, 1947.
Last Tales. New York: Random House, 1957.
Anecdotes of Destiny. New York: Random House, 1958.
Shadows on the Grass. New York: Random House, 1961.
Ehrengard. New York: Random House, 1963.
Carnival: Entertainments and Posthumous Tales. Chicago: University of Chicago Press, 1977.
Daguerreotypes and Other Essays. Chicago: University of Chicago Press, 1979.
On Modern Marriage and Other Observations. New York: St. Martin's Press, 1986.

Collected Letters

Letters from Africa, 1914–1931. Translated by Anne Born, edited by Frans Lasson. Chicago: University of Chicago Press, 1981. Fascinating reading for anyone especially interested in Dinesen's life in Africa. Contains a useful biographical chronology prepared by Frans Lasson.
Karen Blixen i Danmark: Breve, 1931–1962. 2 vols. Edited by Frans Lasson and Tom Engelbrecht. Copenhagen: Gyldendal, 1996. Although the Danish letters have not yet been translated, Dinesen's English correspondence appears here in English.

Bibliographies

Henriksen, Liselotte. *Isak Dinesen: A Bibliography.* Copenhagen: Gyldendal, 1977. Particularly useful for locating older reviews and interviews.
Jørgensen, Aage. *Litteratur om Karen Blixen: En bibliografi.* Århus: Center for Undervisning og Kulturformidling, 1998. Contains more current secondary literature references.

Biographies

Bjørnvig, Torkild. *The Pact: My Friendship with Isak Dinesen.* New York: St. Martin's Press, 1983. A memoir by someone who knew Dinesen well.

Donelson, Linda G. *Out of Isak Dinesen in Africa: Karen Blixen's Untold Story.* Iowa City: Coulsong, 1995. The author is an M.D., and her remarks on Dinesen's failing health in later years are especially interesting.

Hussein, Tove. *Africa's Song of Karen Blixen.* Nairobi: Majestic Printing Works, 1998. Contains biographical follow-up information on the African staff of Dinesen's farm in Kenya.

Migel, Parmenia. *Titania: The Biography of Isak Dinesen.* New York: Random House, 1967. Parmenia Migel was a personal friend of Dinesen's, and the biography shows that influence.

Pelensky, Olga Anastasia. *Isak Dinesen: The Life and Imagination of a Seducer.* Athens: Ohio University Press, 1991. Contains scattered pieces of interesting information.

Svendsen, Clara. *The Life and Destiny of Isak Dinesen.* Edited by Frans Lasson. New York: Random House, 1970. A beautiful book filled with photographs from Dinesen's life.

Svendsen, Clara, ed. *Isak Dinesen: A Memorial.* New York: Random House, 1965. A collection of testimonials from friends and admirers of Dinesen.

Thurman, Judith. *Isak Dinesen: The Life of a Storyteller.* New York: St. Martin's Press, 1982. The standard biography of Isak Dinesen. Contains a useful bibliography of Dinesen's minor works.

Secondary Literature in English

Aiken, Susan Hardy. *Isak Dinesen and the Engendering of Narrative.* Chicago: University of Chicago Press, 1990. A theoretically sophisticated look at Dinesen's authorship from a feminist perspective, which is both lucid and enlightening.

Beard, Peter, ed. *Longing for Darkness: Kamante's Tales.* New York: Harcourt Brace Jovanovich, 1975. An awkward translation and transcription of Kamante's tales of his life on the farm in Africa.

Billy, Ted. "Isak Dinesen's 'Ring': Matrimonial *Götterdämerung.*" In *Karen Blixen/Isak Dinesen: Tradition, Modernity, and Other Ambiguities,* 126–29. University of Minnesota Conference Proceedings, 17–20 April 1985.

———. "Werther Avenged: Isak Dinesen's 'The Poet.'" *West Virginia University Bulletin Philological Papers,* Series 78, vol. 24, no.5–1 (November 1977): 62–67.

Blackwell, Marilyn Johns. "The Transforming Gaze: Identity and Sexuality in the Works of Isak Dinesen." *Scandinavian Studies* 63, no. 1 (1991): 50–65.

Brantly, Susan. "Karen Blixen and the Mystery of *Albondocani*" *Nordica* 9 (1992): 179–88.

Bredsdorff, Elias. "Isak Dinesen v. Karen Blixen: *Seven Gothic Tales* (1934) and *Syv fantastike Fortællinger* (1935)." In *Facets of European Modernism,* edited by Janet Garton, 275–93. Norwich: University of East Anglia, 1985.

Brink, J. R. "Hamlet or Timon: Isak Dinesen's 'Deluge at Norderney.'" *International Fiction Review* 5, no. 2 (July 1978): 148–50.

Burstein, Janet Handler. "Two Locked Caskets: Selfhood and 'Otherness' in the Work of Isak Dinesen." *Texas Studies in Literature and Language* 20, no. 4 (1978): 615–32.

Cooper, Brenda, and David Descutner. "'It Had No Voice to It': Sydney Pollack's Film Translation of Isak Dinesen's *Out of Africa*." *Quarterly Journal of Speech* 82, no. 3 (1996): 228–50.

————. "Strategic Silences and Transgressive Metaphors in *Out of Africa*." *Southern Communication Journal* 62, no. 4 (1997): 333–43.

Danish Literature Information Centre, *Karen Blixen—Out of Denmark, Papers from a Colloquium at the Karen Blixen Museum, April 1997*. Copenhagen: Danish Literature Information Centre, 1997. A collection of essays by various authors.

De Simone, Shirley Clouse. "Alpenglow: Isak Dinesen and the Sense of History." Diss., University of Kentucky, 1977. Contains some useful readings of individual tales by Dinesen.

Froula, Christine. "When Eve Reads Milton: Undoing the Canonical Economy." *Critical Inquiry* 10, no. 2 (December 1982): 321–47.

Gilead, Sarah. "Emigrant Selves: Narrative Strategies in Three Women's Autobiographies." *Criticism* 30, no. 1 (winter 1988): 43–62.

Gossman, Ann. "Sacramental Imagery in Two Stories by Isak Dinesen." *Wisconsin Studies in Contemporary Literature* 4, no. 3 (autumn 1963): 319–26.

Hannah, Donald. *Isak Dinesen and Karen Blixen: The Mask and the Reality*. New York: Random House, 1971. Hannah had early access to Dinesen's Danish archives, and one can find material here in English not available elsewhere, such as a translation of "The Revenge of Truth."

Harrington, David V. "Isak Dinesen's 'Alkmene.'" *Discourse* 9, no. 4 (1966): 471–81.

Hees, Annelies van. *The Ambivalent Venus: Women in Isak Dinesen's Tales*. Minneapolis: Nordic Roundtable Papers, 1991. An abbreviated version of a longer work focusing on the women in Dinesen's authorship from a psychoanalytical perspective.

Heiskanen-Mäkelä, Sirkka. "Isak Dinesen's *Out of Africa*: Regressus ad Origenem." *Neuphilologische Mitteilungen* 75, no. 3 (1974): 453–71.

Henriksen, Aage. "A Portrait of Karen Blixen." *Orbis Litterarum* 22, nos. 1–4 (1967): 319–42.

————. "The Empty Space between Art and the Church." *Scandinavian Studies* 57, no. 4 (1985): 390–99.

————. *Isak Dinesen/Karen Blixen: The Work and the Life*. New York: St. Martin's Press, 1988. Henriksen was a close friend and confidant of Dinesen as well as a highly respected scholar. His observations on her work and life are worthy of note.

Horton, Susan R. *Difficult Women, Artful Lives: Olive Schreiner and Isak Dinesen in and out of Africa*. Baltimore: Johns Hopkins University Press, 1995. A comparison of these two women writers and the impact that living in Africa had upon their identities.

Hutchinson, Sandra. "Frontiers of Imagination: The African Writings of Dorothy Livesay and Karen Blixen." In *Canada and the Nordic Countries,* edited by Jørn Carlsen and Bengt Streijffert, 138–48. Lund Studies in English 78. Lund: Lund University Press, 1988.

James, Sibyl. "Gothic Transformations: Isak Dinesen and the Gothic." In *The Female Gothic,* edited by Juliann E. Fleenor, 138–52. Montreal: Eden Press, 1983.

JanMohamed, Abdul. *Manichean Aesthetics: The Politics of Literature in Colonial Africa.* Amherst: University of Massachusetts Press, 1983. An enlightening look at colonial authors in Africa, Isak Dinesen among them.

———. "The Economy of Manichean Allegory: The Function of Racial Difference in Colonialist Literature." *Critical Inquiry* 12, no. 1 (autumn 1985): 59–87.

Johannesen, Eric O. *The World of Isak Dinesen.* Seattle: University of Washington Press, 1961. Provides a useful overview of various recurring themes in Dinesen's fiction.

———. "Isak Dinesen, Søren Kierkegaard, and the Present Age." *Books Abroad,* winter 1962, 20–24.

Jørgensen, Aage, ed. *Isak Dinesen, Storyteller.* Århus: Akademisk Boghandel, 1972. A collection of essays by various authors.

Juhl, Marianne, and Bo Hakon Jørgensen. *Diana's Revenge: Two Lines in Isak Dinesen's Authorship.* Translated by Anne Born. Odense: Odense University Press, 1985. A look at Dinesen's fiction from a feminist perspective.

Kennedy, Dane. "Isak Dinesen's African Recovery of a European Past." *Clio* 17, no. 1 (fall 1987): 38–50.

Knipp, Thomas R. "Kenya's Literary Ladies and the Mythologizing of the White Highlands." *South Atlantic Review* 55, no. 1 (1990): 1–16.

Landy, Marcia. "Anecdote as Destiny: Isak Dinesen and the Storyteller." *Massachusetts Review,* spring 1978, 389–406.

Langbaum, Robert. *Isak Dinesen's Art: The Gayety of Vision.* Chicago: University of Chicago Press, 1975. Langbaum's book first appeared in 1964 and has endured as perhaps the best introduction to Dinesen's work in English.

Lewis, Florence. "Isak Dinesen and Feminist Criticism." *North American Review,* March 1979, 62–72.

Nixon, Rob. "*Out of Africa.*" *Grand Street* 5, no. 4 (summer 1986): 216–27.

Pelensky, Olga Anastasia, ed. *Isak Dinesen: Critical Views.* Athens: Ohio University Press, 1993. Pelensky has anthologized a number of fine articles that had previously been published in journals. These articles are not listed elsewhere in this bibliography and the volume is worth consulting.

Petersen, Gail J. "Sine Materia: The Imprint of the Human Voice on Narrative." Diss., University of Wisconsin, 1995. A search for the oral quality of Dinesen's fiction, this dissertation focuses primarily on "The Blank Page."

Phillips, Robert S. "Dinesen's 'Monkey' and McCuller's 'Ballad': A Study in Literary Affinity." *Studies in Short Fiction* 1 (1963–64): 70–76.

Riechel, Donald C. "Isak Dinesen's 'Roads Round Nietzsche.'" *Scandinavian Studies* 62, no. 1 (1991): 326–50.

Rouse, H. Blaire. "Isak Dinesen's Africa." *Proceedings of the Sixth Congress of the International Comparative Literature Association,* 649–52. Stuttgart: Erich Bieber, 1975.

Schleifer, Ronald. "The 'Gothic' Flannery O'Connor." *Modern Fiction Studies* 28, no. 3 (autumn 1982): 475–86.

Scholtz, Antonine M. L. Marquart. "From Revenge to Reconciliation: Truth as a Theme in the Work of Isak Dinesen." *Scandinavica* 12, no. 1 (1973): 27–36.

Schow, H. Wayne. "Karen Blixen and Martin A. Hansen: Art, Ethics, and the Human Condition." *Scandinavian Studies* 52, no. 1 (1980): 16–31.

———. *"Out of Africa, The White Album,* and the Possibility of Tragic Affirmation." *English Studies* 67, no. 1 (February 1986): 35–50.

Singh, Rashna B. "Isak Dinesen's *Out of Africa:* A Variation on a Theme." In *Karen Blixen/Isak Dinesen: Tradition, Modernity, and Other Ambiguities,* 60–65. University of Minnesota Conference Proceedings, 17–20 April 1985.

Smith, Sidonie. "The Other Woman and the Racial Politics of Gender: Isak Dinesen and Beryl Markham in Kenya." In *De/Colonizing the Subject: The Politics of Gender in Women's Autobiography,* edited by Sidonie Smith and Julia Watson, 410–35. Minneapolis: University of Minnesota Press, 1992.

Sodowsky, Gargi Roysircar, and Roland Sodowsky. "Myriad Possibilities in Isak Dinesen's 'The Dreamers': An Existential Interpretation." In *Creative and Critical Approaches to the Short Story,* edited by Noel Harold Kaylor, Jr., 329–40. Lewiston: Edwin Mellen Press, 1997.

Stafford, Jean. "Isak Dinesen: Master Teller of Tales." *Horizon* 11, no. 1 (1959): 110–12.

Stambaugh, Sara. "Witch as Quintessential Woman: A Context for Isak Dinesen's Fiction." *Mosaic* 16, no. 3 (1983): 87–100.

———. *The Witch and the Goddess in the Stories of Isak Dinesen: A Feminist Reading.* Ann Arbor: UMI Research Press, 1988. Stambaugh is particularly well versed in the English literature of the Victorian Age, which provides some useful insights into Dinesen's fiction. Stambaugh pays more attention to Dinesen's posthumous collection *Carnival* than many other works.

Stecher-Hansen, Marianne. "Both Sacred and Secretly Gay: Isak Dinesen's 'The Blank Page.'" *Pacific Coast Philology* 29, no. 1 (September 1994): 3–13.

Stephens, Anthony. "Narrative Structures in Karen Blixen's 'The Dreamers.'" In *Festschrift for Ralph Farrell,* edited by Anthony Stephens et al., 121–36. Las Vegas and Frankfurt: Peter Lang, 1977.

———. "The Paradox of the Omnipotent Narrator in the Works of Karen Blixen." *Neophilologicus* 62 (1978): 297–313.

Thiong'o, Ngugi wa. *Detained: A Writer's Prison Diary.* London: Heinemann, 1981.

———. "Interview." *Kunapipi* 3, nos. 1–2 (1981): 110–16, 135–40.

————. "A Tremendous Service in Rectifying the Harm Done to Africa." *Bogens verden* 62, no. 10 (December 1981): 663–65.

Thurman, Judith. "Isak Dinesen/Karen Blixen: A Very Personal Memoir." *Ms.,* September 1973, 72–93.

Walter, Eugene. "The Art of Fiction XIV: Isak Dinesen." *Paris Review,* autumn 1956, 43–59.

————. "Isak Dinesen Conquers Rome." *Harper's Magazine,* February 1965, 46–55.

Westenholz, Anders. *The Power of Aries: Myth and Reality in Karen Blixen's Life,* translated by Lise Kure-Jensen. Baton Rouge: Louisiana State University Press, 1982. Westenholz has some strong opinions about Isak Dinesen.

Whissen, Thomas. *Isak Dinesen's Aesthetics.* Port Washington, N.Y.: Kennikat Press, 1973. A general discussion of Dinesen's aesthetic principles without much close analysis of individual stories.

————. "The Bow of the Lord: Isak Dinesen's 'Portrait of the Artist.'" *Scandinavian Studies* 46, no. 1 (1974): 47–58.

————. "Without Fear: Isak Dinesen's *Winter's Tales* and Occupied Denmark." *International Fiction Review* 3, no. 1 (January 1976): 57–61.

————. "The Magic Circle: The Role of the Prostitute in Isak Dinesen's Gothic Tales." In *The Image of the Prostitute in Modern Literature,* edited by Pierre L. Horn and Mary Beth Pringle. New York: Frederick Ungar Publishing, 1984.

Woods, Gurli A., ed. *Isak Dinesen and Narrativity: Reassessments for the 1990s.* Ottawa: Carleton University Press, 1994. A collection of essays by various authors on various aspects of Dinesen's work, most of which are informed by modern narrative theories.

Zengos, Hariclea. "'A World without Walls': Race, Politics, and Gender in the African Works of Elspeth Huxley, Isak Dinesen, and Beryl Markham." Diss., Tufts University, 1989. A useful look at sensitive political issues involved in Isak Dinesen's role in Africa.

Index